Tenacity

REMARKABLE PEOPLE OF THE FUR WAR

Heroes, Oligarchs, Psychopaths, Survivors, Scoundrels, Observers

DAVID A. BAINBRIDGE

*Rio Redondo Press Mission: Advancing sustainability accounting
and reporting, increasing sustainable management of resources
and people, and protecting future generations.*

THE FUR COAST

James Hanna's ship the *Sea Otter* set sail from Macao under a Portuguese flag on April 15, 1785 on the first trip from the Orient to the Fur Coast. He returned on December 15 with the first sea otter furs to China by direct route. No one could imagine how momentous this trade would become and the catastrophic impact it would have on the communities of the First Nations and the ecosystems of the coast and interior, from Baja California to the Bering Sea. The people swept up in this rush for furs and wealth came from many nations, and represented the full spectrum of human behavior—from heroic to incomprehensible savagery. Here are a few of these remarkable people.

The *Sea Otter*, 1785

Contents

Prelude

*B*efore the fur traders arrived on the West Coast, hundreds of thousands of people lived in the area that would be affected. Some of the highest population densities in North America were found here, just as they are today. Hundreds of tribes and tribelets thrived with the often-rich natural resources. Some were allies while some were enemies, and trading took place across hundreds, and in some cases, thousands of miles. Some tribes relied heavily on slaves, and slave raiding affected many weaker tribes. The first European visitors to the coast were almost invariably treated well by native people who were curious about the new arrivals.

Some people lived in isolated tribelets or villages on inlets or islands with few affiliates, while others could gather hundreds of warriors from a large area to resist European encroachment. The Unangan fought long and hard against the Russians. The Tlingit threw the Russians out of Sitka in 1802 and remained powerful enough to extract high prices for their furs for many years. Tribes like the Chinook manipulated the fur trade to their advantage and gained power and wealth before succumbing to the diseases the fur traders brought.

Who were the First Nations? The many language groups and subgroups of the fur trading areas are continually being revised and disputed as research continues. Some of the more common groupings and tribes included: Wakashan, Quileutae, Nuu-Chah-nulth (Nootka), Salish, Haida, Tlingit, Tsimshian, Kalapuya, Alsea, Suislaw, Kuitsh (Kalawatset), Umpqua, Athapaskan, Sahaptian, Chinookan, Chimakuan, Eyak-Athpaskin, Aleut (more properly Unangan), Haisla, Xaihais, Alutiiq (Sugpiaq), Inupiaq, Yupik, Kootenay, Yurok, Karok, Miwok, Sacian, Huchiun, Huimen, Hupa, Wiyot, Tolowa, Tutuni, Tillamook, Chemakum, Kwalhioqua, Haisla, Tolowa, Penutian, Chumashan, Kumeyaay (Tipai-Ipai), Hokan, Uto-Aztecan, Yuki-Wappo (Yukian), Cochimí, Guaycura, and many more if we consider more distant inland contacts.

The borders, extent, culture, languages and dialects are very uncertain in many cases because the people and tribes were gone before they were studied. Epidemics had made their way to the fur lands from overland to the south and from the sea, even in the protohistoric period. Early visitors like Juan Rodríguez Cabrillo (1542), Sir Francis Drake (1579), Sebastian Vizcaino (1602–1603), and shipwrecks of Spanish treasure ships and Japanese vessels in distress all brought diseases.

The cultural declines accelerated dramatically as Russian explorers and fur traders arrived on the fur coast after the survivors of the Bering Expedition made great profits on their sea otter pelts in 1742. After Captain Cook's expedition reached Canton with sea otter pelts in 1778 and sold their furs at very high prices, the race was on. In 1785, the first non-Russian ship arrived on the northwest coast specifically for furs, and the great struggle for exploitation and dominance of the fur trade had begun.

Few observers were able to spend time with the tribes and provide ethnographic information before they were irrevocably changed. John Jewitt, a captured sailor who became a Nuu-Chah-nulth slave for two years, was one of the few exceptions. By the time more interested and better-trained observers arrived it was too late. These observers were often clueless about how drastic the declines in population had been. They studied and recorded what they could. However, when 90% or more of a tribe is lost, so too are the details of life, history, language, and boundaries. As epidemics swept away whole groups, like the Chinook (1829–1832), others took their place. The expansion of the Klickitat into former Chinook territory in the

1830s was quite remarkable. These epidemics changed boundaries, further confusing and challenging researchers.

Return to the September day in 1785 when the first British fur trader, Captain James Hanna, arrived on the coast in the 60-ton ship *Sea Otter* (formerly *the Harmon*). Before he left he had 560 pelts and had committed the first massacre of native people for petty theft. Who among the observers would have guessed that in just 35 years the sea otters would be almost gone and epidemics would sweep through and devastate native communities.

My goal with this book is to introduce the people from many countries and cultures who were involved in the global race for furs. I also touch upon the economics and politics that drove them, and the cultural and environmental consequences that resulted (more in "Volume 1: The Fur War" and online at www.furwar.com). There are lessons we still need to learn.

This book is divided into four chapters:

1. GEOPOLITICS
It begins with a section on the motivation and actions of the nations involved in the aggressive and competitive pursuit of furs.

2. THE PEOPLE
The heart of this book is about the remarkable men and women who contested for power, money, and survival. There are heroes, oligarchs, psychopaths, survivors, scoundrels and observers. The catastrophic impact the fur trade had on the First Nations communities is detailed in Volume 1. The rapid loss of so many people and community storytellers has erased much of the historical record of the First Nations and the stories of their heroes.

3. MULTI-ETHNIC COMMUNITIES
On a more positive note, I describe some of the early successes of the fur trade such as Kanaka Village at Fort Vancouver and Fort Ross on the California coast.

4. Lessons Not Yet Learned

I conclude with a discussion of what we still need to do to improve our management of the environment and economy and to protect cultural integrity and diversity.

Appendix A. Further Reading

I have read and reviewed hundreds of articles, theses, books and reports. I suggest a few of the best and most readable in Appendix A.

Acknowledgements

Many people have helped me along the way, and for that I give thanks.

A NOTE ON SPELLING: The confusion of spellings in this period adds a great deal to the challenge. From native languages to Cyrillic, Spanish, French, and English (and then retranslated) it becomes very confusing. I have used, to the best of my ability, the more common name. Names are usually left as encountered rather than standardized. Thus, Veniamin instead of Benjamin. To follow trails across time and languages is a challenge. Try following almost any of these characters and you will see what happens. Errors and confusion by earlier writers, and even the subjects themselves, reveal the rich diversity of our historical past.

CHAPTER 1

Geopolitics

The fur trade played a key role in the development and ultimate ownership of lands and resources on the west coast of North America. The struggle played out far from the capitals of power and shifted over time as rulers, governments, tribes, companies, and individuals struggled to get rich or merely to survive. The players in this complex conflict included Russia, Great Britain, America, Spain, Mexico, Hawaii, France, and the many First Nations whose lands it had been. At times, the fur trade was incredibly profitable and helped make some men and women very rich. The economic returns and taxes also helped support governments. But like most "gold rushes," it more often led to suffering, abuse, death, and despair for the sailors, trappers, and fur traders involved.

It was even worse for the many First Nations. Abuse and conflicts led to resistance and warfare that in some cases decimated local communities. More often it was not deliberate genocide, because the natives were used to collect the furs; but they had little or no resistance to introduced diseases. Beginning at first contact, a series of epidemics of smallpox, malaria, influenza, syphilis, and other diseases[1] swept through the region. These killed 50–90% of the people in some tribal groups. The intermittent fever (malaria) of the 1830s was introduced by a fur-trading vessel and spread by natives and Hudson Bay Company trappers. This fever was particularly destructive in Oregon and California and would remain to torment and kill many gold seekers in California during the Gold Rush. The many deaths led to social disruption in even the strongest tribal groups. Many tribes and tribelets were gone before they could be noted in a journal or placed on a map.

Violence against the natives for minor thefts was almost incomprehensible. The theft of a chisel, trap, or gun could lead to indiscriminate killing of many native people with little regard to guilt or innocence; a completely innocent village would often be shot up and many people would be killed. When Captain Gray left the trading port of Clayoquot in 1792, he ordered the destruction of the Nuu-chah-nulth village of Opitsaht. The attack was a retaliation for insults Gray thought he had endured and in response to a rumor of a plot against his men. The plot may have been real but could also have been a misunderstanding. The village of Opitsaht included 200 houses with much carved work and was about a half-mile in diameter. As John Boit said, "This fine village, the Work of Ages, was totally destroyed in a short time."

If trappers or traders were killed (often for cause) the response was horrific - intended as a lesson for all surrounding tribes. After a small group of the Clallum tribe killed four Hudson's Bay Company (HBC) men, Alexander McLeod killed 25+ natives, including women and children; shelled, and then burned the village. All of the tribe's property, stored food, and 46 canoes were destroyed. Two of the murderers were ultimately killed by others in the tribe who found them guilty of bringing tragedy to the tribe. Those suffering this abuse would often then avenge the transgression by attacking an innocent party of trappers or traders.

In 1829, Jedidiah Smith's expedition had 15 men killed on the Umqua River by the Kelawatsets after a chief was ill-treated when an axe was taken. Smith also met with the common reversal of native treatment of trappers. In 1826, Smith was treated very well by the Mojaves along the Colorado River but when he returned in 1827 his party was attacked and men were killed. In the interim, American trappers had mistreated the Mojave and they were seeking revenge.

Native sea otter hunters were often forced to work far from home, leaving the women, children, and elders to survive as best they could. The men might be gone for years, left on some rocky island to hunt for furs and survive if possible. Hunters were often killed by natives in the regions where they were hunting. They also faced great risk from severe storms. In some years, parties of more than 500 *baidarkas* set out upon a perilous journey following the line of the coast of Alaska for more than a thousand miles. In one year, one-third of the fleet was lost on the way. Shelikhov and others also took the excellent fur suits from the natives for their own use or sale and replaced them with Chinese cotton, ill-suited to the cold, wet conditions. In 1799, over 150 hunters were sickened and 100 died from eating poisonous shellfish—they did not encounter this shellfish poison at home. At Kukak, a village opposite Kodiak on the Alaska Peninsula, only 40 out of 1,000 men remained by 1805— just 4% surviving. Some died of disease but over the ten preceding years the Russians had taken the rest of the men away to hunt sea otters and few had returned.

There was almost no one to stand up for the native people. Once the Russian Orthodox Church arrived, it attempted to protect the natives, *kreol* (mixed race), and low status Russian workers. In California, the missionaries were more often a problem than a source of relief. The mission of San Diego de Alcalá was established in 1769, and the missionaries and soldiers so infuriated the Kumeyaay that they attacked and burned the mission in 1775. Resistance continued, but the more effective weapons and soldiers of the Spanish led to more and more natives held, often against their will, on the missions for labor and "conversion." Too often, the conversion was fatal.

While it was not intentional genocide, the results were the same, mirroring the results of the Jewish holocaust or the Palestinian *nakba*.[2] The virtual disappearance of many tribes made future settlement by Europeans and Americans - from California to Alaska - much easier.

In this book I try to provide a new view of the fur trade on the West Coast using the people involved to explore the cultural, political, and environmental consequences of the rush to collect furs—from sea otters to beaver. This new look is important because this period is too often neglected in history books. Educational programs and books about California history typically skip from a brief mention of the natives to a considerable amount about the missions and a little about the Californios (Spanish and Mexican ranchers), and then much more about the Gold Rush. With just a few minor changes in government response or markets we might speak Spanish or Russian on the west coast and Hawaii might be an independent nation or a former Russian, French or Spanish colony.

The seventy-five years from 1765–1840 cover the most critical period of the Fur War. The intensive sea otter slaughter led to their near total destruction by 1830. The beaver fell to the trappers next and many other fur bearers were mercilessly hunted. By 1840 the beaver trade had also collapsed with the advent of the silk top hat. In the same year the first wagon reached Oregon. The Russian fur outpost at Fort Ross was sold to John Sutter in 1841 and the exodus of the HBC from Oregon continued with the creation of Fort Victoria on Vancouver Island in 1843 and the boundary settlement of 1846.

THE FUR TRADE COMPETITORS

The major players in the competition for furs were the Russians, English, and Americans, with lesser but still important players from Hawaii, Spain, and Mexico. Many traders made bold and success-ful journeys, but others made terrible, costly blunders. Leadership problems in distant capitals played a major role in the final out-come. Over these 75 years the Russians had four leaders, the Spanish had five, the British two, the Americans eleven, Hawaii had three; and in just 25 years the Mexicans had more than thirty lead-ers. The fur trade contenders were also engaged in a series of wars involving shifting alliances over this period. Conflicts included the U.S. War of Independence, the Anglo-Dutch War, the Anglo-Spanish War, a series of costly Napoleonic wars, the Anglo-Russian war, the Spanish-Portuguese War, the War of the Oranges, the Haitian

Revolution, the War of 1812, three Russo-Turkish Wars, the Mexican War of Independence, the Portuguese Civil War, the Hawaiian wars of consolidation, a war between England and France, the Russian-Swedish War, and the First Opium War. These all diverted attention, resources, and people from the struggle for domination of the fur trade. At the same time, the fur trade added much needed money to the government coffers.

THE RUSSIANS

The development of the fur trade in the West began with adventurers from Russia after the sea otters of the western Pacific islands became scarce. In 1741 the Danish captain Vitus Bering and the German naturalist Georg Wilhelm Steller reached Alaska on the Russian ship *St. Peter*. They later shipwrecked and Bering died, but the survivors lived on sea cow meat and other mammals and eventually made it back to Kamchatka with 900 sea otter furs. Their fortunes were made and the "soft" gold rush was on.

Russian adventurers, *promyshlenniki*, sailed in increasing numbers to the Aleutian Islands and later, along the coast of Alaska and down to British Columbia and eventually California. From 1743 to the founding of the Russian-American Company in 1799, more than 150 private fur-trading and hunting voyages were made from Kamchatka to North America. These could be very profitable. In 1787 Erasim Gregorian Sin Izmailov returned to Kamchatka with furs worth 172,000 rubles. Although the market was almost entirely in China, Izmailov tried to throw the British off the trail by saying the otters were going to Japan. In total, these voyages brought back furs worth more than eight million silver rubles (perhaps $2 billion in today's dollars).

The *promyshlenniki* fur traders typically operated small ships[3] with crews of 40–70, often with many Siberian or Kamchatkan natives in the crew. The typical fur hunt lasted 2–6 years and required wintering over. The costs and profits were shared in a variety of ways. A typical cruise might offer a share to each Russian participant while the natives might get a half-share and the captain and navigator might get two shares or more. Shelikhov and the other companies typically charged everyone for the food they ate, the clothes they wore out, and more. By the end of a cruise the low-level workers might owe as much or more than they earned.

The *promyshlenniki* often treated the native Alaskans poorly and took women and others as hostages, workers, and sex partners. The local people bravely resisted the abuse of the Russians but faced insurmountable odds against guns, cannons, and ruthless traders. As conflicts with the native people intensified and more Russians were killed, retaliatory massacres took place.

The first permanent Russian settlement was made at Iliuliuk on the island of Unalaska on the north side of the Aleutians in 1768.[4] In 1784, the Shelikhovs set up the second permanent settlement at Three Saints Bay on Kodiak (Koniag) Island. Alexander A. Baranov moved the Kodiak Island settlement from Three Saints Bay to Pavlovsk after the earthquake and tsunami of 1786. In 1793 Baranov founded the port of Voskresensk in Chugach Bay, and then a settlement in Yakutat Bay in 1795.

Natalia Shelikhov and others lobbied tirelessly in St. Petersburg, and their work paid off when the Russian-American Company (RAC) was chartered in 1799. This provided a monopoly on the fur harvest from Alaska. In return, the RAC would provide a better organized and financially stable company to protect Russian national interests, much like the role the Hudson's Bay Company played for England. Alexander Baranov became the manager of the RAC in 1799 and started the New Archangel (later Sitka) settlement on Sitka Sound. In 1812, the RAC established Fort Ross on California's northern coast. A new rule was put in place in 1818 in an effort to reduce abuse of natives and workers; this required the governor of the RAC to be a naval officer. This did improve management in some respects but it diminished the innovation and enterprise of the company.

The Russian fur trade began in the Aleutians and worked its way east, north to the Pribilofs, and south from the Alaska coast as far as central Baja, California. Land furs, including beaver and fox, were collected; but the sea otter was the primary target. Much of the otter hunting was done by native people in specially constructed fur trade *baidarkas*,[5] with fleets of many hundred hunters. This method was later adopted by the Americans, often in cooperation with their Russian rivals.

The Russian settlements were severely hampered by the distance from the sources of supply. The overland journey from St. Petersburg to Okhotsk was 5,000 rugged miles, and then supplies had to cross the treacherous sea of Okhotsk and the North Pacific. The sea routes from the Russian port of Kronstadt were much longer (13,000 miles) but less dangerous. The sea route cost only one-third as much but took much longer. As a result, the Russian fur trading posts were almost always short on supplies. Despite efforts to suppress trade with foreigners, many supplies and ships came from America and England. Sixty-one of the seventy-two ships that visited Russian-America between 1787 and 1806, sailed from Boston. After the Imperial Russian government became alarmed by reports of American influence, the tsar enacted a *ukase*, prohibiting all foreign merchant ships from trading with Russian colonies beginning on September 4, 1821. This led to severe hardship in Alaska and more illegal trading. It was soon ignored and perhaps a million rubles in trade with foreigners was conducted from 1820–1825.

The low numbers of Russians in Alaska and along the southern coast was a persistent problem. By 1817, 450 to 500 *promyshlenniki*, a few Kamchatka natives and *kreols* (mixed race), and 26 sailors lived in sixteen settlements stretching from the western end of the Aleutian Chain at Adak to Russian America's southeastern terminus at Fort Ross. This was fewer people than in a typical coastal tribal village before contact. Some authors suggest there were never more than one thousand Russians in all of Russian-America—an area about as large as the Spanish territories stretching from Mexico to Peru. Efforts to recruit skilled settlers were rarely successful, although some Finnish, Baltic Germans, and European Russian workers were enticed to come to the north in later years. Efforts to send the mixed-race *kreols* to Russia for advanced education and training were met with limited success.

The Russian settlement at Fort Ross was started in 1812 to improve the supply situation. Agricultural production in California helped meet the need for food in the northern settlements. This became a multi-ethnic community that functioned well and was fondly remembered by many of the Russians. The Russians also interacted favorably with local natives and American traders, but not so well with the Spanish and then Mexican governments.

In 1822, the charter for the Russian-American Company permitted the Russians to conscript half of the adult native male population between 18 and 50 years of age to work for up to three years hunting sea otters. This undermined the north coast natives' ability to obtain food for their families.

In 1824, the Russo-American Treaty released Russian claims on the Pacific northwest coast of North America south of parallel 54°40' N to the United States. They maintained Russian rights to trade south of that latitude. In 1825, Russia and England agreed on a follow-up to the Russo-American Treaty that more clearly defined the boundaries between Russian-America and British claims and possessions in the Pacific northwest, again at parallel 54°40' N with associated rights and obligations concerning waters and ports in the region. The treaty established a vague division of coastal Russian interests and inland British interests north from 56°N, and led to conflicting interpretations of the meaning of the treaty's wording which later resulted in the Alaska boundary dispute between the United States, Canada, and Britain.

The treaty also included the right to navigation by British vessels for both commerce in the region and access to rivers crossing the designated boundary. These rights were exercised by the Hudson's Bay Company in 1834 but opposed by the Russian-American Company with warships and a blockade. The Dryad Affair led to a new RAC-HBC Agreement in 1839, with the RAC agreeing to lease the mainland portion of the region south of Cape Spencer at the entrance to Cross Sound, and the HBC promising to supply Russian-America with wheat, flour, salted meat, butter, and other supplies, all at a fixed price. In addition, the HBC waived its demand for payments for damages incurred during the Dryad Affair.

The Russian fur trade declined steadily but remained active. Russian fur hunting ships reached as far south as Baja California through 1830. The *Baikal* for example, was given permission to hunt from Mission San Luis Rey (San Diego County) to Todos Santos in 1826. They got 468 otter furs in three months. In 1842, Lavrentiy Zagoskin led a two-year expedition that investigated the Yukon, Kuskokwim, and Innoko River drainages. This led to more beaver being taken from these northern rivers. His research would later prove useful in the Yukon Gold Rush of 1896. A short-lived RAC fort and outposts were also established in Hawaii.

THE BRITISH

In 1776, Captain James Cook was provided with two ex-coal scows, *HMS Resolution*, and *HMS Discovery*, to continue exploration and survey work in the Pacific. Among the many men on the crew were a handful of Americans, including John Ledyard from Groton, Connecticut. On his third voyage, Cook sailed to the Northwest coast and reached Alaska in 1778. In May they found themselves surrounded by *baidarkas* at their anchorage in Snug Corner Cove on Prince William Sound. This area had not yet been traumatized by the *promyshlenniki*, and Captain Charles Clerke noted, "...*they are a very happy race.*" The crew also picked up some sea otter pelts and fur clothing to help them stay warm on the ship.

Captain Cook was killed in Hawaii in 1779 after a struggle triggered by the theft of a small boat from his ship. Lack of understanding and cultural awareness, and perhaps Cook's frustration after too many years at sea, led to the death of a native chief. This led to the assault that killed Cook. *HMS Endeavor* later fired on the native village, killing many Hawaiians. Cook's ships eventually reached Canton, China and found their sea otter pelts could bring $100 each. Sailors made dramatic profits on the sea otter skins they had picked up and used as blankets onboard the ship. The price for a prime hide represented more than two year's wages (the annual salary for a seaman in the Royal Navy was just £10, about $44). A good pelt was worth the equivalent of about $2,000 in today's dollars (if we consider the value in relation to salary it would be closer to $20,000). The potential for enormous profit was clear.

The first trading vessel on the coast, other than the Russians, was the British *Sea Otter* commanded by James Hanna in 1785. In his brief visit to the coast he obtained 560 pelts worth £7,000 in Canton. George Dixon and Nathaniel Portlock, also former members of Cook's expedition, became partners in the King George's Sound Company (1785) to pursue the fur trade. They sailed from England (with permission) with the *King George* and *Queen Charlotte*. They spent 1786 and 1787 exploring and trading on the northwest coast. British ships from India were also on the coast illegally. In 1787, Charles William Barkley sailed on the *Imperial Eagle* to the Northwest Coast from England via Hawaii under an Austrian flag. In 1787, the *Prince of Wales,* captained by James Colnett, and the sloop *Princess Royal,* with Captain James Duncan at the helm, also made it to the coast.

John Meares resigned from the British navy to form a company to trade furs on the northwest coast. His first trading voyage to Prince William's Sound, Alaska in 1786 was tragic, and many sailors died from scurvy. He returned to Nootka in 1788 with two ships under Portuguese flags. He "bought" some land and built a temporary trading post where his men constructed the *North West America*, the first ship built on Canada's west coast. In 1789, Meares formed a new company with other British entrepreneurs and sent three ships to build a permanent trading post at Nootka and to trade over a large area. They found Nootka occupied by a Spanish naval force which seized the British ships and crews.

The British were hampered by the monopoly of the East India Company and South Sea Company in selling furs and other goods in Canton. These bureaucracies added many costly burdens in fees and graft. The English ships were less efficient than the Americans, with larger crews and less skillful sailors. The British crew and officers were typically salaried instead of being shareholders like the Americans. This reduced hustle, increased cost, and reduced profits.

The English were more active in the inland fur trade, primarily after beaver. This effort was part of a larger goal to develop and protect British interests against both the Russians and Americans. In a February 1822 letter from HBC's Governing Committee to George Simpson, they wrote, "*The Russians are endeavoring to set up claims in the North West Coast of America as low as Latitude 51°, and we think it desirable to extend our trading posts as far to the West and North from Fraser's River in Caledonia, as may be practicable, if there appears any reasonable prospect of doing so profitably.*" The British did set up and manage a very effective group of trading posts for inland furs.

The American fur traders were seen as a threat by the British. In 1824, despite the joint occupation convention signed in 1818, both countries were anxious for clarification of their claims to the region. The British wanted to maintain their claim south to the Columbia River and the Americans wanted to push the British back to the 49th parallel or further north. To slow the American advance, George Simpson directed HBC trapping parties to clear fur-bearing animals from the Snake River region to create a "fur desert." This policy helped fuel growing antagonism between the Americans and British in the Northwest and was attacked in congressional testimony by William Slocum in 1837. The fur desert is an example of international political efforts using the destruction of natural resources as a political weapon. This decision would affect the environment and the local inhabitants: natives, British, and Americans, for generations yet unborn.

THE AMERICANS

John Ledyard was among the first Americans to the fur coast while he was serving as corporal of marines on Cook's momentous third voyage. He learned the value of sea otter fur in Canton. In 1783 he deserted from the British navy, returned to Connecticut, and published his journal about Cook's voyage. He clearly saw the future of the sea otter fur trade and tried very hard to start it by proposing a three-way trade similar to what ultimately developed. He exhausted every avenue of raising funds in the U.S. and Europe to no avail. In talks with Thomas Jefferson in Paris in 1784, Ledyard emphasized the potential value of the fur trade in the West and helped provide the spark that inspired Jefferson to send Lewis and Clark across the country to the Pacific.

After Ledyard's "Journal of Captain Cook's Last Voyage" was published in 1783, the word was out. *"It afterwords happened that skins which did not cost the purchaser sixpence sterling sold in China for 100 dollars. Neither did we purchase a quarter of the beaver and other furr skins we have done, and most certainly should have done had we known of meeting the opportunity of disposing of them to such an astonishing profit."*

Although several members of Cook's expedition returned to the coast first, Boston ships were not far behind. In 1787, *Columbia Rediviva* under John Kendrick and Robert Gray in *Lady Washington* left Boston for the fur coast. They traded, explored, spent much of the winter ashore, and encountered other traders, including the British operating under a Portuguese flag. With a load of otter pelts, *Columbia* set off for China in July 1789. When questioned by a Spanish vessel, this was nominally land and water owned by Spain at the time, the Americans claimed they were merely "explorers."

Captain Gray stopped in Hawaii, replenished his provisions, and then sailed to Canton where he sold 1,250 sea otter pelts for $21,400. It was in Hawaii that he met and became familiar with the native men, or *kanakas*, who would play an important role in the fur trade all along the west coast from Alaska to Baja California and far into the interior. Almost half of the money he made was needed to refit[6] the ship for the voyage home. With a modest cargo of tea and other goods, the *Columbia* reached Boston in 1790 and was the first American ship to circumnavigate the world.

Gray persuaded investors to finance another trip and he was back on the coast by 1792. In a confrontation with natives, he used the ship's cannons to kill two tribal leaders over a minor transgression. On this voyage, Gray wintered on the coast instead of going to Hawaii. His crew built a house, dubbed Fort Defiance, in Clayoquot Sound. They also built the first American vessel on the Northwest Coast. Gray concentrated on the southern part of the Northwest Coast, including the Columbia River, which he discovered and named.

This trip was successful, as were others, and soon many American ships were trading on the golden round from Boston to Hawaii to the Northwest coast to Canton, China to Boston. During the peak years (1790s-1810) the trade on the southern part of the Northwest Coast had so largely fallen into the hands of Boston traders that the Indians called all Americans *Boston men* to distinguish them from the British, known as *King George's men*. Nootka Sound was humorously referred to as a suburb of Boston. Trade increased rapidly along the full coast, wherever sea otters could be found. The Yankee traders found the native people to be shrewd and aggressive bargainers and eventually learned of the extensive inter-tribal trade that had been carried out before the Europeans arrived.

From 1790–1810 as many as 100 American ships reached the Northwest Coast. They were unparalleled in their success because they had strong financial incentives, total flexibility, efficient ships and skilled sailors. The most generous ship's owners split shares at 50% for the owner, 10% captain, 7% supercargo (sales agent), with the rest to be split between the mates and crew. In some cases, the captain and officers were also allowed to do some trading of their own and allowed some cargo space. Other captains only gained a share of 1–6% with the crew paid a flat rate and charged heavily for all supplies. Sometimes the shares applied only to the Canton sales, and in other cases they applied to all sales, including the Northwest Coast, China, and Boston.

The most noteworthy captains, like William Sturgis, respected the native people and traded for years without incident. Others treated the natives like animals and stole furs, held hostages for fur ransoms, shot people with no provocation, blasted and burned villages, and otherwise laid what would become fatal traps for future visitors.

The American ships covered the coast up to and past Russian holdings and far to the south along the Baja Coast and islands. As the northern otter populations declined under enormous hunting pressure, the ships moved further south. In 1804, Joseph O'Cain, with an American ship and Russian-supplied native hunters and *baidarkas,* cleaned the otters from the Baja Coast from Rosario to Santa Domingo. These southern otter pelts were not as good, but good enough. When O'Cain arrived back at Kodiak to meet the Russians he had 11,000 otter pelts his hunters had taken and 700 he had purchased and traded (illegally) from the Spanish. In 1839, otter pelts were still being collected as far south as Cedros Island (300 miles south of San Diego).

American statutory claims to the west coast were weak. The Russians, British and Spanish had been more active on the coast. America's claims included Gray's discovery of the Columbia River in 1792, Lewis and Clark's visit in 1805, and John Jacob Astor's funding of the construction of Fort Astoria in 1811. Astoria was sold to the British during the War of 1812 but was ultimately reclaimed by the Treaty of Ghent in 1818. But the Americans won by "eminent domain." Overland fur traders and settlers from America tilted the balance of the land conflict. A provisional Oregon government was established by local residents in 1841.

Further north, the American presence faded when the sea otter trade declined and sealing and whaling became more profitable. Interest in the North Coast and Alaska was modest even after the purchase of Alaska in 1867, until the discovery of gold in the Yukon (1896) changed everything.

THE SPANISH & MEXICANS

The Treaties of Tordesillas (1494) and Zaragoza (1529) divided the world between Spain and Portugal. This split gave what is now Mexico and the Americas almost entirely to Spain. Exploration and exploitation were well underway by the time the second treaty was signed. The first explorers of the West Coast were Spanish sailors with a Portuguese captain, Juan Rodríguez Cabrillo, in 1542. Spanish treasure ships also stopped and were shipwrecked in Baja and California during the late 1500s and 1600s. Sebastian Vizcaino sailed the coast in 1602 looking for Monterey Bay and other places where the Philippine treasure ships could find refuge. Japanese trading vessels also visited the southern coast.

Increasing activity by the English and Russian traders and explorers, led the Spanish to move north out of the Missions in Baja California. The Jesuit priest Miguel Venegas emphasized the Russian risk in a book published in Madrid in 1757, "...*the Russians in future voyages, will come down as low as Cape Blanco: and if California be abandoned by the Spaniards even as far as Cape San Lucas.*" San Diego was started as a Mission and military installation in 1769, with San Francisco following in 1776, and Santa Barbara in 1782. The primary goals were colonization; blocking the Russians, Americans and English; income for Spain and the church; and conversion of natives to the Catholic faith, not necessarily in that order.

To further affirm claims on the northern coast, the Spanish naval officer Esteban José Martínez arrived at Nootka Sound in May 1789 and built Fort San Miguel. When the British ship *Argonaut* arrived, a dispute arose between Captain Colnett (who had planned to build a British outpost in the same place) and Martínez. This led to the seizure of several British ships. When the news reached Europe, Britain requested compensation but the Spanish government refused. Both sides prepared for war and sought assistance from allies. The crisis was resolved peacefully but with difficulty through a set of three agreements, known collectively as the Nootka Conventions (1790–1794). Spain agreed to share some rights to settle along the Pacific coast but kept its main Pacific claims; this facilitated British expansion since Spain no longer played a role north of California.

Despite the efforts of Vicente Vasadre, the Spanish failed to understand the potential value of furs. Bureaucracy raised its ugly head and the fur trade on the coast went underground; in California it was almost all illegal. In fact, a royal *cedula* of 1785 forbade all private trade in furs. American traders (smugglers) were particularly active and found willing customers. They tormented the Spanish administration from 1797–1821, and later, the Mexican government. The American ships were well led and armed and felt little fear of the Spanish. In a particularly bold move, the *Lelia Byrd* reached San Diego Bay after buying many furs illegally along the Baja coast in 1803. The *commandante* in San Diego was incensed when the Americans bought still more illegal furs in San Diego. He tried to keep the ship in port, but the *Leila Bird* exchanged cannon fire with Fort Guijarros on Point Loma and escaped to sea unharmed.

Spain eventually transferred many of its historic territorial claims to the United States in the Adams-Onís Treaty of 1819. Spain continued to control present-day California until 1821, when Mexico proclaimed independence on September 27. Mexican independence changed things yet again. Land grants to officers enabled a lucky few to become ranchers and men of means. In addition, the mission system had almost 400,000 cattle, 320,000 sheep, and 60,000 horses by 1830. In 1833, a new governor for California, Jose Figueroa, brought new energy to the area and accelerated the privatization of mission lands. In response, the missions slaughtered more than 100,000 cattle in 1834 to sell the hides and tallow, cashing out before privatization.

American ships transported most of the hides, and along with them, a few furs. Richard Henry Dana was in California in 1835 at the peak of the cowhide trade (see *Two Years Before the Mast*). He employed a mixed group of workers and noted in passing that twelve Hawaiians were living in a huge Russian bread oven at the beach in San Diego. Point Loma had a large hide preparation area and much firewood was consumed in drying the hides. This is probably when the pine trees were stripped from the point. Hides were the currency of exchange for a time and became known as "California banknotes." The maritime trade brought in foreigners and led to settlement pressure from Americans. Some jumped ship, became Catholic, took up Mexican citizenship, and married local women.

By the 1830s a steamship (the *Beaver*) was working the coast out of Astoria, Oregon for the HBC. It was trading on the Hawaii, NW coast, and Southern California routes along with sailing ships. Much trade was also going from Hawaii to China, but diseases from Asia were brought east as well.

THE HAWAIIAN KINGDOMS

Fur trade ships and explorers from all nations stopped to get water, food, companionship, and supplies in Hawaii, often paying a high price. The fur ships and traders also hired *kanakas* to work on ships and land operations throughout the fur lands. Women were sometimes romanced, purchased, or abducted for on-board exploitation. Trading companies established bases in Hawaii, most on the main island at Honolulu and on Oahu, but there were also short-lived Russian outposts on Oahu and Kauai.

Beginning in 1795, King Kamehameha consolidated power in a series of wars, and by 1810 he was the undisputed leader of Hawaii. The men, ships, and armaments of the fur trade were intimately involved in the tribal wars. Cannons, muskets, and sailing ships changed the balance of power and increased the lethality of war. Diseases including venereal disease, measles, and smallpox were brought to Hawaii. Communities that had once been very healthful were beset with death and disfiguring diseases. When King Kamehameha II (*Kalaninui kua Liholiho i ke kapu 'Iolani*) traveled to

England in 1824 on a whaling ship, one of his goals was to arrange for British protection for his kingdom. His death from the measles in London limited the negotiations and further destabilized the political situation at home when Kamehameha III. assumed the throne at age 10.

CHANGES IN THE LAND AND SEA

The remarkable Steller's sea cow was extinct within 27 years of the first Russian fur trade in Alaska. The removal of the beaver and otters initiated profound changes in the rivers and coastal waters, as ecosystem function and structure were radically changed (see more in Chapter 4 of Volume 1: *Fur War*). Increasing visits by ships led to tree cutting for masts, spars, ship repair, and firewood. Cattle and horse drives spread weed seeds across hundreds of new miles of trail. In California, hundreds of thousands of cattle were wild and uncounted. In the drought of 1828–29 an estimated 40,000 mission livestock starved to death. They devastated the rangeland but became food for a much-enlarged grizzly bear population. No market for the meat existed but the hides were worth exporting and were collected, dried, baled, and shipped. More than 1.25 million hides were shipped from California between 1820 and 1845. Tallow was also collected and shipped. Many of the fur traders switched to carrying Hawaiian sandalwood to China after the sea otter populations were decimated. Traders played off the rivalry among chiefs to get the best prices. Large profits were made, and by 1830 the trade in sandalwood had completely collapsed as the best trees were all gone.

AND THE WINNER IS...

America clearly won while everyone else lost. The natives lost the most as the stories of these individuals and details about the community and tribal level in Volume 1 showed. The First Nations and international traders and explorers pursued different strategies, but most decisions were made on the ground by the remarkable people you will read about in the following chapter. As the old Chinese proverb puts it, "The mountains are high and the emperor is far away." Many critical actions were decided upon by the people who were on the coast.

The US Army Barracks look down on the Hudson's Bay Company Fort Vancouver in this 1854 lithograph by Gustavas Sohon. Most HBC operations had already shifted to Fort Victoria. They would leave for good in 1860.

CHAPTER 2

The People

The remarkable people who contested for power, money, and survival included heroes, oligarchs, scoundrels, survivors, psychopaths, and observers. The choice of the title "Tenacity" reflects the often seemingly impossible odds these individuals overcame. Physical and mental toughness and indomitable will contributed to their survival and their stories. They are arranged by date of birth in each group. Some, as you will see, were involved for a short time, while others were active for several decades. Many, like William Sturgis, led exemplary lives and deserve much greater recognition.

As you read, consider yourself in their shoes. Could you command a ship around the world at the age of nineteen with twenty-two men (most of them older than you) as crew? Could you survive being constantly wet and cold for weeks at a time? Could you hike, ride, and camp in the snow for five months every year while caring for several children under the age of 15, preparing food, skinning beaver, and perhaps giving birth and nursing an infant? Could you continue after nine out of ten people in your family and village died of new diseases? Could you endure a winter shipwreck in Alaska, salvage the wreckage, and build a new vessel? Could you survive a 14-month drift across the north Pacific only to shipwreck on the coast — and be made a slave?

NOTE:
The people of the fur trade are arranged by category but there are overlaps. Dates of native birth and deaths are uncertain; most of the

others are well-reported but inconsistent. Exhaustive searches provided images for most of the key people. Where no original image could be found the search was made for descendants or relatives. Failing that, an image was developed based on names, ethnicity, and places. Such images are indicated by the symbol ❖.

HEROES

K'ALYÁAN, SKILLFUL TLINGIT WAR CHIEF

K'alyáan[1] was probably born about 1775. We don't know about K'alyáan's childhood, but the early years for a future chief would be demanding and hard. Young men were rigorously trained for battle. He must have already proved himself to be a strong warrior to play a leadership role in the wars with the Russians at Sitka. The Russians under Baranov had arrived about 1795. They were unable to negotiate use of the hill where the village was located, but concluded a treaty of sorts with the Kiks.ádi band of Tlingit before starting construction in 1799 of a fort a short distance away they called St. Mikhailovskii.

Relations soon soured after the Russians and their allies from Fort St. Mikhailovskii killed Chief Kuiu k̲wáan, his wife, and children. They also kept a nephew of another chief in chains for a minor theft. The Aleuts working for the Russians were plundering native graves and taking stores of food. Captain Sturgis noted that the Russian *promlysenniki* and Aleuts often killed natives with little or no provocation. Revenge was not long in coming, and in 1802, after Ivan Urbanova's trade party (about 190 Aleuts) and a small work group under Alexey Evglevsky and Alexey Baturin left the fort, there were probably 26 Russians, six Americans (serving on Russian

K'alyáan

ships), 20–30 Koniag, and around fifty women and children at the fort.

The Tlingit had asked the Russians to leave, but their request was ignored. The Tlingit sought help from their allies and then attacked simultaneously from the forest and the sea.[2] Many of their allies had arrived in battle canoes. K'alyáan played a key role in the assault. The armed crowd of several hundred quickly overran the fort and killed more than twenty men. The women and children were captured to be sold for slaves. The two hunting parties were both later surrounded and attacked, and many were killed.

Several days after the attack, two American ships and a British ship arrived and picked up a few survivors. Henry Barber, skipper of the British *Unicorn*, seized two Tlingit chiefs, including K'alyáan, for ransom. If they weren't ransomed with furs and the return of the survivors of the attack, the chiefs would be hung. To clarify his intent, he shot several canoes to pieces with cannon fire, killing many natives. Eventually Barber ended up with 28 survivors—8 men, 17 women, and 3 children, and the penalty of many furs was paid. Barber kept the furs as a fee for service.

Expecting the Russians would return, K'alyáan heeded the prophetic visionary Shaman Stoonookw's and rallied the clans to construct a fort. This was built of many layers of green sapling and logs and named Shís'gi Noow. The captured cannon were well placed and the fort was nearly impregnable. It was placed near shoal water to prevent the Russians from moving the *Neva* and her cannon too close.

Baranov bided his time and gathered his sailors, workers, and Aleut and Alutiiq hunters. With added money and supplies from successful fur trading he set out in the fall of 1804 to retake Sitka. Baranov's war party from Kodiak met Commander Urey Lisianskii and the *Neva* in Port Krestof and sailed into Sitka Sound on September 28th. The Tlingit in the fort used delaying tactics to hamper the Russian advance, expecting that their clan allies were on their way. When their allies did not arrive, the shamans reported that they had no vision of reinforcements arriving and that there was a "dark force" in the future.

The Russians landed in front of the fort on the first of October 1804. Baranov led the assault of Russians with 400 Aleut and Alutiiq natives. Ten were killed and 26 wounded after the Tlingit waited until the Russians came very close before opening fire. The Aleut and Alutiiq hunters broke and ran for their *baidarkas*. K'alyáan and an elite group of Tlingit warriors attacked the Russian's right flank and Baranov was shot in the chest. Timely cannon fire from the *Neva* prevented the destruction of the entire Russian landing party. The Tlingit had defeated the Russians again.

Unfortunately for the Tlingit, their gunpowder was lost in an explosion of a canoe even before the battle began; without sufficient gunpowder they couldn't defend their fort effectively. Although the *Neva*'s cannon did little damage to the fort, the Kiks.ádi realized they were beaten. They stalled and negotiated until slipping away in the night. They would not be back to Sitka for 18 years.

In 1805, K'alyáan visited Sitka and attempted to negotiate a peace but was not successful. The Tlingit rebuilt an abandoned fort to the south on Point Craven. From here they could see any canoe or ship heading toward Sitka and warn them to stay away. Their blockade was effective, and fewer and fewer boats attempted to reach Sitka. This hurt Russian trade but helped the Americans, who soon established a trading operation at Trader's Bay across from the Tlingit fort. Natives from around southeast Alaska could then trade with the Americans instead of the Russians. This worked well because the Americans would pay more and were willing to sell firearms, lead, and gun powder. One of the Russians grumbled that the Tlingit were better armed than they were. This further under-mined Russian control of the southern coast. The Tlingit continued to attack isolated groups of Russian fur hunters.

The Tlingit were never defeated. The power of the Tlingit tribes enabled them to get premium prices for their furs, sometimes three times the price paid to Koniag or Aleut hunters. In 1818, when

K'alyáan was painted by Mikhail Tikhanov, he appears to be of middle age. No record of his death is available, but it is likely that he succumbed to the flu or measles epidemic brought by the *Finlandia* in 1819.

In the 1880s, the new Chief Katlian[3] negotiated a payment of $200 each for five Kiks.ádi lost when a schooner sank in the Bering Sea. He succeeded in getting an award but lawyers and others took all the money and none reached the Tlingit families. They were furious and threatened trouble, but the chief helped calm the waters. There is a Katlian Bay north of Sitka that may once have been the site of the Kiks.ádi summer village of Chief K'alyáan.

THE HIEROMONK MAKARII, ADVOCATE FOR THE NATIVE PEOPLE

Alaskan natives were treated better by the Russian Orthodox Church than by the fur traders. When natives and workers were mistreated, the clergy were usually the first and only people to come to their defense. But they didn't have much power, as many clergy were illiterate themselves and poorly supplied; they spent much of their time meeting their own needs for daily living. Eventually the church became a powerful, if not always effective, check on the brutal treatment of both natives and common laborers.

Hieromonk[4] Makarii was a hero when it came to standing up for

the disadvantaged. He was born a serf somewhere around 1770, and he received religious training in Karelia at the Konevskii Monastery on Konevets Island in the western part of Lake Ladoga (not far from St. Petersburg). He reached Alaska in 1794 and put his ship in at Unalaska, where the priests baptized more than 100 people. On September 24,

Hieromonk Makarii

1794, the mission reached St. Paul, Kodiak Island. Makarii was dispatched with an interpreter to the Unalaska region north of the Aleutian Islands in the summer of 1795, and also traveled to a few islands, including Unga and Akun. He reached Unalaska on the *Phoenix* on May 25, 1795.

Wherever Makarii stopped, he performed the sacraments of baptism, confirmation, and marriage. He was observant, and by the time he reached Unalaska he realized the treatment of the natives by the Russians of the Golikov-Shelikhov Company was appalling. As a former serf who had come as a volunteer to serve the natives and "spread the Word" this was unacceptable. In 1796, Hieromonk Makarii sent a letter of complaint westward. It was quite specific as to both the nature of the abuses and who was carrying them out:

"They send out the men to hunt sea otter from the earliest spring, healthy or ailing, it does not matter. Some of those who are ill, die en route. They keep the men hunting until fall and there is no time to put up food for themselves and their families, nor get materials for clothing. They starve to death and suffer from cold because of lack of clothing. When they are subjected to severe floggings, they commit suicide. If an Aleut does not bring in plenty of fox pelts, they strip him and pin him to the ground and beat him with sinew cords, all the time chanting that 'we do not tolerate laziness.'"

According to a report Makarii submitted to Bishop Veniamin of Irkutsk in 1797, there were fifty settlements in the eastern Aleutians in which 2,472 persons (1,149 men and 1,323 women) were baptized. Makarii arranged transport back to Russia with members of a rival fur trade company, the Kiselev Brothers Company. He and six Unangax *toions* (leaders) set out, intending to present their complaints of mistreatment to government officials in Okhotsk. The Okhotsk office did not take Makarii seriously and they attempted to detain him; no doubt with the goal of protecting the rich fur companies. So Makarii took his complaint to the Bishop of Irkutsk and Nerchinsk. After meeting with officials, he was told to take his appeal directly to Tsarina Katherine.

Makarii was a monastic without title and would have had few sources of financial support. Worse yet, he probably lacked authority to travel and may well have departed his post in Alaska without proper authorization. This journey revealed both his resourcefulness and determination. The long and dangerous journey was difficult for the *toions*; one died in the Kurils and two returned home from the islands after falling ill. However, three men—Ielisei Popachev, Nikolai Lukanin, and Nikifor Svin'in, continued on and two made it to St. Petersburg alive in the spring of 1798. This followed an arduous journey of more than 7,000 miles. While they were making their way across Eurasia to St. Petersburg, Katherine, who had respected native people, died, and her son Paul assumed the throne. The new monarch was heavily lobbied by the Shelikhov fur company and was not sympathetic to the pleas of the natives. Instead, Makarii was rebuked for leaving his post. The *toions* interceded on his behalf to minimize his punishment. Makarii remained vocal in his defense of the native people and his criticism of the *promyshlenniki*. He refused to recognize the authority of the freshly appointed Bishop Ioasaf, whom he accused of turning his back on the natives and being motivated by greed.

On their return journey eastward, Lukanin and Svin'in died on the demanding overland route. Makarii and Bishop Ioasaf were lost in the shipwreck of the *Phoenix* in 1799 before reaching the colony. Their deaths temporarily drove the mission into quiescence, but Makarii's testimony probably helped support the effort to create the Russian-American Company and to add demands supporting better treatment of the native people.

WILLIAM F. STURGIS, A MOST REMARKABLE MAN

One of the most successful and enterprising men of the fur trade on the west coast was born in Barnstable, Massachusetts to Hannah Mills and Captain William E. Sturgis in 1782. William Jr. joined the counting house of his uncle Russell Sturgis at the age of 14. A year and a half later William started working with James and

Thomas Handasyd Perkins' maritime fur trade between the Pacific Northwest coast and China. Sturgis received a good education and mastered celestial navigation under the tutelage of Osgood Carlton. When his father was killed by pirates in 1797, Sturgis, at age 15, went to sea in exchange for seven dollars a month as sailor and assistant trader on the *Eliza* under Captain James Rowan. They were bound for the Northwest Coast and his first contact with the first nations.

William Sturgis proved adept at trading and, unlike many of his contemporaries, he respected the natives and worked hard to

learn their languages and customs. From the very beginning he established his reputation as an honest trader who treated the native people well. He also had the opportunity to demonstrate his leadership skills. At Kaigani, the crew of the *Ulysses* had mutinied to protest the cruel treatment they received from Captain David Lamb.

William F. Sturgis

Captain Rowan and the captain of a third ship managed to talk the mutineers down without violence but the *Ulysses* was left without a navigator or mate. Sturgis accepted the difficult task of working with this detested and feared captain as chief mate, navigator, and trading assistant in return for a good salary and percentage of the profit—a bold and courageous move for a 17-year-old, like many he would make throughout his life. The cruise and trading were successful and the *Ulysses* continued to Canton, where they met the *Eliza*. Sturgis rejoined the *Eliza* and reached Boston in 1800, after more than two years at sea.

His next position was as mate for Captain Charles Derby on the *Caroline*. Derby was ill when they left port and as he became more and more incapacitated Sturgis became the de facto captain. Derby's illness worsened and he officially transferred command to

Sturgis, left the ship, and died in Hawaii. Now Captain Sturgis, age 19, led a cruise that was a complete success. This was followed by a 1803–1804 voyage on the *Catherine* where he managed to collect 4,900 sea otter skins. With sales that year in Canton at $50 each, this would be a gross return of $245,000 for a cruise costing perhaps $30,000–40,000. These voyages made it clear that he was both an excellent commander and trader. One of his voyages netted Sturgis the profit from more than 6,000 sea otter skins.

Sturgis was also an innovator and marketing genius who listened to his customers. In 1802, at the suggestion of native friends, Sturgis sent home a fine ermine (a weasel with white fur in winter) pelt known as a *click* by the local tribes. He asked his company to buy as many as possible at the annual Leipsic, Delaware fur fair. About 5,000 were procured and taken to the coast in 1804. The clicks were highly valued and Sturgis managed to purchase 560 prime sea-otter skins worth $50 each in Canton for five ermine skins each, costing less than 30 cents apiece. He succeeded in trading all of his ermines at the same rate. Others tried to match him later, but in less than two years one hundred clicks wouldn't buy a single otter skin.

After returning to Boston, the ship was refitted and returned to the coast for another successful cruise, this time returning in 1806. In that same year his command was increased to a new ship, the *Atahualpa*, and supervision of two other ships. Sturgis was lucky to hit the coast at the peak of the sea otter harvest and with good prices in China. He returned to Boston in June 1808, completing his fourth round-the-world voyage, just 26 years old.

In 1809, Captain Sturgis commanded the *Atahualpa* on a trip direct to Canton with 300,000 Spanish dollars for trade. They were attacked by Chinese pirates while moored at Macau Road, but Sturgis managed to get the ship underway and fought off the pirates using four small cannons he had brought on board (against the wishes of the ship's owner). They fought the pirates off long enough to sail within protection of the Portuguese harbor guns. The pirates were captured and their commander, Apootsae, was killed by the Chinese authorities.

In 1810, Sturgis returned to Boston with a now substantial fortune. On shore to stay, he married Elizabeth M. Davis. They had one son, who unfortunately was later killed in a sailing accident, and five daughters. Sturgis formed a trading partnership with John Bryant as Bryant & Sturgis. From 1810 to 1850 more than half of the trade carried on between the Pacific Northwest coast and China was under their direction. His firm controlled an even larger part of the trade to California including much of the cowhide trade. Richard Henry Dana, author of *Two Years Before the Mast*, sailed on a Bryant and Sturgis ship.

Sturgis established a remarkable record. His fair-trading practices earned him many friends in the native communities and he never had to suffer or resort to violence; it was one of his proudest achievements. He was a capable commander who was well regarded by his crews and managed many successful round-the-world voyages. As an owner, he was careful with his budgets and expenses and tried hard to ensure good working conditions for the crews of his ships. Dana remarked on the care and consideration of this owner, who visited the ship before it sailed and told the sailors what to expect and what to bring with them.

Captain Sturgis was notable for his successful interactions with many tribes. He rightly pointed out that the violence against fur ships on the Northwest Coast was commonly the result of cruel and often vicious treatment of the native communities by ship captains operating with greed, terror, and violence. This, in many cases, led to revenge being taken on the next ship in — often innocent. He also argued that the coast should be owned and governed by the native people. *"If, by negotiation, the whole extent of the coast from Mendocino in latitude 40, to Prince William Sound, latitude 60, could be left in quiet possession of the native and rightful proprietors of the soil, it would be better for the civilized world, even in a political point of view, to say nothing of these moral considerations..."*—Editorial letter to the newspaper in Boston, 1822. Sturgis always took a keen interest in the Oregon question, and published several articles and pamphlets in favor of the American claim. His familiarity with the coast led Sturgis to propose the border line for the U.S./Canada boundary that was eventually adopted.

Although a wealthy man, he lived in near-spartan simplicity. His dress was always simple and unpretentious, his furniture and trappings without ostentation. Sturgis was elected to the Massachusetts Legislature in 1814 and he would serve as a member of the Massachusetts House and Senate much of the time for more than 30 years. Too honorable to be a successful politician, Sturgis was nevertheless a good representative of the people. On one occasion a learned member of the assembly endeavored to confuse him with a string of Latin and Greek quotations, to which Mr. Sturgis, who was self-educated beyond the point attained by most college graduates, replied in a native language of the Northwest Coast. He said his comments were quite as much to the point, and doubtless as intelligible and convincing to most of those present as the classical quotations they had just heard.

Dying in 1863 after 81 years of adventure and service, Sturgis donated his childhood home to become the Barnstable Public Library. Now known as the Sturgis Library, it holds a collection of his papers. The records of Bryant & Sturgis are preserved at the Bryant Library of the Harvard Business School.

WICKANINNISH, KING OF THE TLA-O-QUI-AHT

Chief Wickaninnish[5] was born about 1750, probably to a royal family, with his mother being from a nearby tribe. His early years are a mystery but it is likely he grew up in Opitsaht and the other villages on the yearly rounds of Clayoquot Sound. Wickaninnish was described as being tall (over 6 feet), athletic, and active but tending to be fat. He was a skilled leader, whaler, and warrior. Wickaninnish was an effective and aggressive chief, and consolidated power over a large area through brutal raids. By the time of the fur trade, the community of Opitsaht was estimated to have about 4,000 people[6] and Wickaninnish said his control extended over 13,000 people. A

Chief Wickaninnish

visitor described his house as 40 by 80 feet and 12 feet high.

The first recorded trades of the Tla-o-qui-aht[7] were made with the British Captain John Meares in 1788. Meares noted, *"There lived the chief in a state of magnificence much superior to any of his neighbours, both loved and dreaded by other chiefs."* Meares and later visitors were astonished by the size and finish of the buildings on Clayoqout Sound. While Meares was visiting with the neighboring Chief Maquinna, Wickaninnish paddled in for a visit. He later piloted Meare's ship to his village on Clayoquot Sound. Meares presented Wickaninnish with a number of gifts and received 50 large sea otter pelts in return. Wickaninnish also managed to obtain a musket, pistol, powder, and ball. He would later make great use of European weapons. In addition to direct fur trading, Wickaninnish claimed a role as middleman between the Europeans and other tribal groups. Hopeful traders arrived at other villages only to find that Wickaninnish's agents had already stripped them of furs.

In 1789, the Spanish captain Esteban José Martinez arrived and built a small fort on the rocky point at Friendly Cove, Nootka Sound. On June 6th of that same year, Wickaninnish arrived in style from Clayoquot for a visit after returning from a raid with slaves, otter skins, and other spoils in tow. Martinez traded with the Tla-o-qui-aht and all went well. It is noted that Martinez bought an 8-year-old slave girl. The Spanish left for the winter but returned in April 1790. Francisco de Eliza was tasked with maintaining the little fort at Friendly Cove to support Spanish claims. His ships also explored the area. In one case, Wickaninnish noticed the trouble the Spanish ships were having when trying to maneuver, and he directed his men to use their seagoing canoes to tow the Spanish ship into position. Trading again went well, although the cost of furs was going up and requests for favors were increasing. One of the Spaniards described Wickaninnish at this time as a heavy man with a serious, good face, about 40 years of age.

In October of 1790, British captain James Colnett arrived on the coast with his ship in distress. He soon got into further trouble with lost boats, missing men, and general confusion. Colnett suspected the Tla-o-qui-aht had taken his boats and took one of the king's brothers hostage. Tensions were high but eventually calmed after the Spanish and survivors of Colnett's boats confirmed the stories the natives had told Colnett. Wickaninnish was angered by this mistreatment and launched a night raid on the ship. Quick reaction by the crew and the ship's cannons kept them off, but one of the king's brothers was killed and the village was bombarded. Trading resumed, but with caution.

In March of 1791, the Spaniards returned to explore and were well received. Eighty canoes arrived to welcome the *San Carlos*. The king was now described as being about 50 years old, and fat but robust. Relations were good and Francisco de Eliza described an amazing show put on in Wickaninnish's home, including an estimated 600 singers. Wickaninnish's children later had dinner on Eliza's ship. A big celebration was made for the birth of a child. A tenuous peace was maintained with Maquinna, whose favorite wife came from Wickaninnish's family. Wickaninnish had a 12-year-old son who became eligible to lead a whaling boat.

Relations deteriorated with the arrival of the Americans, Robert Gray and John Kendrick. They built a small outpost about three miles from Opitsaht called Fort Defiance, complete with six cannons. Kendrick claimed he had "purchased" 300+ square miles of Clayoquot Sound, centered on Opitsaht, from Wickaninnish for trade goods (firearms and powder). They added a two-story log building to the fort and built a small sloop using a prefabricated frame. The Tla-o-qui-aht were curious about the ship-building and brought food and wood for the carpenters.

Gray killed two natives who had been making threatening sounds and gestures near his ship. After a purported plot to seize the ship was uncovered, Captain Gray had Opitsaht destroyed by firing on it and burning it. John Boit, the sixteen-year-old fifth mate, described the tragic scene as a fine village of more than 200 homes, boats, equipment and food were burned.

John Kendrick pre-purchased furs to thwart British traders; this resulted in a tragedy in 1792 when Captain William Brown of the *Butterworth* became infuriated by the sharp trading practices and high prices for furs. In frustration, he had his crew seize furs, literally stripping them from the native people. Brown himself pointed a gun at Wickaninnish and demanded more furs. After the Tla-o-qui-aht killed a sailor in revenge, trading stopped. Brown seized nine natives, whipped them, and tossed them into the sea for target practice. Four chiefs were killed, including another of Wickaninnish's brothers. In May 1793, when American trader Josiah Roberts arrived in Clayoquot Sound on the *Jefferson*, Wickaninnish would only agree to trade with the Americans if two of the ship's officers remained ashore as hostages while trading took place aboard ship. Anger continued to build in 1794 when Josiah Roberts destroyed the seasonal village of Sechart with swivel guns after one of his men was killed.

In 1793–1794, the two powerful chiefs, Wickaninnish and Maquinna, got into a conflict over the marriage plans of their children. As tempers flared, Maquinna asked the Spanish for protection. Eventually it was apparently resolved and Wickaninnish's son married Maquinna's daughter.

Wickaninnish now had 200 muskets and two barrels of powder and was not afraid to use them. In August 1794, Wickaninnish visited a Spanish ship after another successful raid. More than 70 people had been killed and many slaves and goods had been taken and were displayed. The Spanish bought several slaves in order to free them.

In 1795, Captain Charles Bishop arrived from the north on the *Ruby* after a visit with Maquinna. Trading went well and to the captain's surprise, Wickaninnish asked if the ship was for sale. It wasn't, but Wickaninnish gave Bishop a down-payment for the purchase of a 54-foot ship with six carriage guns. Apparently it never arrived. In October, Wickaninnish was called away by the death of Maquinna (whose successor would also be named Maquinna). In 1803, when the *Boston* was taken by Maquinna, Wickaninnish tried to buy the armorer John R. Jewitt, but was unable to make a deal.

We next hear of Wickaninnish and Opitsaht in May of 1813. After further abuses by American and British ships, the anger of the Tla-o-qui-aht had grown. At least two of Wickaninnish's brothers had been killed by traders, his villages had been bombarded and destroyed, and he himself had been mistreated. The most recent insult had been the taking of a dozen hunters by Captain George Eayres. He left them on the Farallon Islands off San Francisco to hunt seals, and never returned to pick them up. Only two of the twelve survived the 800-mile journey home and swore they would take revenge.

The arrival of the *Tonquin* and Captain Thorn provided the spark needed for an attack. Thorn was a martinet—abusive, quick to temper, and demeaning toward natives. He lost his temper and ended an attempt to bargain with an important chief by rubbing his face in the fur. Wickaninnish had had enough. They boarded the vessel with concealed weapons and on command took the ship killing most of the crew. The next day the ship blew up, killing and maiming many people involved in stripping the ship. The blast may have been touched off by Lewis, the wounded armorer, hiding below deck, or by accident. Only the interpreter Lamayzie was left alive and made a slave. He eventually reached Astoria to tell the story.

The Nuu-chah-nulth continued to suffer from diseases and ill-treatment. A trading ship that had been selling alcohol and taking native women was captured and destroyed in 1864. The innocent paid with their lives yet again as the largest single naval attack in British Columbia history destroyed nine Ahousat villages. The Royal Navy bombardment killed one hundred[8] men, 69 canoes were destroyed, and houses, equipment and supplies were burned. A land assault killed more native men.

Today, the Tla-o-qui-aht have a registered population of more than 1,000 members. Most live off the reservation but the tribe still occupies three main sites: TyHistanis, Opitsaht, and Esowista. The language, Nuučaan'uɬ, is endangered with only 20 to 30 fluent speakers, but efforts are underway to preserve and promote the traditional language. Efforts have also been made to protect the environment and Clayoquot Sound was designated a UNESCO Biosphere Reserve in May of 2000.

JOHN BOIT, JR., CAPTAIN/JOURNALIST/POET/ADVENTURER

John Boit, Jr. was born on October 15, 1774 in Boston to John and Sarah Boit. It is believed he attended the Boston Latin School. He

wrote well and kept journals of his adventures that were more open and honest than most. He was fond of literature and did a great deal of reading on his long voyages. He also had a taste for poetry and in addition to copying verses in his logbooks, he wrote many lines of his own.

In 1787, the American ships *Columbia Rediviva*[9] (Capt. Kendrick) and the *Lady Washington* (Capt. Gray) departed for the

Captain John Boit, Jr.   Northwest Coast. They would eventually trade ships. Kendrick stayed while Gray went on to Canton and then returned to Boston. This helped mark the birth of the highly profitable triangular Golden Round for ships, from Boston to the Northwest Coast, then (Hawaii) on to Canton and back to Boston. The *Columbia* returned to Boston in August 1790, becoming the first American-flagged ship to circumnavigate the globe. This voyage was not very profitable, but the merchants immediately launched a second voyage of the *Columbia* with Captain Gray, in September of 1790.

John Boit, Jr., age 16, was onboard. He had begged his father and brother-in-law to let him go on the *Columbia*; they could do this because they were fitting out the ship. They decided not to permit him to go as a seaman, where he might be picked on, and instead had him appointed as fifth mate.[10] What Captain Gray thought of this we can only imagine, but John turned out to be a good sailor and leader.

We get a good sense of the man through his notes. One of my favorites is from April 23, 1791: *"Between the hours of three and four p.m. departed this life our dear friend Nancy the Goat, having been the Captain's companion on a former voyage round the Globe; but her spirited disposition for adventure led her to undertake a second voyage of circumnavigation. But the various changes of climate, and sudden transition from the Polar colds to the Tropical heats of the Torrid Zone, proved too much for a constitution naturally delicate. At 5 pm committed her body to the deep. She was lamented by those who got a share of her milk!"*

The sloop *Union*

The trading went reasonably well but Gray was quick to anger and did not hesitate to fire upon natives. There was violence on both sides, and on January 27, 1792, Gray ordered Boit to punish the natives. *"I am sorry to be under the necessity of remarking that this day I was sent, with three boats all well man'd and arm'd, to destroy the village of Opitsatah. It was a Command I was no ways tenacious of, and am grieved to think Capt. Gray shou'd let his passions go so far. This village was about half a mile in diameter, and contained upwards of 200 Houses, generally well built for Indians; every door that you enter'd was in resemblance to a human and Beast's head, the passage being through the mouth. Besides which there was much more carved work about the dwellings some of which was by no means inelegant. This fine village, the work of Ages, was in a short time totally destroy'd."*

Also on this trip, Gray explored the Columbia River (named after his ship) and established a claim on behalf of the United States to the surrounding territory. In May of 1792, John Boit again reports: *"On the 15th took up the Anchor, and stood up River but soon found the water to be shoal so that the Ship took the Ground, after proceeding 7 or 8 miles from our 1st station, however soon got off again. Sent the Cutter and found the main Channel was on the South side, and that there was a sand bank in the middle, as we did not expect to procure Otter furs at any distance from the Sea, we contented ourselves in our present situation which was a very pleasant one. This River in my opinion, wou'd be a fine place for to sett up a Factory [Trading Post]. The Indians are very numerous, and appear'd very civill (not even offering to steal), during our short stay we collected 150 Otter, 300 Beaver, and twice the Number of other land furs. the river abounds with excellent Salmon, and most other River fish, and the Woods with plenty of Moose and Deer, the skins of which was brought us in great plenty, and the Banks produces a ground Nut, which is an excellent substitute for either bread or Potatoes."*

In September he noted, *"the Spaniards* [at Neah Bay] *had erected a Cross upon the beach, and had about 10 Houses and several good gardens."*

Gray ordered several other attacks on natives during the 1792 voyage, including one at Chicklisaht, a Nuu-chah-nulth village north of Nootka Sound, killing seven and seizing the natives' sea otter furs. The Chicklisaht took their wounded to the Spanish post at Nootka Sound and asked the *commandante,* Bodega Quadra, to punish Gray.

Boit was to witness more usually unwarranted killing of natives on this voyage. In what is now called Grays Harbor, Captain Gray fired on a group of Chinooks, killing twenty. In Clayoquot Sound, he killed or wounded at least 25 natives who were approaching his ship in a war canoe during the night. He battled a group of Kwakiutls in late 1792. Gray left North America on October 3, 1792, arriving in the Hawaiian Islands on October 29, and in Macao on December 8. The expense accruing to the *Columbia* at Canton was $7,000. The otter furs were landed at Canton and delivered to the Hong Merchants for $90,000, averaging $45 each. The land furs were much less valuable. The ship was then loaded with a full cargo of teas and nankeen[11] cloth, sugar, and China porcelain and sent off to Boston.

In July of 1794, the nineteen-year-old Captain Boit took charge of the sloop *Union,* laying at Newport, Rhode Island. He set out for the NW Coast of America, China, Isle of France, and back to Boston after overhauling the ship in July and August. They then loaded stores and provisions for three years and cargo to trade with the natives including sheet copper, bar iron, blue cloth, blankets, and trinkets of various kinds. The sloop was well fitted with a crew of 22, ten carriage guns and eight swivel guns on the rails.

Captain Boit successfully traded on the northwest coast and circumnavigated the globe in less than two years. His crew had beaten off an Indian attack. It was said that they found "the females were quite amorous" in Hawaii. They exchanged their sea otter skins for silks at Canton and successfully weathered a four-day gale en route to the Cape of Good Hope. The ship was temporarily seized and then released by a French cruiser and later fired upon by a British frigate. Once safely home, Boit would captain other ships. He cared for his men as we learn from the memorial stone for a young sailor in the Central Burying Ground on the Boston Common. The epitaph reads: *Here lies Inter'd the body of Chow[12] Mandarin, a native of China, aged 19 years; whose death was occasioned by the fall from the mast of the ship, Mac of Boston (1798). This stone is erected in his memory by his affectionate master* (as in captain, not slave owner) *John Boit, Jr.*

In 1799, Boit married Eleanor Auchmuty Jones in Newport, RI. They had seven children, including Caroline, Julia Overing (1820), Ellen Maria (1803–1821), Henrietta Auchmuty Howard (1812), and Edward (1813).

He captained many other ships, including the *Mac* and *Mount Hope*. The *Mount Hope* was built at Newport for Gibbs & Channing. At 570 tons, she carried ten guns, six- and nine-pounders, and 45 men. She sailed for Batavia in July of 1801 under the command of Captain Boit. In October 1806, she entered from the Isle of Bourbon, having completed her fifth voyage to the East Indies without having lost a man or being detained or interfered with in any way despite wars between other countries.

Boit gave up the sea when he was about forty years old. He retained his interest in ships but became a successful and well-regarded Boston merchant. He died on March 8, 1829 and was buried at King's Chapel. In the old credit books of Baring Brothers & Company in London stands the name of Captain John Boit, with the record, *"His word is as good as his bond."*

DIONISIO ALCALÁ GALIANO, HYDROGRAPHER[13]

Dionisio Alcalá Galiano was born in Cabra, southern Spain in 1760. His parents were Alcalá-Galiano Pareja y Valero de la Serna and Antonio Alcalá-Galiano. He entered the navy in 1771 (at age 11) and naval school in 1775. He graduated and began active service in 1779. He became a midshipman as a teenager and worked as an assistant hydrographer. He later studied astronomy at the Royal Observatory in Cádiz under Admiral Vicente Tofiño de San Miguel. He first assisted with survey work charting the Spanish coastline, resulting in the atlas *Maritímo de España*, published in 1789. He continued to work with Tofiño for a number of years and conducted surveys in the Azores, other islands, and the South American Coast.

In 1785, Galiano married María de la Consolación Villavicencio. Soon after the marriage he left to survey the Strait of Magellan—no easy task.

In 1789, at the age of 27, he was selected for Malaspina's planned global circumnavigation and sailed aboard the *Atrevida*. Galiano completed work in Mexico while the Malaspina expedition trav-

Dionisio Alcalá Galiano

elled to the northern Pacific. Malaspina failed to find the mythical Northwest Passage, and the viceroy decided to send a new expedition with ships better suited for coastal exploration. The *Sutil* and *Mexicana* were brig-rigged schooners (in Spanish, a *goleta*) built by the Spanish Navy yard at San Blas, New Spain.

On Malaspina's recommendation, Lieutenants Alcalá-Galiano (on the *Sutil*) and Cayetano Valdés y Flores Bazán (on the *Mexicana*) were sent north. Tacking up to the north against the wind was challenging but they made it to Nootka Sound in May. The Spanish post at Friendly Cove, under the command of Juan Francisco de la Bodega y Quadra, was now well developed. Galiano also noted the friendly relations prevailing with the Nootkas. Maquinna often ate with the commander using a knife and fork, like most polite Europeans, and contributing to the good humor of his fellow diners.

Galiano maintained equally friendly relations with the British survey ships, meeting Captains William Broughton and George Vancouver. On June 23, the *Discovery*, *Chatham*, *Sutil*, and *Mexicana* sailed together north along the Sunshine Coast through Welcome Pass and Malaspina Strait up to their next anchorage in Desolation Sound. At the entrance of Jervis Inlet on June 24, the British and

Spanish officers assembled onboard *Discovery* for "a meal in the English style." The two sides worked together until July, when they resumed circumnavigation of Vancouver Island separately. José Cardero was a seaman-turned-artist who illustrated parts of the journey.

The Spanish ships had trouble with scurvy and disease, so it appears likely Joseph Burling O'Cain and other American and English sailors were taken aboard to help sail south.[14] The captain of the *Sutil* was severely reprimanded for allowing them onboard, but O'Cain was noted as the *pilotin hablitado*. Most Spanish exploration was kept virtually secret, but Galiano began editing reports and charts of the voyage and they were published in 1802. Galiano saw the economic potential of the area but felt the sea otter trade would not be economically viable for the long term. He suggested buying all the furs to displace the British and American traders, believing it would be in the national interest to continue scientific experiments and exploration to help make Spanish sovereignty permanent.

He returned to Spain in 1794 and rose through the ranks, eventually becoming a brigadier. He commanded naval escort vessels convoying silver treasure fleets from Veracruz to Cadiz. He died in battle in 1805 when he was hit by a cannon ball as captain of the *Bahama* in the Battle of Trafalgar.

Julia Rivet Ogden, courageous mother on the move

Julia Rivet was a Salish (Selin) woman born about 1790. Her father was half Absaroka and half Salish, and a Salish chief. Therese, her widowed mother, married Francois Rivet. Her stepfather was an interpreter who accompanied Lewis and Clark up to the Mandan Villages. Like her mother, Julia spoke English, French, Salish, Chinook wawa, and other native languages. Peter Skene Ogden may have first met her at Spokane House in 1819. His first country wife,[15] a Cree woman named Marie Comptois, was left behind when he came west to the Columbia. Julia's first husband had been killed, and Peter was impressed with her and wanted to form a partnership.

As a Salish woman and daughter of a chief, Julia expected a proper marriage, and according to one tale, Peter ended up spending much of his savings to assemble a herd of 50 horses in 1821. It was only with the delivery of the 50th horse, a magnificent gold and cream mare, to her tent that she accepted his proposal. She rode out in a white buckskin dress and beadwork and they paraded together around the fort and through the camp. They would be together for 31 years and have seven children. Their first child, Cecilia, was born in 1822. Peter had been combative in his youth and was shifted to the West, in part to outrun a violent event in the fur war (when under the influence of a much older boss, he killed a native who was trading with the competing fur company).

Julia Rivet Ogden

He was later described as an excellent leader, respected by his men; a witty conversationalist with a good sense of humor and a fondness for practical jokes. His letters to his children reflect his love for them and his wife (affectionately called "the old lady" as she was four years older than he).

In April 1824, with Julia pregnant at Fort Spokane, Ogden left for Fort George. He found her in good health when he returned home in August. At almost the same time a messenger brought word that the HBC ship *Valiant* had arrived at Fort George, so Peter repacked and headed downriver for another 1500-mile roundtrip. He was back at Fort Spokane in October to meet his newborn son, Michael.

The 1824–1825 fur brigade for the Snake Country left the Flat Head post on December 20, 1824, with Peter as the leader. The brigade included Julia and their children, as well as 55 men and boys and 29 other women with their children. On Christmas Eve they camped on Wild Horse River and feasted on horse meat. The next day a baby was born, holding up the party for a day. On the 28th, with thankfully only ten inches of snow on the ground, they met Jedidiah Smith, the American fur explorer, and his party coming from the south. Smith would stay with them for safety until March 19th. Guarding and sharing information around the campfire may have fueled the desire for the HBC fur trappers to go further south in California. The trapping party met limited success but kept moving.

On Good Friday, Julia was faced with a sick child after three months of tough winter travel. Six-year-old Charles (from her first husband) had a chest cold and was feverish. She vowed to prepare a special goose broth and goose grease for his chest. She carried him wrapped in her blanket until they reached the Snake River. Late in the afternoon while Charles was napping fitfully, Peter heard a gunshot. Kittson told him that he had seen Julia swimming in the river. He rushed down to the river to find Julia's clothes on the bank and one of the hunters with a rifle. She was out in the current and swimming strongly. After reaching the opposite shore she picked up the dead goose; swimming a little slower with the goose in her hand, she made it back across the river. The stalwart Julia emerged with steaming breath, an ice necklace, and frozen hair. Charles benefitted from the goose broth and was soon well again.

Julia was present at the contentious meeting with Johnston Gardiner and the desertion of the HBC freemen. While she was busy rounding up her children, several of the deserters (or Americans) stampeded the horses outside her tent. Her eight-month-old son Michael had already been tied to the saddle of one of the mares that raced out of camp. She quickly grabbed a horse and rode into the American camp, where she managed to recover the mare and baby. She also collected several company horses loaded with furs. The Americans and the HBC were amazed by her courage.

Julia was pregnant again in the fall of 1825 and stayed at Fort Vancouver while Ogden undertook his third Snake Country expedition. This time, the company ruled that no women were allowed,

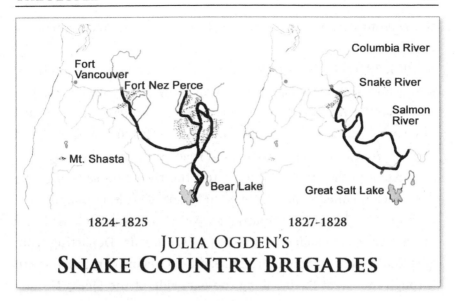

Fort Vancouver
Fort Nez Perce
Columbia River
Snake River
Salmon River
Mt. Shasta
Bear Lake
Great Salt Lake

1824-1825   1827-1828

JULIA OGDEN'S
SNAKE COUNTRY BRIGADES

but some snuck out of the post and showed up a couple of days into the trip. The men would be happy to see them as it took at least a half-hour to prepare a skin, and the men sometimes got 75, or more, beaver a day. By June 7th, the party had 2000 beaver pelts. Julia gave birth to Sarah Julia on January 1, 1826 at Fort Vancouver (or Fort Nez Perce with her mother) and she quickly became a favorite. When Ogden returned, he had a couple of months to spend with his family, a rarity.

When Peter arrived at Fort Nez Perce in September 1827 to prepare for his fourth expedition into the Snake River country, Julia was four months pregnant and caring for her five children: Peter (then about 10), Charles (8), Cecilia (6), Michael (4), and Sarah Julia (2). Imagine the fortitude it takes to walk, ride and camp for 9 months, first pregnant and almost all in winter snow with such a large family. A baby named David was born in the snowy wilderness but sadly died soon after in fierce cold and winds as hunger stalked the brigade. He was buried in a willow grove, and the other children in the family and brigade put tokens on his lonely grave. Ogden read a service, a cross was set, and then the party continued on. By April 24th, the group had collected their 2000th beaver pelt. On July 19th, they

returned to Fort Nez Perce and Ogden went on to Fort Vancouver
with the furs.

In 1828, on Ogden's fifth Snake Country brigade, Julia and the
family once again travelled together. Leaving on September 22, they
would not return until July. They reached as far down as Bear Lake
(a favorite wintering spot), saw the Great Salt Lake, and explored
Ogden's Hole, now home to Ogden, Provo, and Salt Lake City. They
also explored the Humboldt Sink and the river that sank into the
desert. They called it Mary's River, in honor of Ogden's daughter.

In 1829, Julia and the children stayed at Fort Nez Perce with her
mother as Peter headed to the Gulf of California. Departing from
Fort Nez Perce, he worked through eastern Oregon, continued south
through the Great Basin, along the east side of the Sierra Nevada

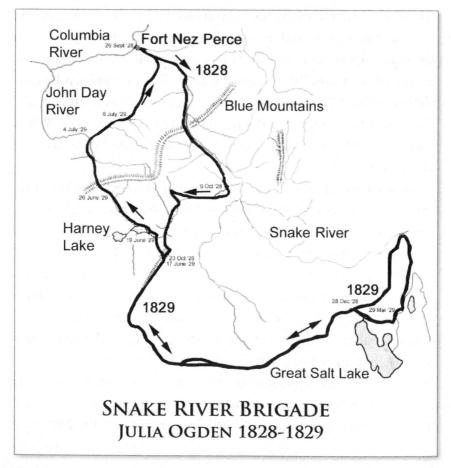

SNAKE RIVER BRIGADE
JULIA OGDEN 1828-1829

Mountains. They finally struck the Colorado River and followed it to the Sea of Cortez before returning through the Mojave Desert to California's Central Valley. They visited San Francisco before following the Sacramento River north into the Humboldt Country, back through eastern Oregon, and on to the Columbia River. On the way back in 1830, a canoeing accident at the rapids on the Columbia called the Dalles cost nine lives in Peter's party, including Julia's half-brother Francois, Jr. Many furs and the journal of the trip were also lost.

After retiring from the Snake River effort, Ogden was in charge at Fort Colville for a while in 1830–1831. While they were there, a male child succumbed to a stomach abscess in January 1831. Ogden was tasked with setting up a new northern outpost at the mouth of the Nass River. Again, Julia and children went with him. Fort Simpson quickly took shape and trading was good. In mid-August, Governor Simpson arrived for a visit. Fish, sea mammals, shellfish, and other foods were abundant and the winter passed quietly. Action picked up when the natives gathered to harvest the eulachon fish, arriving in the millions. By the end of the season Peter had 3,000 skins, but they had paid higher prices for them than they had expected.

In the spring of 1834, Peter was called back to venture north on the *Dryad* to deal with the Russians. Julia and family were left behind. In a clear case of confused language and misunderstanding, the Russians said they would resist a settlement with force. The HBC eventually tried to recover the cost of the expedition from the RAC. Negotiations led to a contract to supply Russian-America with food and supplies in exchange for a lease on the Alaska panhandle. The *Dryad* returned to Fort Simpson and the men devoted their efforts to finding a more protected spot and moving the fort. Despite some trouble with the natives, this was accomplished, and Peter and family returned to Fort Vancouver.

In 1835, Ogden was promoted to chief factor and assigned to Fort Saint James on Stuart Lake, in what is now northern British Columbia, where he would remain for almost a decade. This was a lovely spot and the family settled in for almost the first time. In 1839, Julia was pregnant again, this time waiting at home while Ogden led the New Caledonia brigade from Fort St. James to Fort Vancouver. His daughter Sarah Julia, 13, accompanied him on the trip. When he returned, 51-year-old Julia had successfully delivered another son, Isaac. In 1840, the whole family accompanied Ogden from Fort St. James to Fort Vancouver. The improved route to Fort Vancouver involved roughly one-thousand miles of river and over-land carry by horses and took from mid-April to mid-June but was much better than the previous method of taking furs 3500 miles east to Montreal.

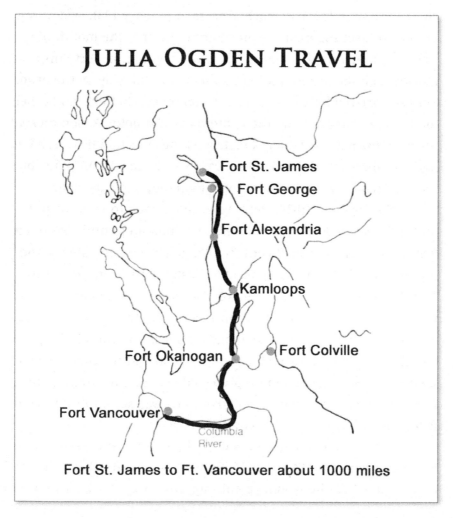

JULIA OGDEN TRAVEL

Fort St. James
Fort George
Fort Alexandria
Kamloops
Fort Okanogan
Fort Colville
Fort Vancouver
Columbia River

Fort St. James to Ft. Vancouver about 1000 miles

In 1844, Julia and the children stayed at Fort Vancouver while Peter crossed the continent to eastern Canada and sailed to England to visit family members and company headquarters in London. Traveling with British officers on the way back, Lieutenant Warre found Ogden *"a fat jolly good fellow reminding me of Falstaff both in appearance & in wit always talking..."* In 1847, he was appointed co-leader of Fort Vancouver when Dr. McLoughlin retired. Ogden enjoyed parts of this work and presumably Julia finally enjoyed some rest with the children growing up and going to school. Isaac, the youngest, would have been eight. Fort Vancouver was a lively multicultural center with much always going on and as many as thirty languages being spoken. But the demand for beaver for hats was down and the fur trade was declining. At the same time, the growing number of American immigrants were not happy with the British presence. Many of the former fur trade workers had settled around French Prairie (later Champoeg) but many also would move to Vancouver Island.

Julia was not listed as living with Peter in the 1850 census, but she may well have been traveling to visit her daughter or mother. Peter had two young Rivet children and two Hawaiians (a cook and a steward) living with him. He was granted a paid year-long furlough in 1852, and then retired. In 1854, the couple was living with daughter Sarah McKinley in either Oregon City or Champoeg. Isaac, the youngest child, was 15.

Peter died in 1854. Julia and Peter were never officially married, but he had made an effort to ensure that she and the children would be fairly treated. She and the children were mentioned in the will, dated June 15, 1851 and probated May 15, 1855. The executors were Sir George Simpson, governor of Rupert's Land; Archibald McKinley of the Hudson's Bay Co. (his son-in-law), and Thomas B. Anderson of Montreal. The will dispersed about £4,600, as well as Montreal Bank stock and shares in Puget's Sound Agricultural Company. Peter's siblings contested the will and won a bigger share of the money.

In 1860 the census found Julia living with her daughter Sarah in Champoeg, Oregon. After Champoeg was washed away in the great Willamette flood of 1861, the McKinley family moved to Lac La Hache (Axe Lake), British Columbia. She is listed there in the Canadian census of 1881. Julia died at her daughter's home in Lac La Hache, British Columbia in 1886 at the age of 98. She had walked, canoed, and ridden thousands of miles around the West while caring for her husband and children. Truly a remarkable woman.

Today there are 6,800 Salish, with about 4,000 living on the reservation. A few elders are truly fluent in Salish, and there are many more people learning the language today. For online resources visit http://www.thesalishinstitute.org/home. There are also classroom programs and many conferences and training efforts.

ALEXANDER KASHEVAROV: NAVIGATOR, MAP MAKER, AND DEFENDER OF *KREOLS*, NATIVES, AND NATURE

Alexander Kashevarov was born in 1809 on Kodiak Island. His father Filipp Kashevaroff had come to Kodiak from Russia on the *Three Saints*. In 1794, Filipp, as he was known, was a fifteen-year-old serf assigned as an apprentice to the RAC shipwright James Shields[16] to learn more about ship building and navigation. Filipp married Aleksandra Petrovna Chechenova, an Alutiiq woman, and their children became officially recognized as *kreols* in 1821.

Alexander Kashevarov

The *kreol* classification was created in the Russian system to accommodate the children resulting from mixed marriages. They were granted special economic privileges, including being exempt from state taxes, and were educated at the expense of the RAC. Filipp went on to command many vessels, and three of his sons became seafarers. By

1818, he had been transferred to New Archangel (now Sitka, Alaska) where his sons would have many opportunities to learn more about seamanship, the Russians, *kreols*, and the native people of Alaska. This would include the Tlingit and their strategies for native subsistence and the hunting of marine mammals.

When he was twelve, Alexander was sent to St. Petersburg under the patronage of RAC merchant Ivan Vasilyevich Prokofiev. On the long journey there he rounded Cape Horn and docked at Rio de Janeiro and Copenhagen. He was first placed in a private boarding school[17] in St. Petersburg to learn Russian, math, and other subjects. He then entered the Kronstadt Navigation School and graduated in 1828 at age 20. His schooling included navigation, seamanship, and cartography.

Kashevarov shipped out on the RAC *Elenea* and spent two years sailing a circuitous route to Alaska, seeing much of the Pacific Ocean on this cruise. The ship stopped in Australia, then Micronesia and the Marshall Islands. Here he was given his first task of producing new maps on his own. He sailed around the world again in 1831 on the company transport *Amerika* and was promoted to ensign. They visited Australia again, saw new parts of Polynesia and Melanesia, undertook an in-depth study of the equatorial Gilbert Islands, and again stopped in Brazil. By the time he returned to Alaska in 1832, Alexander had seen a great deal of the world and learned much about ship handling, navigation, mapping, and Russian and foreign cultures.

After his return to Alaska, Alexander served as captain on several company ships (1833–1837), usually sailing between Sitka and Kodiak Island, but also occasionally to other ports. In 1834 he married 16-year-old Serafima Alekseeva Sokolof in Sitka, with his father as a witness. They went on to have three children, Mariia Aleksandrova (1832), Anna Aleksandrova (1835), and Aleksandr Aleksandrov (1836).

Kashevarov carried a fleet of Aleuts and *baidarkas* south to Fort Ross (California) in 1835, where he was to *"find out how best to conduct the hunt.*" He was promoted to second lieutenant in 1837. His superiors must have been impressed with his skill as a navigator and chart maker, for he was chosen to lead a coastal expedition to explore and chart the north shore of Alaska. During the summer of 1838 he traveled more than 300 miles in a larger skin boat (*baydar*) from Cape Lisburne to a point east of Point Barrow. They travelled in a single *baydar* with five *baidarkas* for support. In Sitka, warm clothing and small wooden and leather food containers were designed specifically for use in the *baidarkas* in case the expedition got lost or was forced to abandon its larger skin boat. The most modern instruments for surveying and observation were included and put to use. Kashevarov's journal of his explorations provides excellent information on this time and place.

Between 1839 and 1843, Kashevarov commanded RAC ships sailing between Sitka, Petropavlovsk, Okhotsk, and California. He

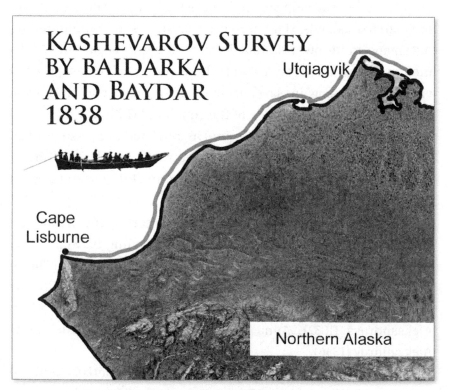

Exploration of the North Coast by Baydar and Baidarka

continued sailing, training new navigators, and making hydro-graphic, geographic, and ethnographic observations around Kodiak Island, the Aleutian Islands, Bristol Bay, the Pribilofs, the Alexander Archipelago, and the Yukon Delta. He sometimes transported Aleut hunters to their hunting grounds and these trips provided new opportunities to observe the sea otter hunt.

Kashevarov's first brief report on his coastal explorations was published in 1840, followed five years later by the publication of his more detailed diary covering this work. This provided additional information including anthropological reference to tribal life, clas-sification, and distribution. He was promoted to lieutenant in 1841. In that same year he carried sea otter hunters to Kamchatka and checked their prowess with rifles. In 1842, he published the ethno-graphic account *"Zametki ob eskimosakh v Russkoy Amerike"* (Notes on the Eskimos in Russian-America).

In 1845, Kashevarov returned to St. Petersburg where he was released by the RAC and joined the Hydrographic Department of the Naval Ministry to work on his atlas of the North Pacific Ocean. He was promoted to captain of the second rank, and in 1850 he returned to the Russian-American Company as a captain-lieutenant. He was then appointed commander of the port of Ayan on the Okhotsk Sea. At the end of June 1855, an enemy flotilla led by the frigate *Barracuda* attacked Ayan, whose residents had been evacuated. Kashevarov was awarded the order of St. Vladimir 4th class for his actions in defense. Kashevarov remained at Ayan until 1855 when he was once again discharged from the RAC and returned to St. Petersburg to serve in the Hydrographic Department. He was appointed chief draftsman of the department in 1858 and served in that capacity until 1862 when he was assigned to the reserves.

Alexander's commentaries on native life, ecological knowl-edge, and resource management were some of the most important resources for the time. In 1860, two inspectors were sent to review the RAC operations. Both Kostlivtsev and Captain P. N. Golovin pre-pared reports, but Golovin died suddenly. Both reported that the company should continue but that improvements should be made. Aleksander, then living in Saint Petersburg where he was working on his atlas of the Pacific Ocean, offered his own critiques describing the company's mistreatment of natives and natural resources. He revealed abuses that had never before been made public. After Golovin died, Alexander rewrote his report out of respect. Former Governor Wrangell declared Kashevarov's accusations were based on fact.

His thoughts about reforming the Russian-American Company appeared in several articles for the Russian naval journal *Morskoi Sbornik*. It had not escaped his notice that the directors of the company who met in St. Petersburg, most of whom knew little about Russian-America, were more concerned about stockholders' profits than they were about the welfare of the inhabitants of Alaska, both Russian and native.

Despite company claims of conservation successes, Alexander felt the company had misunderstood the environment in Alaska and had mismanaged its fur resources. He had seen the decline of the sea otter and other fur bearers firsthand. As early as 1817, when Adelbert von Chamisso stopped at the Pribilof Islands, he remarked that sea otters had been in such abundance thirty years prior that a man could catch 200–300 of them in an hour, and now they were gone. Alexander argued that the company's attempts to create *zapusks* (closed seasons) had not worked. The RAC claimed success but Kashevarov disputed their reports of unqualified success in the Pribilofs. He noted that the numbers of fur seals taken from the islands were down, and that there were fewer fur seals. Sea lion numbers had declined to an even greater extent and sea otters were entirely gone. Before the arrival of the Russians, all of these animals had thrived and multiplied. Alexander argued that only the natives understood the animals well enough to manage them and thus should be ceded control over Alaska's environment. Although these radical claims were met with company derision, Kashevarov's pleas for ecological sophistication and ecological justice provide a glimpse into the desires of the native people shortly before the colony's demise and sale to the U.S.

He also commented on the beaver slaughter. Lavrenty Zagoskin, a Russian naval officer, reported that new ways of hunting were causing serious problems for the beaver. Hunters were destroying beaver lodges to get at their prey, a method that usually netted only the male, while the female and young were left homeless to perish. Kashevarov thought beaver conservation was inherently impossible with the current situation: *"One cannot even think about creating zapusks (temporary hunting restrictions),"* because the beavers were being caught by "independent natives" who recognized no power over them.

Kashevarov's advocacy for native hunting incorporated another equally radical claim. He noted that the Aleuts had been deprived of their traditional means of subsistence and argued, *"It is somehow strange to keep from the inhabitants of this maritime colony the right to freely use the products of their home sea, given to them by God for their well-being!"* Fur tribute demands took sea otters and fur seals out of the natives' hands and the RAC claimed ownership of all marine mammals. Kashevarov argued that placing restrictions on the numbers of animals that could be caught would only perpetuate the injustice because many natives still depended on these animals for almost all of their daily needs.

Golovin had been very critical of the natives but even more condescending to the *kreols* in his report. He described them as entitled, overly proud, too sensitive, inclined towards hooliganism, primitive, dishonest, and lazy. He summed it up by saying that to the present time the *kreols* had not been of any use. As a *kreol* himself, Alexander felt compelled to respond to Golovin's slanders, and informed him that he disagreed with many of his viewpoints. He finished with a personal plea: *"We [kreols and natives] are people just like everyone else. If we don't know foreign ways, we know our own very well, and understand that, for the perfection of our own lives, we had to see much, learn and imitate new, useful things from others. Just let it be that others can be fair with us."*

Kashevarov's notes on Alaska's Arctic Inuit end with this poignant observation: *"the savage is unquestioningly servile to the customs of his ancestors. Destruction of these customs, even through education, would mean his destruction if this enlightenment would disenchant the (resulting) half-savage with his past and leave him alone to struggle with ... new needs."* Kashevarov could not have known just how prophetic his words would prove.

All in all, Kashevarov spent what he described as *"eleven years of service in the colonies."* In 1863, he was brought out of the reserves in an unsuccessful attempt to apprehend Eskimos who had attacked the Russian settlement of Mikhailovskii Redoubt on the Yukon River.[18] He retired in 1865 with the rank of brigadier general. He died on September 25, 1866 after a most remarkable life. His parents would have been amazed by the arc of his career and life. His accomplishments deserve to be known to all historians and anthropologists concerned with Alaska, as well as the Arctic and its native inhabitants. Kashevarov's journals, articles, books, and charts were important sources of information for navigators. His works include *the Atlas of the Eastern Ocean, Coastal Exploration in Northwest Alaska,* and many more.

BODEGA QUADRA: PERUVIAN BASQUE
EXPLORER, NEGOTIATOR

Juan Francisco de Bodega Quadra[19] y Mollinedo was born on May 22, 1744 in Lima, Peru to Tomás de la Bodega y de las Llanas of Biscay, Spain and Francisca de Mollinedo y Losada of Lima, Peru (her Peruvian family was originally from Bilbao, Spain). He was baptized June 3, 1744 at the Parroquia El Sagrario of the Lima Cathedral. His father was a businessman and deputy of the Spanish consulate in Cuzco and later Lima. Juan studied at the Jesuit College of San Marcos in Lima and then entered the Naval Academy in Cadiz, Spain at age 19.

Bodega graduated in four years with the title of officer of the Royal Navy. After graduating in 1765 he made several cruises through the Mediterranean. He returned to Callao, Peru in 1767. A mutiny over lack of pay was harshly put down with seven executions and many floggings on the ship where he was a junior officer. He was back in Spain in 1773 and rose to the rank of ship's lieutenant in 1774. By then, both of his parents had died. As a Basque born in Peru, his advance was perhaps slowed by class prejudice, common in Spain and colonial America.

Bodega Quadra

In 1775, the Spanish sent the *Santiago*[20] commanded by Bruno Heceta, and the schooner *Sonora*[21] commanded by Bodega, north from San Blas to explore the northwest coast and to counter the Russian advance. The ships left in March, but illnesses (particularly scurvy), storms, the poor sailing capacities of the *Sonora*, and other incidents slowed their progress. In July, Bodega accidentally sailed over what is now called Sonora Reef (off Gray's Harbor. Washington) and was trapped there for a while by wind and tide.

The *Santiago* anchored a few miles to the south. Many friendly Quinault visited the schooner and traded with the crew and gifted them with food. The next day, an armed party from the *Santiago* went ashore and conducted a possession ceremony that was observed by some of the Quinaults. When six sailors from the *Sonora* went ashore later to collect water and wood they were attacked and killed. Bodega was unable to help because the shore party had taken the schooner's only boat. Nine large canoes carrying about thirty Quinaults carrying bows and shields then came alongside the *Sonora*. They made signs of friendship but when the natives approached in an apparent attempt to board the ship, Bodega fired two swivel guns and muskets killing many of them. Bodega wanted to further avenge his lost sailors but was overruled by Heceta, who reminded him of their orders to use force only in self-defense. Quinault elders today believe the attack took place because the natives understood full well what the land-claiming ceremony and placement of a large cross on the beach meant.

Bodega was able to get past the reef and continue on. Heceta, along with his sick sailors, decided to return to San Blas. Bodega continued northward on the *Sonora* and got close to Sitka, Alaska at 59° north latitude. He failed to find any Russians and returned southward, landing again to claim the coast for Spain. After his journey and surveys, he was able to draw a more accurate map of the west coast of North America.

In 1776, Bodega was sent back to Peru to retrieve a new vessel for use on the Northwest Coast. He returned to San Blas with the Callao-built frigate *Favorita*. He was recognized as a courageous and competent officer and was awarded the military title of Knight of the Order of Santiago in 1776. In February of 1779, the *Princesa* and *Favorita*, under the commands of Lieutenants Ignacio de Arteaga and Bodega respectively, headed north again. They surveyed inlets and bays while looking for the Northwest Passage, reaching 58°30' before bad weather forced them to turn back.

They made further efforts to solidify Spain's claim of the Pacific Northwest with a formal possession ceremony at Port Etches.[22] The officers and chaplains went ashore in a procession and then raised a large cross with cannon and musket salutes. The *Te Deum* was then sung, followed by a litany and prayers. After a sermon, a formal deed of possession was drawn up and signed by the officers and chaplains. The land title to what they called Puerto de Santiago formed a part of Spain's claim to sovereignty in the North Pacific up to 61°17'N.

Bodega was promoted to Frigate Captain in 1780 in recognition of his achievements during the 1779 voyage. In 1784, he requested and received permission to travel to Spain, and he made it there in

1785. He spent four years in Spain and the king approved his promotion to Ship's Captain in November 1786; this was the highest naval rank below flag officer ranks. He was also knighted as a full-fledged Knight of the Order of Santiago.

In 1789, the hot-headed Esteban Jose Martínez was sent north to improve Spain's claim. He built Fort San Miguel in Friendly Cove as instructed; but then, in an attempt to enforce Spanish claims on the Northwest Coast, he seized a number of British vessels in Nootka Sound. Bodega had been appointed commandant of the Naval Department of San Blas and sailed to America on the same ship that was carrying the new viceroy, the Count of Revillagigedo. The viceroy and Bodega arrived to find themselves embroiled in the Nootka Crisis. A new expedition had to be immediately organized to re-occupy and reinforce Nootka Sound.

In 1790, a new Spanish expedition under Francisco de Eliza reoccupied Nootka Sound. The expedition was organized very quickly. Three ships, *Concepción*, *San Carlos*, and *Princesa Real*, sailed from San Blas and arrived at Nootka Sound in early April with Francisco de Eliza appointed commandant of the base. The First Company of the Free Company of Volunteers of Catalonia, under Pedro de Alberni, sailed with Eliza to garrison the Nootka establishment. The logistical challenge had been enormous, but Bodega's careful choice of subordinates had made it possible. The expedition had needed not only cannons and munitions, but also food, warm clothes, new equipment for the soldiers, materials for constructing buildings and improving Fort San Miguel, materials to maintain and repair ships, copper sheets to trade or give to the natives, and many other supplies. This rapid deployment was a remarkable achievement since San Blas was chronically under-supplied and under-funded. Alessandro Malaspina would come up to the fort in 1791.

In 1791 Bodega was appointed the Spanish commissioner for the negotiation and administration of the Nootka Conventions between England and Spain. He sailed to Nootka in 1792 to take command of the situation involving the trading post of Santa Cruz de Nutka and Fort San Miguel. With its barracks, hospital, and flourishing gardens, this was the sole European outpost between California and Russian-Alaska. The genial commandant from Lima earned the respect and admiration of his men, the British and American fur-traders, and the Nootkas.

Bodega made a point of hosting and entertaining every visitor, indigenous and European. He held feasts for the officers of every ship that arrived at Nootka Sound, including the French fur-trading ship *La Flavie*, the "Portuguese" ship *Feliz Aventureira* (a British ship under a Portuguese flag), the American ships *Columbia* (Captain Robert Gray) and the *Hope* (Captain Joseph Ingraham), Captain Vancouver's ships *Discovery* and *Chatham*, and many others. Their journals record their amazement at the glorious dinners he provided, often with more than fifty people served multiple courses on 300 pieces of silver. Bodega also offered help with ship repairs to any vessel in need. During his single summer in command at Nootka he also facilitated construction of a second, short-lived base at *Núñez Gaona* (now Neah Bay, Washington).

Captains Vancouver and Bodega remained on friendly terms but they were unable to reconcile the conflicts in instructions from their respective governments. Bodega was uncertain about the depth of his superiors' wish to maintain Spanish sovereignty for a part of the world that had limited strategic value. He improvised, and by chance, asked for exactly the condition that both the king and viceroy later communicated to him. Vancouver was equally handicapped by lack of instructions and maintained a strictly literal interpretation of Article I. of the Nootka Convention. Having reached an impasse, the two agreed to refer the points at issue back to their respective governments in Madrid and London. Quadra arranged passage for Vancouver's envoy, William Robert Broughton, through Mexico. Eventually, Spain and Great Britain signed an agreement on January 11, 1794, in which they agreed to abandon the region (the third Nootka Convention). Bodega kept a journal of the trip and it offers insight into the characters and the nature of their interactions.

Bodega did well in his rise from Lima to naval commander, but his career was marked by discord and complaints by him of his staff and colleagues. They may have treated him poorly because he was of Basque descent and a colonial. Perhaps many of his complaints were justified, but he must have been considered a problem child at times.

At some point in 1789 Bodega married Maria Marin de Valle. She was the daughter of the commander of the troops in Tepic and militia in San Blas. She and her servants added to his household expenses and stress. He married with a priest but without royal permission (most likely due to poor timing), and this made his situation awkward. They had a son, but little was recorded of their life together because he had not had permission to marry. His finances collapsed in 1793 when he was audited and found to be overcharging the government for his household. He was allowed two servants but expensed for six extra, probably adding his wife, his son (Juan Francisco), his wife's servant, his sister, perhaps his mother, and a cook.

He suffered from chronic headaches and medical historians suggest Bodega may have developed a cerebral tumor. He requested a medical leave in April 1793 to restore his health. He did not improve and tried to set his affairs in order. He left a remarkable collection of letters, reports, and charts, but not much for his family. He left San Blas for Guadalajara and Mexico City, but suffered a "strong hemorrhage" in Guadalajara and then had a seizure in Mexico City, where he died on March 26, 1794 at the age of 50. In 1815, his wife appeared before a notary in Guadalajara to draw up her will.

VICENTE VASADRE Y VEGA: VISIONARY ECONOMIST, ABLE ADMINISTRATOR, POLITICAL PRISONER

Vicente Vasadre[23] was an energetic, innovative economist, entrepreneur, author, administrator; and less successful revolutionary. He was a *gallego* (Galician) born around 1750 in La Coruña, Spain.[24] He was well-educated and may have lived in several towns in the north and east of Spain before he began to leave a paper trail. The University

Vicente Vasadre y Vega

of Santiago de Compestella, which Carlos III[25] had granted the title of *Regia* (Royal), was not far away and he may have attended. He was related to Pedro Varela y Ulloa, later a secretary of the Spanish navy.

He was very business oriented and always trying to improve the management of people and resources. Vasadre wrote many monographs on the economy and politics; these deserve greater recognition, as he was very knowledgeable about societal problems and the flaws in the Spanish and colonial economies. He was a forthright advocate for free markets and fair treatment. In 1799 he noted that free trade would mark a glorious epoch for posterity. Hacienda Secretary Gardoqui found Vasadre to be *"a man of talent and willing to work"* as well as *"one of the most skilled and knowledgeable men in commerce and in the things of America that I have dealt with."*

News of Captain Cook's voyage to the Northwest Coast in 1778–1779 led the Spanish to try fur trading in California. Vicente was, by some accounts, a merchant in New Spain[26] in the 1780s, but he must also have developed some very good connections in court. In 1784[27] he proposed a plan to the viceroy and King Carlos III that would exchange Chinese quicksilver (mercury used for gold refining) for California furs. China had good mercury supplies and a seemingly insatiable demand for sea otter furs, while California and Mexico were short of mercury. Vasadre also highlighted the risk from the growing push to the south by the Russians and English. Instead of returning empty to San Blas from California each year, the ships could bring sea otter pelts to Acapulco for reshipment on the Manila galleons, and from Manila to China for mercury or money.

His arguments were well received, and on June 2, 1785, King Carlos III ordered that the plan be given careful consideration. Provincial mining directors regarded it with favor, and on January 22, 1786, the viceroy of New Spain, Bernardo de Gálvez,[28] decreed that it be executed. He, in turn, notified Governor Pedro Fages and Father Fermín Francisco de Lasuén and asked for their cooperation.

Vicente traveled up to Monterey on a ship from San Blas in June 1786. Under his plan, he was to manage the government monopoly of the fur trade that he had negotiated (much like HBC, RAC). The transport ship also brought his credentials and Viceroy Galvez's instructions to Governor Pedro Fages. These were made public in a proclamation on August 29, 1786. In addition to his own salary of $4,000, Vasarde had $8,000 with which to begin buying furs. Father Lasuén and Governor Fages had high hopes for the project. Vicente was still in Monterey when the French explorer the Count de La Perouse passed by on his world cruise of exploration and had a good visit with Vicente and the governor. La Perouse noted that Governor Fages said he would be able to ship 20,000 skins a year from California and an additional 10,000 as soon as two or three settlements were founded north of San Francisco.[29]

Christianized natives learned to bring their furs to mission padres to exchange for cloth and other Mexican articles. Soldiers and residents of the pueblos who purchased skins from the unconverted natives had to turn them over to a corporal or alcalde to be forwarded to the commander of the nearest presidio. Prices offered ranged from ten pesos for first-class skins, those of at least one and one-fourth varas (about 42"), black in color and cured; to two pesos for those of the third-class skins of three-fourths of a vara, brown and raw.

Vasadre's first collection was encouraging, and in just three months of traveling on land and sea he visited nine missions, four presidios, and two pueblos. By the time he left San Diego for San

Blas on November 28 he had 1,060 skins. Missions Rosario and San Fernando in Lower California sent a consignment worth $2,000. Missions in upper California that contributed the most furs included San Carlos, San Antonio, San Luis Obispo, San Buenaventura, and San Diego.

In addition to granting Vasadre's monopoly, which had been designed to benefit the Crown more than the missions, a liberalization of rules forbidding private trading via the San Blas vessels allowed trade goods to be carried when there was room. The sole restriction forbade the introduction of foreign goods to California. Officers and crew members brought articles on their own accounts for barter with soldiers and missionaries. By 1803, it became evident that the original intent of the concession was being subverted and a vice regal decree in April prohibited officers and crews from trading or refusing to carry goods consigned by private persons.

Vasadre wanted additional resources for his trip to China and argued that he needed twelve to fifteen thousand pesos to curry favor with the Chinese mandarins. He also said he would need silver gifts for the emperor. He added that his small annual allowance of four thousand pesos was insufficient for traveling and working effectively with the leaders and businessmen of the Philippines and China and asked for a raise.

Vasadre's request fell on deaf ears. His salary was frozen, but "if" the governor and administrator of the Philippines considered costly gifts necessary, Vasadre could be supplied with sufficient funds after "a judicious examination..." He did get some support in a letter from José de Gálvez, minister of the Indies, to the governor of the Philippines that expressly stated that the officials in Manila were not to interfere with Vasadre's operations and that he was directly responsible only to the Spanish government. Financially limited but protected, he hoped, from bureaucratic meddling, he sailed on the *San Andrés* in the spring of 1787.

It was clear the fur collection had been handicapped by lack of skilled hunters, and the ensign (*alférez*) of San Francisco suggested that hunters should be brought from Europe. Otter hunting had also been limited by the lack of suitable materials for barter. The natives would not hunt sea otters unless they were compensated and the padres would not work on the fur collection without some returns. There had also been a problem of soldiers leaving the service, seizing furs by force from the natives, and then requesting payment from the missions.

Vasadre had argued the fur trade should be run through the missions even before he went to California, and upon his return to México City he wrote, *"With the practical knowledge which I have acquired and which I lacked before, I am of the same opinion."* He also submitted detailed instructions for suitable merchandise for barter and requested these to be delivered to the missions. Vasadre hoped to include San Vicente, Santo Domingo, Rosario, San Fernando, and San Francisco de Borja in the plan because of the abundance of otters along the southern coast.

Vasadre's suggestions were approved and in March of 1787, a copy of the new regulations was sent to Father Lasuén who was asked to circulate it with his full support. In September 1787, Governor Fages published a proclamation on the subject and Lasuén circulated the rules to his missions. For the next two years (1787–1789) the California otter trade proceeded according to Vasadre's revised plan. In November 1787, the *Favorita* and the *San Carlos* took 1,750 skins to San Blas; over one thousand were sent to San Diego from the lower California missions. In the north, Monterey added 220 skins and Santa Barbara sent 166. These were the largest contributors in upper California.

From San Blas, the California skins were sent overland to México City to be dressed, if they had not been treated in the north. They were then placed in pitch-covered boxes to preserve them from moths and then transported back over the highlands to the waiting Manila galleon at Acapulco. Because the supply vessels from the north arrived late in 1787, the galleon *San José* had to be held over until March. This was deemed unacceptable, so the request went out for the collections of skins to continue throughout the year so the pelts should be ready for the galleon's departure without delay.

The good news did not last long, and in 1788 very few skins were contributed to the Spanish missions. In October, Father Lasuén delivered only 76 skins to the *hablitado*,[30] and Father Cambón of San Francisco, 116 furs. In 1789, between 200 and 300 were collected from the missions of San Carlos, Santa Barbara, La Purísima, and San Buenaventura.

Some of the officials in New Spain felt the price schedule was set too high and felt the business would be a losing proposition if they paid seven to ten pesos[31] for first-class skins. In March 1787, the governor and mission fathers were asked to suggest a lower rate that would still provide some incentive for hunters. Father Lasuén argued that the schedule was fair and that as soon as the exchange of quicksilver in China was affected, it would be possible to pay even more. He concluded by saying that until a final decision was rendered, the missions would deliver skins without statement of their value, but with careful account of their number, quality, and size. When he was instructed to determine, according to the schedule of Vasadre, the worth of those skins he had sent the previous year, he again protested directly to the viceroy that values had risen.

The goods promised by Vasadre in return for the first skin collections were very slow in arriving and it appeared many skins were slipping down to San Blas on private accounts. But the biggest obstacle was an order issued in June of 1787, restricting mission control of trade. Merchandise destined for the purchase of skins was to be sent to the presidios where the *hablitados* could trade goods for furs. In addition, soldiers were to be allowed to barter and trade in furs. Father Palóu had recommended these changes to stop complaints directed by the soldiers against the missions and to reduce theft and destruction of property by soldiers engaged in the illegal sea otter trade. Sadly, his recommendations made things worse. Father Cambón described the situation to Palóu. Of the *hablitados* he said, *"They will pay the soldier well, and always will retain a profit; but to the*

Indian they will give a vara of flannel and six threads or a few beads for a large and fine skin, worth eight pesos, which the king will give them, and which will remain in their pockets." Cambón closed his letter to Palóu by appealing to him as an old friend to do all he could to have the new trade regulations repealed.

In 1790 legislative action was taken by the officials in Mexico City to offer lower prices. For example, skins of the first class that once could be purchased for seven to ten pesos, now brought only five to seven pesos. This effectively ended the Spanish sea otter trade and shifted sales to the American and British *contrabandistas*. The Spanish king ordered the Vasadre project discontinued, and the news reached Mexico City in July and California in December.

The odds had been against Vasadre from the first, and despite his letter of support from the administration, he was done in by the Philippine Company officials in Manila. They had opposed his plan from the beginning. Two years before they had been given the right to bring quicksilver from China. In 1786 and 1787, representatives of the company were in Madrid negotiating for permission to exchange mercury for California sea otter skins. In addition, the administrator of the Philippines, Ciríaco González de Carvajal, had also made a proposal to bring the California otter trade more directly under the control of the Philippine Company.

With no luck and likely growing despair, Vasadre arrived in Canton in November 1787. Through lavish spending in high society, he managed to make connections and sell his otter furs. However, there had been a slump in price as a result of a glut of skins brought from the Northwest Coast. Vasadre succeeded in getting a comparable price for his furs even though his southern skins were inferior in quality.

The Philippine officials were vexed by Vasadre's independence. They completely derailed his project when the *San José* arrived at Manila with 1,750 skins for Vasadre. The governor remitted the entire lot of furs to the Philippine Company office at Canton, not to Vasadre. Vasadre was advised that the sale of the new consignment was to be arranged jointly with the proceeds remaining in the care of the Company. He was also instructed to hand over the money or quicksilver he had received for the first lot of California skins.

Vasadre wrote a terse reply. He denied the right of the Philippine governor to have anything to do with the first consignment of skins and indicated he would follow up his original plan and push through his negotiations for quicksilver. To his critics, he was clearly *"one of those proud men foolishly pleased with their own judgment who aspire to independence."* In December 1788, the Philippine Company factors asked him to hand over either the first consignment of skins or the equivalent value in cash. Vasadre finally admitted defeat, turned over all his business affairs to the company, and left for Spain.

Vasadre lost but he had correctly seen the market opportunity. Sea otter skins did help obtain quicksilver for New Spain. Jars of Chinese mercury, obtained in exchange for otter skins, arrived on the Manila galleons from 1789 to 1793. Between 1786 and 1790, 9,729 sea otter and some seal skins were sent to China. Vasadre claimed they brought $3,120,000 to the treasury (but it was more likely closer to just a million).

English and American ships began to appear in California after 1790 and they could offer better goods and higher prices for furs. Before long they were taking 2–3,000 furs a year from California. Spain had made a bold move to limit the activities of foreign vessels in the North Pacific by occupying Nootka Sound in 1789, but when this threatened to lead to war it was not supported. Two other proposals for larger commercial fur ventures in the Pacific were outlined; but both, as presented to the king, failed to materialize.

If Vasadre's plans had been supported, the Russian outpost at Fort Ross might have been a Spanish fur trade fort instead. Adding outposts in Humboldt Bay and on the Columbia to *Núñez Gaona* on the Olympic Peninsula and Fort San Miguel in Nootka Sound might well have kept the Russians, British, and Americans at bay. In addition, his liberal economic instincts and entrepreneurial instincts might well have enabled the California economy to develop and remain in the Spanish fold.

In 1789 Vicente settled in Madrid, where he was appointed Member of the Board of Commissioners of the Company of the Philippines,[32] a position he held for six years. On December 5, 1794 he was made the secretary of the newly created Consulate of Veracruz, where he performed his duties with great success. He was sick in 1797 and asked to be transferred to the less stressful post of treasurer. In 1802, he wrote a position paper on a solution to the annual trans-Pacific outflow of about a million pesos from New Spain to China for raw and finished silk. He proposed *"in the pueblos of the jurisdiction of Veracruz the cultivation of silkworms"* to establish a local silk industry. His request for a transfer was finally honored in 1802 and he became treasurer. He continued in that role until 1806, when he was granted permission to spend two years at home in Spain to restore his health.

In the rebellion of 1808, Vicente sided with Napoleon, like many other Galicians. In this effort he collaborated with minister José Miguel de Azanza, a man he knew from Mexico. Azanza entrusted Vicente with a secret mission to Mexico to swing the vice royalty to Napoleon. His mission was to be camouflaged by Vicente's appointment as Minister of the Board of Commerce and Currency. He was given a passport from Joachim-Napoléon Murat (King of Naples) and sent toward Cadiz but captured by the Spanish loyalists and taken to Seville. After he recanted his support for Napoleon before the Junta de Sevilla he was appointed Secretary of Commerce and Business of the Indies (August 21, 1808), a position he continued to hold until he was appointed governor of Venezuela on January 7, 1809. He traveled to Guaira[33] and started work. He did well and he sent a large donation of money and cacao for the war against Napoleon.

On April 19, 1810, an initial declaration of Venezuela's semi-independence from Spain was signed.[34] Vasadre was brought before the revolutionary Cabildo and forced to resign. He returned to Spain as the first Spanish official deposed by the Spanish-American revolutions. In 1814 he was appointed administrator of Guadalajara and returned to Mexico but was unable to take up his position because the papers showing his collaboration with the French government had been found. He was ordered to Spain and imprisoned. After a long prison stay in Cádiz, he was tried and found guilty. He was eventually released but prohibited from residing in the capital, in a border area, or in a port. In 1824 he was accused of being a constitutionalist, found guilty, and jailed. He spent his last years in a La Coruña prison begging for his case to be reviewed. His last letter was addressed to the Secretary of State and Office of the Overseas Treasury in La Coruña on May 11, 1828 shortly before he died.

We know little of his family except that he had a son, Juan Vasadre. In 1832 Juan requested a position in the Indies; he may have been a ship captain or soldier. In 1839 the guide to non-natives living in Madrid includes Colonel Juan Vasadre. A man called Ignacio Vasadre, born in Veracruz, was involved in politics around Mexican Independence.

NIKOLAI PETROVICH REZANOV, STRATEGIC THINKER AND ROMANTIC

Nikolai Rezanov's father, Pyotr Gavrilovich, was registrar in the Imperial Senate in St. Petersburg when Nikolai was born in 1764. An attorney and judge, his father had also been president of the Equity Court in Irkutsk, so the family was familiar with life in the wilderness of Siberia. The family was in the ranks of the untitled nobility and few would have imagined how far Nikolai would rise during his career.

Katherine The Second's turn toward liberal and modern Europe helped create an international court that was alive with new ideas. Nikolai learned his lessons in French, but also knew Russian, German, and some Spanish. He was a musician and became friends with leading poets and writers. He was described as tall, smart, able, and courageous; but also, either cold and arrogant or warm and gracious. His rapid rise suggests that he was ambitious, able to get things done, and could work with people from many walks of life.

Nikolai Petrovich Rezanov

Nikolai joined the Izmaylovsky regiment of the Imperial Guard at the age of 14 and was a captain by the time he was 19. He was responsible for the protection of Katherine the Great during her trip to Crimea in 1780. After fulfilling his duty as a court officer, he joined the staff of the Bureau of Petitions to the tsarina at age 27. This bureau was effectively the nerve center of the empire.

In 1793 Nikolai assumed responsibility for overseeing developments in Alaska and reached Irkutsk in 1794. He also probably visited the Mongolian fur transfer town of Kyakhta, where furs entered China. In 1795 he married fur oligarch Natalia Shelikov's daughter Anna. Her dowry, shares in the family fur company, tied his fortunes to the fate of the fur trade in the Pacific. This probably led to his management role in the fur trading company and a not-always-easy relationship with his mother-in-law Natalia. Rezanov developed the Regulations of Prices in 1797 and managed land taxation in St. Petersburg and Moscow. He was awarded the Order of Saint Anna of the 2nd Class and 2000 rubles a year for his service.

Nikolai and Natalia probably worked out plans for the new fur company together. Her experience in the fur trade was much greater, but his understanding of the Hudson's Bay Company, East India Company, and international politics was better. Their wealth, noble connections, and political skills enabled them to obtain a monopoly on the fur trade through the *ukase* of 1799 and the creation of the Russian-American Company. It is probably not a coincidence that the approval was granted on Rezanov's birthday. Final results were not clear until Tsar Paul I. was assassinated in 1801 and the new Tsar Alexander confirmed the fur company monopoly.

The death of his wife[35] in childbirth in 1802 may have contributed to Nikolai's willingness to travel around the world with a Russian fleet in 1804. Hailed at the time as "the Columbus of Russia" he was much impressed with the agricultural potential of Hawaii. From Hawaii the warship *Neva* rushed to Sitka to combat the Tlingit revolt. Rezanov went to Petropavlovsk in Kamchatka instead, then sailed south to Japan. His goal of opening trade with Japan failed and he returned to Kamchatka in 1805 and headed to Alaska. He carried extra books with him and founded the first library at Kodiak. He supported improved educational efforts for natives and workers alike.

Maria de la Concepcion
Marcela Arguello

He was given greater responsibility for governance of Alaska in 1805 and he made an effort to reduce abuse of natives and workers and to protect the fur resource. Supply ships failed to arrive for four years and conditions grew increasingly difficult. "*There is no bread,*" wrote Rezanov in 1806, and he added that the Tlingit were well armed and that even fishing had to be done under threat. Rezanov took action and sailed to California for supplies even though the Spanish government prohibited foreign trade. The commander of San Francisco, José Dario Arguello,[36] was cordial but firm. After a complex strategic game of regulations, rules, foreign power legalities, and perhaps a few bribes, the needed supplies were made available for the Russians. This initiated a lively illegal exchange that benefitted both sides for many years. The Californios supplied the Russians with wheat, fruit, fruit trees, cattle and horses, and the Russians helped bring in manufactured goods.

The 41-year-old Nikolai fell in love with Maria de la Concepcion Marcela Arguello, the 15-year-old daughter of the commander of the Presidio of San Francisco. After a whirlwind romance he pledged to marry her. They celebrated the betrothal with a grand party. He wanted an immediate marriage, noting that he would soon have to return to St. Petersburg and he wished to take his bride with him. Their age difference and differing religions and languages were an obstacle to approval, but Rezanov's skill as a negotiator won them over. The only caveat was that the pope and the king of Spain must approve. Letters were sent. He may well have viewed his marriage in a dynastic light (as perhaps he had with his wife Anna Shelikov). He noted that the poor defense of California could easily have been overwhelmed by the Russians during a European crisis. He could easily foresee a Russian/Spanish empire symbolized by his marriage.

Rezanov was a big picture, long-game thinker, and his plans could have changed the future of the west coast from Mexico to California, Alaska to Hawaii. He also saw the potential value of bringing Chinese coolies to California to solve the persistent labor shortage. Sadly, he never made it back to St. Petersburg; he died of injuries sustained in a fall from his horse on the notoriously difficult trail between Irkutsk and Krasnoy in 1807.

No one in St. Petersburg came close to his energy, initiative, or grasp of the problems in the Pacific from Russia's standpoint. A remarkable opportunity was lost. Had Rezanov lived, we might speak Russian or Spanish in California today. He would never return to marry his love, Maria Conchita. Although myth says she waited for him faithfully for 40 years, the truth is equally sad. After Baranov told her brother (the first Spanish visitor to Russian Fort Ross in 1812) about his death, she would not marry. In 1852 she took a perpetual vow as Sister Maria Dominga, becoming one of California's first nuns.

JEDIDIAH STRONG SMITH, EXPLORER

Jedidiah S. Smith was born in July 1798 in Jericho, New York. He would spend his first ten years in this frontier town on the Susquehanna River, set in the rolling hills of central New York. His father, a store-keeper (also named Jedidiah), and mother Sally Strong, managed a

Jedidiah Strong Smith

family of 14 children. The Smiths had restless feet and the family moved on to Pennsylvania and then Ohio. As a boy, "Diah" was tutored by a friendly doctor and learned to read and write (along with a little Latin). His tutor and lifelong friend gave the young Smith a copy of Lewis and Clark's 1814 book, and it captured his imagination. He enjoyed hunt-

ing, fishing, and rambling through the woods and wilderness. At age 13 he started his first job, clerking on a freight boat on the Great Lakes, where he met fur traders and voyageurs. This suggests he was already able to do bookkeeping—perhaps he had learned in the family store.

In 1822 he heeded General William Ashley's call for enterprising young men to work north in the Missouri country. Even as a young man he had an aura of quiet competence, strength, and will. He was soon hired on as a hunter. In the next nine years he would cover more ground than anyone else in the exploration of the West, ful-filling his intended role, "I wanted to be the first to view a country on which the eyes of a white man had never gazed and to follow the course of rivers that run through a new land."

A passport bearing the signature of Secretary of State Martin Van Buren was issued to William Sublette for "Diah" on April 9, 1831, noting that he was 6'2" in height, with a "straight and open" fore-head, light blue eyes and a Roman nose, with "Light or Sandy hair," and a fair complexion. It was also noted that his face was "long &

expressive with a scar on the left chin." He was most unusual for a mountain man, trapper, trader, and explorer. He was religious (a devout Methodist), and therefore drank very little, did not smoke, did not consort with women, and he shaved daily. He was serious and found little humor in life. He preferred a black silk bandana and was seemingly concerned about his looks and tried to hide his mangled right ear. After engaging a grizzly bear in hand-to-paw combat the bear lifted his scalp and tore off his ear. Smith had the presence of mind to have James Clyman sew his scalp back on and then persuaded him to sew up the ear as best he could. Smith was tough. He then mounted up on his horse and rode back to camp.

In 1824, he bought out Major Andrew Henry's share to became a company partner with William Ashley. He led a party of men north and west from the Missouri, met Alexander Ross and Peter Skene Ogden from the HBC, and followed them all the way up to the Flathead Post. They traveled together for protection. We can also imagine Smith pumping the trappers for information, scouting the country, and assaying their willingness to work for someone other than the HBC.

In 1825, Smith was at the mountain man rendezvous near Green River and began a new partnership with William Sublette and David Jackson. He then returned to St. Louis. In 1826 he started what would be almost three years of continuous travel; first, back to the known areas of Wyoming and Utah, and then leaving Bear River on August 7th he headed down the Colorado River and across parts of the old Spanish trail to California to arrive at the San Gabriel Mission on November 27th. They were fed and cared for, but tensions were clear. Fortunately, they were eventually allowed to leave, and headed north over the Tehachapi Range to trap the San Joaquin River and the tributaries flowing from the Sierra Nevada Mountains.

Here Smith left most of his trappers while he and two others returned to Wyoming for the next rendezvous, arriving on July 3. While there, he dispatched a letter about his travels and discoveries to William Clark, now the Superintendent of Indian Affairs. With new supplies and men, he returned down the Colorado to California, where several of his men were killed by the Mojave people. He collected his remaining men and then headed north through Oregon where most in his group were killed on the Umpqua River. The survivors made it north to Fort Vancouver. The HBC didn't charge him for their efforts in recovering his furs and equipment from the Umpqua but made up for it by offering a low price for his furs. After recovering for part of the winter at Fort Vancouver, Smith headed east to Fort Colville and on to the Flathead Post before returning south to the Wind River area and the rendezvous. He sold out of his company and headed down the river to St. Louis for the last time.

Smith had negotiated his way out of trouble with the Spanish authorities in California, thanks in part to a friendly American ship captain. He had traveled and observed the HBC brigades twice, spent

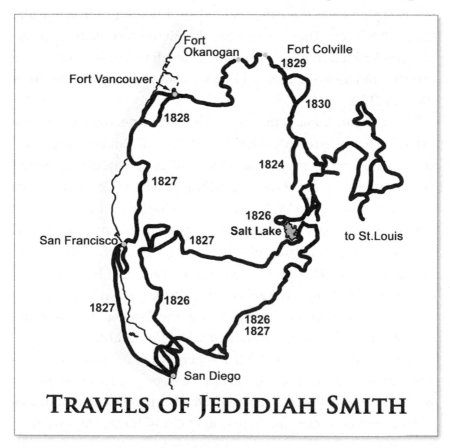

TRAVELS OF JEDIDIAH SMITH

several months at Fort Vancouver after the Umpqua massacre, and contemplated crossing Canada at the invitation of George Simpson, the governor of the HBC. He had observed and mapped new lands and wrote letters about what he had learned to the appropriate government entities back home. He finally returned to St. Louis after three exhausting years.

Smith had proved himself to be a fighter early on and his bravery was never questioned. No matter how difficult the journey, he was always in the lead. He had remarkable stamina (and will) and seemed to function better than anyone else with little or no water, food, or sleep. His men appreciated his skills and leadership, but he proved to be a dangerous man to travel with. He was the leader of parties that cost many trappers' lives.

He had wanted to explore and map new territory, and he did. At the time of his death he had both a book and giant map underway. Unfortunately, his large map of several sheets was lost, but notations from the Smith map(s) improved many others, including the 1836 map of the West by Albert Gallatin, the 1839 map of the United States by David Burr, and two 1841 maps of the Oregon Country. Lt. John C. Fremont's 1845 map of the West includes notes detailing routes and landmarks in descriptive language that could only have come from Jedediah Smith.

He was a reasonably good businessman, though his partners might have preferred to see more trapping and less traveling. He amassed a considerable fortune for his hard work and risk taking. When the Jackson, Smith, and Sublette furs were sold in 1830 they returned $84,499. His share after expenses might have been more than $25,000 (more than a half-million dollars today).

Smith kept busy when he got home, purchasing a townhouse on Federal Street in St. Louis to share with his brothers Ira, Peter, and Austin. He also bought two house slaves. In addition, he sent money for his brother Ralph to purchase 261 acres for him in Wayne County, Ohio. He wrote to the Secretary of War to describe the South Pass that would make the Oregon Trail feasible. In March 1831, he

asked the Secretary of War John H. Eaton to fund a federal exploration of the West, but to no avail. He could not settle, and invested in
and left on a trading party to Santa Fe with 24 wagons and 78 men,
including two of his brothers. While looking for water on the driest
part of the Santa Fe Trail he was surprised and killed by a group of
Comanche warriors in May.

In less than ten years Smith had covered a remarkable stretch
of ground and proven himself under the most trying conditions. He
had been lonely and sometimes felt unworthy if we can believe his
letters home. He had one close friend, Robert Campbell. Although
William H. Ashley was to be the executor of his estate, his brother
Ira challenged the appointment and won, taking over in 1833. Ashley
turned over $9,000 in assets. His brother Ralph retained the farm-
land. Robert Campbell apparently helped with accounts. His father
was to get $200 a year for life and the rest was split among his many
siblings.

He summed up his life, "I started into the mountains, with the
determination of becoming a first-rate hunter, of making myself
thoroughly acquainted with the character and habits of the Indians,
of tracing out the sources of the Columbia River and following it to
its mouth; and of making the whole profitable to me, and I have per-
fectly succeeded."

OLIGARCHS

NATALIA SHELIKHOVA, FUR OLIGARCH

Natalia Alexeyevna Kozhevina was born about 1762 in Okhotsk to
Aleksei Kozhevin, a prominent navigator, adventurer, and explorer,
and his wife Fiokla. The couple could not have guessed how far their
daughter would travel and how far she would rise. In 1775, Gregorii
Shelikhov (age 28) married Natalia (age thirteen and a half). It
would be a successful, if at times turbulent, partnership. Natalia
proved to be a tough and adventurous traveler, effective administrator, and a very successful businesswoman and politician.

In late August 1783, Natalia, Gregorii, and their young son left Okhotsk for Alaska in a newly built galiot christened *The Three Saints*. Adverse weather and sea conditions forced them to winter over on Bering Island, and they did not reach Kodiak Island until late the next summer. Working along with their crew, Natalia and Gregorii collected pelts, started the first homes, improved the settlement's defenses, and built a second outpost at Kenai Bay (now Cook Inlet). While returning to Russia in early August 1786, the Shelikhov's ship made landfall near Bolshaya Rechka in Kamchatka. While Gregorii and a small shore party were searching for fresh water and food, a gale struck and *The Three Saints* dragged anchor. The ship was blown

Natalia Shelikhova

to the south with Natalia and the children onboard. The crew was unable to sail back to pick up the shore party. Gregorii and his men made their way overland to Petropavlovsk and waited for the ship. As winter set in Gregorii realized that the storm must have pushed *The Three Saints* far to the south and he set out overland with dog teams. He caught up with his family in Okhotsk two and a half months later, after covering 1200 miles. He rested only eight days before the family set out on the next leg of the journey to Yakutsk, and then on to Irkutsk.

The Shelikhovs would gain power, money, and fame from their fur trading. The risk and reward might be compared to the narco-cartels today. The danger was very great but so was the potential profit. There were six primary Russian joint-stock enterprises active in Alaska in the 1780s but the Shelikhov company was the richest. Altogether they would sponsor or participate in 21 trips and bring in furs worth 2.5 million rubles. The Shelikhovs also learned that establishing settlements in Alaska would not be easy but that the profits could be worth the cost. They hoped to use the results of this trip to convince Tsarina Katherine II. to invest.

Extending their business and the Russian empire to a new continent posed immense problems of supply and communication. St. Petersburg was nearly half a world and many months to a year of travel away. A fragile lifeline extended across more than five thousand miles of Eurasia and three thousand more of the dangerous North Pacific. The Shelikhovs' experiences in sailing to Alaska and back demonstrated how tenuous the connection could be. Under the best conditions it took less than two months to travel from Irkutsk to Okhotsk and another three to sail to Alaska. Yet it took the Shelikhovs nearly a year to reach Alaska and only a few weeks less to return to Irkutsk after fighting storms at sea and blizzards on land.

Natalia Shelikhova became a critical person in the fur trading empire. While Gregorii was absent from Irkutsk, Natalia was in charge of all the business affairs. In her letters, she kept Grigorii well-informed, consulted with him, and repeatedly told him that she and the children missed him. But there were also undercurrents of anger, apology, and frustration. Gregorii was busy supervising shipbuilding in Okhotsk, watching developments at the fur trading point to China at Kyakhta, and making appearances in the salons of St. Petersburg. He pushed the Company's expansion in every possible quarter.

Natalia, with her ledgers, keys, and scales, kept the vast operation going and earned her share of the company. She sent goods to markets and fairs, dealt with debtors and creditors, gave orders to salesmen, dealt with the powerful merchants in town, and many other things. At the same time, she was also the family matriarch and took care of the house and family. She managed to deliver eight[37] children and took care of several Aleut children they brought back from Alaska for further education. The Irkutsk merchants and her sons-in-law addressed her as *matushka* (little mother), a respectful term reserved for priests' wives and the tsarina. Even so, it was undoubtedly quite difficult to be a female in charge of a company in a frontier town.

Gregorii died in Irkutsk in 1795 after experiencing severe stomach pain. Given his many enemies, it is possible that he was poisoned. Rumors that it might have been his wife who poisoned him, or that it was perhaps a suicide, circulated. More likely, it was appendicitis or one of any number of diseases. In any case, Natalia was widowed and left to manage on her own. She went to work immediately, and by 1797 she was able to invest in the Russian-American enterprise. In the reorganization of July 19, 1797 in Irkutsk she noted, *"I give exactly my entire half of that which belongs to me and my children to the company of Mylnikov and his partners for 600,000 rubles."* This was the equivalent of about $300,000 then (roughly $50 million today). Her wealth enabled her to be equally successful at court intrigue. She became a fur oligarch but was probably never fully accepted by the nobles in St. Petersburg, given her lowly birth.

Competitors and rivals tried to usurp Shelikhov's vast holdings, but Natalia emerged victorious thanks to a series of petitions, letters, and bribes to both the court and highly placed regional officials. Nikolai Rezanov, her son-in-law, was a high-ranking government official and this helped. Tsarina Katherine II. was encouraged to support Natalia's efforts and granted her hereditary nobility in 1796, giving Natalia a status above other merchants, allowing her greater access to those in power. After Katherine's death, her son Paul I. helped protect Natalia's interests with support for the Russian-American Company.

Rezanov was appointed chief secretary of the Senate in 1797 and was a representative for the United American Company. In the same year Golikov tried to break off business with Natalia by withdrawing his half of the capital. But Natalia had invested wisely, preserving the value of her shares and making her a continuing major player in the fur trade. Golikov and Shelikhov merged with the Myl'nikovs to create the United American Company, and a charter for this new company was granted by imperial decree and under imperial protection in 1798. Natalia's position was strong, as she owned a third of the shares and had the contractual right to help choose the director and edit company proposals.

Natalia developed and presented many proposals to St. Petersburg about the best organizational strategies to employ in order for a company to effectively operate in the North Pacific and world markets. Natalia presented a thirty-paragraph plan that was included in the charter of the new Russian-American Company (RAC) on July 8, 1799. The RAC supplanted the United America Company. Among other things, her proposal recommended a self-sufficient agricultural supply in America (later partially realized at Fort Ross) and the translation of Russian passports into Spanish and other languages so Russian boats could be better received in foreign ports and encounters. Natalia's influence gradually diminished, although she still retained many shares of the RAC. Natalia's two sons-in-law became prominent in the directorship. Her son-in-law Nikolai Rezanov held many shares and traveled widely through Russia, Alaska, and California promoting the company's interests. Support for this low-cost soft-power approach to Russian territorial expansion paid good dividends for the government.

Natalia might have been just a wife and homemaker in Irkutsk but instead she became an international businesswoman, merchant, politician, and fur oligarch. The fur profits from Alaska were never a significant part of the Russian treasury but fed directly into the royal budget. Natalia's concern for the welfare and education of the native people was notable. She had a number of native god daughters[38] and her efforts helped promote education, intercultural, and interpersonal understanding. Natalia died in 1810 at the age of 48 after a remarkable life.

MAQUINNA: EMPEROR, TACTICIAN, TRADER

Maquinna[39] was the name of the ranking chief of the Mowachaht group of the Nuu-chah-nulth. During the early period of discovery on the west coast of Vancouver Island, Maquinna, born about 1750, was one of the most powerful leaders. He was chief from 1778–1795, and was succeeded by his brother Quatlazape', who also took up the name Maquinna. Maquinna II. led from 1796–1825. The Mowachaht made a yearly round from the summer village at Yuquot to a salmon harvesting village at Tahsis,[40] and on to the winter village at Coopte[41] for herring.

The population of the Yuquot village was perhaps 2,000 people with 500 warriors. About a third of the village may have been slaves captured in raids or purchased; Maquinna alone was reported to have had 50. He was the dominant leader of Nootka Sound and his control extended over a large area with possibly more than ten thousand people in his sphere of influence. His most powerful rival, Wickaninnish, lived to the south at Clayoquot Sound, but peace was maintained through intermarriage.

Maquinna met Captain James Cook in 1778 when his ship spent about a month near the village of Yuquot. It is thought that the native people told Cook to "come around" to the cove. Thinking they were saying their tribal name, they became the Nootka and are so called in most accounts. This name was subsequently inappropriately extended to all the tribes speaking a similar Wakashan language extending from Cook Creek to the north to beyond Port San Juan, and sometimes including the Makah of Flattery Creek, Washington.

Maquinna

Cook's crew established friendly trading relations with the people of Yuquot, and many items changed hands, including sea otter pelts. Cook's crew later sold these for great profits in Canton, and this changed the future course of life on the Northwest Coast. Cook's crew may also have left behind diseases that afflicted the Mowachaht. The cove Cook stayed at became known as

Friendly Cove. The large bay became known as Nootka Sound, and after the friendly reception by Maquinna and the Mowachahts it became an important port of call for traders. For a while it was the center of the sea otter trade and then became the center of conflict between foreign powers.

The next contact was probably James Hanna in the sailing ship *Sea Otter* in 1785. Maquinna was invited onboard and sat on a seat the sailors had placed gunpowder on and touched it off. He later showed scars to the Spanish and complained about the ill nature of Hanna. Trade disputes over pricing arose as well, and after a chisel was stolen from the ship, a conflict erupted. Hanna's muskets and swivel guns may have killed as many as fifty Mowachaht who attacked the ship.

In 1786, when Alexander Walker visited Nootka Sound with the expedition of James Charles Stuart Strange, he noted that Maquinna the elder was "blind with age" and that Maquinna the younger had assumed leadership. Walker described him as "*a stout handsome young man, with a fine manly countenance,*" and added, "*he was the most intelligent Indian I met.*" When British captain John Meares arrived in 1788, Maquinna allowed him to erect a small building on some land at Yuquot, an action that would embroil his people in international politics. Meares describes Maquinna as being "*of a middle size, but extremely well made, and possessing a countenance that was formed to interest all who saw him.*"

The Yuquot were skilled traders and equal matches for the foreigners, often to the European's frustration. From the time of Cook's visit, Maquinna and the people of Yuquot expanded their efforts to control contacts between Europeans and other tribes. Furs from a large area would have to pass through Maquinna's hands to reach the traders. By 1792 he also controlled a trading network with the Kwakiutl group at the mouth of the Nimpkish River (on the east coast of Vancouver Island). Trade routes across the island were used to transfer furs from the east coast of the island and then sold to ships visiting Yuquot and Nootka sound. Like the European captains, Maquinna understood price differentials, and the trader John Hoskins reported that he was a very successful broker and intermediary.

The Spanish sent a frigate north in 1789 to reinforce Spanish land claims to the area and Esteban José Martínez claimed the area for King Charles III. When a force under Francisco de Eliza y Reventa arrived at Yuquot in April and began to build a small settlement, the Mowachaht left the cove. The Spanish settlement and fort were rebuilt a year later by Francisco de Eliza and Pere d'Alberní i Teixidor after Spain decided to firm up claims to Nootka Sound. The Mowachaht's fears were not allayed by Eliza's theft of valuable and difficult to replace planks from their village. Maquinna was also concerned because Eliza, having heard about ritual cannibalism, had threatened to destroy Yuquot if the act was repeated.

British trader James Colnett arrived at Yuquot in January 1791 and tried to win Maquinna back to the British side. Maquinna asked "to see a larger ship" because he wanted to remain on good terms with the Spaniards or to side with the team with the biggest, best armed ships. Martínez arrested Colnett for infringing on Spanish sovereignty. This was seen as a threat to profitable trade by the Mowachaht and other tribes, and Maquinna's brother, Chief Callicum, paddled out to berate the Spanish for their ill treatment of Colnett. He was subsequently shot and killed.

Maquinna temporarily moved to Opitsaht, Wickaninnish's village in Clayoquot Sound. He was welcome because Wickaninnish was the father of Callicum's wife. Maquinna kept a close eye on events at Yuquot, and when a rival chief visited Martínez in August, Maquinna made sure to appear as well. He was at Yuquot again in September and promised Martínez, then departing, to take care of the buildings of the small post they had established.

In June, Maquinna met an exploring mission under Manuel Quimper at Opitsaht, and relations stabilized enough to allow him to help search for survivors of a shipwreck. Maquinna then moved back to his village of Tahsis. When Alexandro Malaspina visited there in August, Maquinna ratified the cession to the Spanish of land at Yuquot made in 1790.

Maquinna's diplomatic skills, which were honed in intertribal relations, proved useful when Juan Francisco de la Bodega Quadra and Captain George Vancouver arrived at Yuquot in 1792 to arrange implementation of the terms of the Nootka Convention. This was intended to end the conflict over the ownership of the coast. It was said that Maquinna played a key role in smoothing relations between them; both enjoyed Maquinna's hospitality, and he was a frequent dinner guest onboard ship. He and his brother apparently performed a masquerade for Vancouver and Bodega Quadra in which the noble brothers acted out a pantomime of European dress and manners, improvising mock-Spanish and mock-English dialogue, all set in the customary style of the great potlatch theatre-dance culture of the Northwest Coast.

When Bodega Quadra left Nootka Sound in September, Yuquot was still in Spanish hands, but it was abandoned in March 1795 after further negotiations between Spain and Britain. Maquinna's people tore down the buildings, reclaimed their planks, and rebuilt their homes. Charles Bishop reported that the village had been reestablished at Yuquot when he visited in September. The elder Maquinna died about this time and his brother Quatlazape' took his place and assumed the name, Maquinna. The new chief faced the more difficult task of trying to maintain his people's prosperity in the face of declining fur sources and increasingly violent conflict between the Mowachaht and Europeans

Relations deteriorated along the coast. Villages were shot and burned, furs were taken from homes and people by force, hostages were taken and abused, diseases struck; and casual murders had been committed for little or no reason by fur traders. Continuing insults and violence against the local people led to the attack on the trading vessel *Boston* in March of 1803. The *Boston* had been in Nootka Sound for several days and was about to leave when Maquinna complained to Captain Salter about a defective gun.

Salter cussed him out, little realizing that Maquinna knew English, including swear words, very well. The fresh insults and long string of grievances were too much and had to be avenged. The vessel was taken and accidentally burned, but most of the goods and guns had been salvaged and moved to the village.

The armorer (blacksmith) John Rodgers Jewitt and the sail-maker John Thompson were spared. Jewitt had been wounded with an axe blow to the head but Maquinna appreciated his skills and character and spared his life. Jewitt interceded on behalf of the older sailmaker, saying he was his father. Jewitt possessed skills that were valuable to Maquinna, and for the next two years the captives lived as the chief's slaves. Jewitt crafted daggers and harpoons, including a new design. Jewitt learned the language and integrated nicely with the village, marrying, and fathering a child. Jewitt provided the most accurate accounts of village life with Maquinna before the catastrophes of disease and further conflict disrupted the community.

According to Jewitt's records, Maquinna held a potlatch in 1803 where he distributed 200 muskets and seven barrels of gunpowder, as well as other goods. Jewitt also tells how Maquinna's life was threatened by those who resented the fact that fur traders no longer came to Nootka Sound after the story of the taking of the *Boston* circulated. Sea otter furs had also become scarce. Maquinna had to intercede to keep people concerned about the possibility of retribution by the Europeans for the attack on the *Boston* from killing Jewitt, the witness.

Wickaninnish offered to purchase Jewitt, but Maquinna refused. The *Lydia* was the first ship to arrive in 1805. A letter from Jewitt had been carried to the north and was picked up, so the captain knew about the captives. Jewitt wrote a "safe pass letter" for Maquinna that was actually a request to hold him for ransom. The captain invited Maquinna aboard and took him as a hostage for Jewitt and Thompson. This temporary capture further damaged his prestige. Jewitt thought well enough of Maquinna to keep the *Lydia* from hanging him and blasting the village to bits. When he left, Maquinna promised to look after Jewitt's son.

Maquinna probably found his later years fraught with tension and difficulty as the otter fur trade declined; diseases like smallpox swept through the villages and the old ways faded. When the *William & Ann* arrived in 1825 they visited and entertained Chief Maquinna. "*Before venturing on board the old man inquired from what country we had come, & on being informed that we were English, he & his people clapped their hands & seemed highly delighted. On showing him a portrait of Mr. Mears he soon recognized his old friend, & had not forgot the Spaniards or C. Vancouver. When we showed him the portraits of himself & Calleum, he easily found out the unfortunate chief & told us that Komkela was dead for many years. In the evening he & his people left us, much pleased with the reception they had experienced.*"

The Mowachahts have endured, and they still live on Vancouver Island. Mike Maquinna assumed leadership of the tribe in 1998. As of 2015 there were only 20 fluent speakers left, but efforts are underway to preserve and reintroduce the language. The Mowachaht and Muchalaht merged in 1950. The combined Nuu-chah-nulth First Nations people currently number about 1,000 and are scattered throughout northern Vancouver Island, with villages located at Espinoza Inlet (Ocluje), near the Village of Zeballos (Ehatis), and Gold River (Tsaxana).

KING COMCOMLY: TRIUMPH AND TRAGEDY

Comcomly was born about 1765 and was active for almost the entire period of the sea otter fur trade. He met and dealt with nearly all the important players, including Lewis and Clark. His skill as a statesman, businessman, and tactician led to great triumphs. At his peak he was referred to as "Chief" or "King" Comcomly and was a key leader of the Chinook people along the lower Columbia River. In large part due to his acumen and drive, the common language of the period was Chinook based.

His parents are thought to have been Chief Komkomis and Tama-I-Tami, and he may also have had Willapa, Chehalis, and Quinault relatives. His summer village of Kwatsa'mts was on the north bank

King Comcomly

of the Columbia River near the mouth of the Chinook River and Chinook Point. Up until 1824, the summer village had been at Point Ellice (Ellis), but this site was abandoned out of grief for the many family members who had succumbed to smallpox and other introduced diseases, and were buried there.

The size of the original Chinook population is unknown but was certainly in the many thousands. The Chinooks told Lewis and Clark of deadly smallpox outbreaks in 1776 and 1801. Other diseases also took their toll and many villages had been depopulated by 1800. The population distribution in different clans is not known either, but perhaps 400 were under Comcomly when Lewis and Clark arrived. His sphere of influence grew quickly and several thousand people were under his leadership at his peak.

Comcomly met fur traders from many ships in the late 1700s. In 1795, the British ship *Ruby,* under Captain Charles Bishop, sailed into the Columbia and traded for furs for eleven days. The captain noted: "*The Sea Otter skins procured here, are of an Excellent Quality and large size, but they are not in abundance and the Natives themselves set great value on them.*" Captain Bishop invited Chief Comcomly to spend the night aboard the ship and provided him with a fine coat and trousers. When the Chinooks ran out of furs, the British traded for clamons (body armor), which were in high demand further up the coast. Recognizing the demand and value associated with clamons, Comcomly then led a Chinook expedition 300 miles upriver to obtain more.

Chief Comcomly encountered Lewis and Clark and the other overland traders on the coast as well. This one-eyed statesman was mentioned as a secondary chief in 1795 but had become tribal leader by the time the Corps of Discovery arrived in late 1805. On November 17th, as the party struggled to complete the last stretch of their journey down the Columbia, William Clark wrote, *"The Chief of the nation below us Came up to See us the name of the nation is (Chinnoo) Chin-nook and is noumerous live principally on fish roots a few Elk and fowls. they are well armed with good Fusees."* Comcomly was wearing a stylish cloth coat when they met.

When the Astorians arrived on the *Tonquin* in 1811, two of the American partners, Duncan McDougal and David Stuart, came ashore in a small boat and met with Chief Comcomly. He was agreeable to the idea of a trading post. When they set out to return to their ship Comcomly pointed out the rough conditions on the river and told them the trip would be too dangerous. The traders were perhaps afraid of staying and set out anyway. Comcomly followed in his large canoe and rescued them when their boat capsized. He took the wet men ashore, built a fire, dried their clothes, and hosted them at his village for three days until conditions improved. He then took them back to their ship in his canoe.

In 1792 John Boit commented, *"The Men, at Columbia's River, are strait limb'd, fine looking fellows, and the Women are very pretty. They are all in a state of Nature, except the females, who wear a leaf Apron."* Gabriel Franchère later wrote, *"They possess, in an eminent degree, the qualities opposed to indolence, improvidence, and stupidity: the chiefs, above all, are distinguished for their good sense and intelligence. Generally speaking, they have a ready intellect and a tenacious memory. Thus, old Comcomly recognized the mate of the Albatross as having visited the country sixteen years before, and recalled to the latter the name of the captain under whom he had sailed at that period."* David Thompson in 1811 found Comcomly to be *"a strong, well-made man, his hair short, of dark brown, and naked except a short kilt around his waist to the middle of the thigh.*" He was later described as a short elderly man, but the richest and most powerful chief on the river.

When the fur traders arrived, the people of the lower Columbia region already possessed a sprawling, competitive, and successful trade system exchanging many items, including slaves. Rather than attempting to supplant it, the fur traders endeavored to work their way into the existing networks. Comcomly was a shrewd politician, tactician, trader, diplomat, and a key player in the trade. He befriended almost all the British and Euro-American explorers he encountered, including Robert Gray and George Vancouver. He was given peace medals by Lewis and Clark and assisted the Pacific Fur Company (the Astor Expedition) when they arrived in 1811. Comcomly made near-daily visits to Fort Astoria, where he was admitted to the most intimate councils of his son-in-law. He was also given his own quarters in the fort. Like many other native people, he probably developed a good working knowledge of English.

Comcomly dominated the trade with Euro-Americans by being an aggressive middleman with reported profits of 50% in many trades. Charles Bishop, trading at the mouth of the Columbia in 1795–1796, noted that Comcomly discouraged other native groups from trading directly with the foreigners by portraying each side as a threat to the other. As George Simpson noted, "*The Chinooks [are] keen traders and through their hands nearly the whole of our Furs pass, indeed so tenacious are they of this Monopoly that their jealousy would carry them the length of pillaging or even murdering strangers who come to the Establishment if we did not protect them. To the other tribes on the Coast they represent us as Cannibals and every thing that is bad in order to deter them from visiting the Fort.*" His understanding of the traders and his many slaves and relations gave him an advantage in the movement of goods and interactions with customers.

Comcomly generously offered 800 warriors to help the Americans fight the British during the War of 1812 and was disappointed that no war broke out (as was captain William Black of the British warship *HMS Raccoon*). He piloted ships upriver and was often entertained at Fort Vancouver by the Hudson Bay Company's Factor John McLoughlin.

At his peak power he was a primary figure in the Columbia River area. He retained his leadership role until 1824, when, at the age of about sixty, he retired and conferred his name and the chieftainship on one of his sons. He had a number of wives, children, and slaves. His daughters were married strategically to maintain relations with other tribes and traders; one married Coalpo, a powerful leader of a Clatsop village on the south side of the Columbia near Fort Astoria. In 1811, his daughter Ilchee (nicknamed the Princess of Wales) married Astorian Duncan McDougal, chief factor of John Jacob Astor's Pacific Fur Company. After he left, she married the upper river Chinook Chief Casino. Marrying his daughters to fur traders brought more foreign goods and access to power.

Comcomly had many other children. Sadly, his favorite sons Chalakan and Choulits died in 1824, probably from smallpox. Casacas (nicknamed the Prince of Wales) possibly took over as leader. Another son, Selechel (nicknamed the Duke of York) was also a leader.

Introduced diseases continued to kill the Chinook people. Comcomly died in 1830 when a malarial fever virtually wiped out the remainder of his tribe. The HBC Chief Factor Dr. McLoughlin stated that ninety percent of the Chinook people had died by the end of the epidemic. Comcomly was noted as sitting forlornly at Fort Vancouver before his death.

Comcomly's grandson, Ranald MacDonald, had a very remarkable life and was the first person to teach English in Japan, from 1847 to 1848. Descendants of Comcomly include Chinook elder and historian Catherine Troeh (1911–2007) and Ambassador J. Christopher Stevens who perished in Benghazi.

By 1840 there were very few Chinook left and the population sank so low that the tribe was not recognized by the federal government. A new case against the head of the Department of Interior, Ryan Zinke, was started by the Chinook Indian Nation in 2017.

DR. JOHN MCLOUGHLIN, EMPEROR OF THE OREGON TERRITORY

John "Jean" Baptiste McLoughlin was born in Quebec in 1784 to a farmer also named John and mother Angélique. He began his medical apprenticeship at the age of 14 and earned his physician's license in 1803 but did not practice medicine. Instead, he signed on with partners of the North West Company of fur traders as a clerk and trader the same year, perhaps to flee problems resulting from a fight with an army officer. He was a towering man of six-foot-four, and he did well as a trader, serving a number of posts in the north central fur trade areas.

Dr. John McLoughlin

He re-upped with the NWC in 1808 to help support his brother's medical studies in Scotland. He served at several posts before arriving at Fort William in 1815. He was implicated and arrested for his role in the Red River Massacre,[42] but was eventually cleared. In fact, he helped prevent the massacre of the men at Fort William. He became convinced that the war between the NWC and HBC would bankrupt them both, and he played an important role in the discussions that led to negotiations and a merger in 1821. He travelled to London but became sick and spent some time under his brother's care.

Upon his return to Canada, John took over as Chief Factor for the Rainy Lake District. He was soon moved to Fort George (Astoria), arriving in the fall of 1824 to manage the Columbia District. It was a mess, with many things to be fixed and the added uncertainty of U.S.-Britain border disputes. HBC Governor George Simpson granted him special authority and freedom to make decisions and improve profits. Operations were moved to the new Fort Vancouver location, much better situated than Fort George. The first site they chose for the fort was up on the bluff but it was too far from the river and the fort was relocated to the flat area near the river in 1828. The mandate to create a "fur desert" guided some of his decisions regarding the allocation of men and resources. Progress was quick, with a sawmill, flour mill, and salmon salting underway. The cost of collecting furs was down as demand drove prices up.

McLoughlin was known to have a violent temper but was recognized as being fair to all, whether native, mixed race, British, or American. This helped lead to the success of both the fort and the adjacent Kanaka Village. Tall and muscular with steely blue eyes, he cut quite a figure. Premature white hair added to his look and some natives called him "White Eagle." He enjoyed entertaining visitors and even treated competitors surprisingly well. He helped Jedidiah Smith recover some of his lost property and hosted him while the effort was underway.

When George Simpson visited in 1829, he was delighted with the progress that had been made and the two discussed ways to improve and extend the coastal trade. Sea otters had become scarce, leading to a greater effort to collect land furs from native tribes. They decided to try some trading posts on the coast and hoped negotiations with the Russians would secure supply contracts to displace American traders. New fur outposts were built and the farming center at Fort Nisqually was developing. An effort to build a post on the Stikine River was dashed by the Russians. The "Dryad Incident" proved costly, with a claimed loss of £22,000.

Conflict with the Americans heated up in 1832 with the arrival of Nathaniel Jarvis Wyeth. His first supply ship was lost (as were many of McLoughlin's) but he persisted. In 1833, Wyeth suggested a partnership with the HBC but it was rejected by the HBC partners. Wyeth went east and returned in 1834 with the Methodist missionary Jason Lee. McLoughlin bought Wyeth out but the HBC partners were not happy about it. The American pressure continued to build, and in 1838, Dr. McLoughlin was called to London for a meeting.

In 1839 the negotiations with the RAC paid off and HBC got a lease for the Alaska Panhandle in exchange for providing supplies for the RAC. The farm base at the Puget Sound Agricultural Company was able to supply much of the food. Simpson's added responsibility for this effort led to a £500 salary increase. He returned west in 1841 and told McLoughlin to close most of the posts and to rely on the steamship *Beaver* instead. They first met at Fort Vancouver, and later in Hawaii at the new HBC post. He was also ordered to find a new base of operations safe from the Americans in case there was an adverse ruling on boundary lines and territorial ownership. This led to the creation of Fort Victoria in 1843.

In 1842, he developed a design for a city at the falls on the Willamette River. In 1845, he paid for the land claim on what would later become Oregon City, the terminus of the Oregon Trail. He was demoted that same year in what appeared to be an effort to get him to quit—which he did. He then moved to Oregon City in 1846. The company rewarded him handsomely for his service, with a two-year leave of absence, a full share for a year, and half a share for five more years beyond that. By one estimate, he had a net worth of $142,585 (more than $20 million today) when he retired. McLoughlin became a citizen of the United States in 1849, built a sawmill and grist mill, was active as a merchant, and served as mayor in 1851.

McLoughlin married Marguerite Wadin (Wadden) McKay, a half-Cree, around 1810 *à la façon du pays*. He officially married her in 1842. She had four children from her previous relationship, and they had two (or three) sons and two daughters together. One son, a manager, was murdered at Fort Stikine. John McLoughlin died of diabetic gangrene in 1857 at the age of 73, following a monumental life. It took five years to transfer his property to his heirs. The Americans continued to chip away at the HBC and Canadians in Oregon; but in 1957, the Oregon legislature passed a bill calling John McLoughlin "the father of Oregon."

Aleksandr Baranov, king of the north

Aleksandr Baranov was born in 1747 in Kargopol, an important trading center with some textile works on the Olnega River, 500 miles north of Moscow. Aleksandr was small of build, fair-haired, and said to be quick of mind, alert, friendly, and clever with his hands. He received some education in Kargopol but moved to Moscow at the age of fifteen to apprentice with a German textile merchant.

Baranov returned home to marry and become a merchant, but in pursuit of greater success the couple moved to Siberia in 1780. He started out as the manager of a glass factory at Irkutsk but then built his own glass factory at the confluence of the Tal'tsinka and Angara rivers to make bottles, flat glass, and beads for the fur trade. He also distilled vodka and made candles. Baranov was elected as a participating member of the St. Petersburg Imperial Free Economic Society about this time. He also worked as an alcohol tax collector, receiving a share of the taxes collected in his work.

John Ledyard probably dined with Baranov in August 1787, as he noted, *"Dined with a gentleman at his glass manufactory and returned in the evening to Irkutsk."* Ledyard would almost certainly have described the potential value of sea otter furs in Alaska. For uncertain reasons, Baranov borrowed a great deal of money in 1787 and

was unable to repay it. He may have suffered trading losses when the Chinese emperor closed the fur market in Kyakhta from 1785 to 1792. Even after Baranov left for Alaska in 1790, he continued investing in the glass company until 1799.

Baranov was also diverting some of his time, capital, and energy to a fur trade operation to the Chukchi people with his brother. The Baranovs' principal

Aleksandr Baranov

post was 600 miles east of Okhotsk at Ishiginsk. Many of their goods and furs were plundered by the Chukchi.

Gregorii Shelikhov had purchased beads (and probably vodka) from Baranov and very likely met with him to discuss other issues. He had offered Baranov the post of manager for the Golikov-Shelikhov firm at Three Saints Bay on Kodiak Island earlier, but Baranov had refused. Now deep in debt and encouraged by both Shelikhov and Ivan Koch, the commandant of Okhotsk, he agreed to go for five years (he ended up staying for 28). His salary would start as the revenue from ten shares in the company. His wife and children returned to Kargopol with some life insurance from the company against Baranov's death. He would never see them again.

The galiot *Three Saints* sailed August 31, 1790 but had a difficult crossing with leaks and slow progress. After successfully reaching Unalaska, the ship was forced ashore by a gale-force wind and broke up. The winter conditions were terrible but Baranov set to work learning the Aleut language, how to paddle a *baidarka*, and how to hunt. Unalaska's Aleuts proved friendly, and by making generous gifts from the remnants of his cargo, Baranov gained their help and advice. Baranov's calm intelligence helped the men under his command survive. Their hope for rescue eventually waned, and they built skin boats to sail to Kodiak. They made it after two challenging months. This must have been hard for the middle-aged Baranov (age 43), as he arrived sick and exhausted. He must have wondered about the wisdom of accepting the position.

To his dismay, Baranov found the settlement in disarray. Between Three Saints Bay and Fort Alexander there were no more than 150 Russians, only half of what he expected. Morale was low due to Shelikhov's failure to keep a range of promises. Shelikhov's former staff members were also jealous of the great authority granted to Baranov and thwarted his authority at first.

But Baranov turned out to be the perfect choice for general manager of the company. He gained the respect of his workers and established good relations with the Aleuts. He put his skills to work in bargaining with the village elders (perhaps using hostages to improve their cooperation) to arrange for 1,200 men and 600 *baidarkas* for the summer sea otter hunt of 1792. A tsunami caused considerable damage in the area and the effort was reduced to 900 men and 450 *baidarkas*. The tsunami also led him to shift the Russian base to St. Paul.

The next season, four hundred *baidarkas*, in groups of two hundred, were sent to hunt the southern coast as far as Yakutat and explore for a future colony; the other 200 went north. Baranov also explored the area, and during a night camp on Mantague Island, he and his men were set upon and almost wiped out by a war party of Tlingits from the Yakutat region. The attack was beaten off, but it was clear that the Tlingits would be much more difficult to work with than the Aleuts. The Aleuts were rightfully afraid of the Tlingits.

Baranov was a ruthless competitor and established his reputation by making money despite the many challenges presented by his employees, the natives, other companies, and the weather. He was soon presented with an Inuit girl by one of the native chiefs; and later, after his Russian wife died, he married a local Inuit woman who bore him two children.

With effective lobbying from Natalia Shelikhov and others, Tsar Paul I. and his Board of Commerce agreed to create a monopoly for a fur company in Russian-America. They felt this would make it easier to resist foreign penetration by the British, Spanish, and Americans, and perhaps lead to better treatment for the natives. Much like the Hudson's Bay Company, the Russian-American Company was to provide soft power at low cost to the government. An imperial charter gave them a monopoly from Latitude 55° to the Bering Strait, including the northern islands.

Baranov exercised a great deal of independent authority as a result of the enormous travel time to St. Petersburg. He was inventive and thoughtful and brought new energy to the operations. He organized new outposts and trading practices. One of his innovations was linking up with the American fur traders, like Joseph

O'Cain, to send *baidarka* hunters on American ships south as far as Cedros Island, off Baja California. These combined operations would scour the coast for sea otter pelts.

Baranov created a new outpost near today's Sitka in 1799, calling it St. Mikhailovsky Redoubt. It later was moved a few miles to become Novo-Arkhangelsk (New Archangel). The local Tlingit were mistreated and objected to the loss of their land, the taking of furs from their grave sites, and other abuses, and sacked the settlement in 1802. An estimated 600 warriors armed with guns destroyed the fort and may have killed 20 Russians and many more Unangan.

Two years later, the Russians returned with four ships, including the warship *Neva*. The Russians destroyed two Tlingit villages. At the site of New Archangel, the Russians attacked the Tlingit-built fort. The cannons were unable to cause much damage to the sturdy fort and the initial attack was easily repelled. Baranov had led the charge and was wounded in the chest. But the Tlingit had lost all their gun powder in a boat accident and were unable to fight for long. They had to abandon their land, their homes, their possessions, and much of their clan regalia to withdraw. They melted away and moved to the other side of the island. They set up a blockade and established Trader's Bay, where Tlingit people from around southeast Alaska could trade with the Americans instead of the Russians at Sitka. Baranov tried to engineer an end to the blockade, but the Tlingit held steady for 18 years, not returning to New Archangel until 1822.

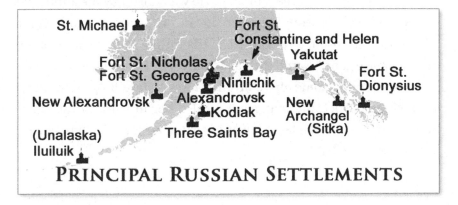

St. Michael
Fort St. Constantine and Helen
Yakutat
Fort St. Nicholas
Fort St. George
Ninilchik
Fort St. Dionysius
New Alexandrovsk
Alexandrovsk
New Archangel (Sitka)
Kodiak
(Unalaska) Iliuliuk
Three Saints Bay

PRINCIPAL RUSSIAN SETTLEMENTS

This was not the only fighting. The next year the Tlingit attacked and destroyed the Russian fort at Yakutat. Independent parties were also attacked, and Aleut and Koniag hunters were killed. In 1808, Baranov transferred company headquarters from Kodiak Island to New Archangel (Sitka). There was timber for ships and buildings at Sitka, and a better climate in which to grow food. In 1836, smallpox struck New Archangel and killed about half of the Tlingit.

Baranov was faced with many significant problems throughout his career. Nasty weather, dangerous seas, hostile natives (well-armed with guns from American and British traders), and the high costs and difficulties of shipping food, people, and supplies in and sending furs out to market made his life a challenge. He was an effective leader and well-liked by most of his men.

After 19 years in Alaska, Baranov requested a replacement. Two men, sent by the Company to succeed him, had both died on the way; one had been his old friend General Ivan Koch, and the second man went down with the *Neva*. His replacement didn't arrive for nine years. Baranov finally left Alaska in November 1818 on a ship bound for European Russia. He became ill after living ashore for a few weeks at Batavia (now Jakarta) and was buried at sea when he died a month later on April 16, 1819. His son Antipater died in St. Petersburg in 1821.

SIR GEORGE SIMPSON, THE BIRCHBARK EMPEROR

George Simpson was born in 1787 in Lochbroom, Scotland as the illegitimate son of George Simpson. He was raised by his aunts and grandmother, and would rise far beyond expectations to become Sir George Simpson, a fur oligarch. His formal education does not seem to have gone beyond the parochial level. He probably first ventured to London somewhere around 1805, where he proved adept at business, especially management. He began work in the sugar trade with his uncle in 1808; it was here that he came in contact with investors in the HBC.

Andrew Colvile apparently employed George Simpson in some HBC matters as early as 1818, but on the whole, Simpson knew lit-

tle about the North American fur trade. Regardless, he must have made quite an impression, for in 1820 he was appointed Governor-in-Chief of Rupert's Land.[43] This involved managing thousands of square miles, hundreds of men, and all outposts and materials. The man he was sent to replace had been threatened with arrest at the request of the NWC, but in the final event he was not arrested

Sir George Simpson

and Simpson started out as his assistant. He learned the fur trade quickly and demonstrated his ability to improve management and control costs.

Simpson sailed to New York and then made his way by boat and wagon to Montreal. From there he went west and north to York Factory on Hudson's Bay. He met his boss at Rock Depot on the Hayes River and was then sent west to Fort Wedderburn on Lake Athabaska. He spent the winter learning about, thinking about, and reorganizing the fur trade. He devoted his energies to promoting thrift and discipline. His dedication to these principles earned him the admiration (and sometimes frustration) of his employees. He showed a remarkable ability to master problems of trade and managing men. He was very skilled in both strategic and tactical decision making. Soon after his arrival in Rupert's Land in 1820 he "married" his first country wife Elizabeth Sinclair. They would have a daughter, Maria.[44]

Returning to Montreal in 1821, Simpson learned that the vicious war between the NWC and HBC had ended with a merger. The combined company had 173 posts (76 HBC and 97 NWC). Many were inefficient and unprofitable; other posts existed in direct competition with each other. Personal enmity and anger between employees of the two firms remained a challenge.

Simpson's first task was to reorganize fur trade operations from top to bottom. In a short time, order and efficiency replaced chaos in the company's affairs, and profits began to soar. He followed the year's furs down the Hayes River to Rock Depot, and then returned to Norway House for the first meeting of the Northern Council, where he learned that he had been made governor of the Northern Department.

Most of the profitable fur areas were in the Northern Department, which covered the region westward from Rainy Lake (on the border of modern-day Ontario and Minnesota) and Fort Albany (present-day Ontario) west to the Rockies. In December 1821, the HBC monopoly was extended to the Pacific and his area of influence grew ever larger. With his new authority, Simpson aimed to economize by making extensive cutbacks in various areas of operations. He reduced the size of the Saskatchewan District workforce from 171 to 53. Promotion was contingent on performance under Simpson, and he carefully reviewed and reflected on the individual abilities of his fur traders. He methodically recorded these in his "Character Book," an often-blunt journal with harsh, snarky reviews of his employees. Men soon learned that insubordination could affect their career prospects for years, and in some cases, decades.

After the council meeting, Simpson traveled back to York Factory. He made a midwinter snowshoe trip of more than 500 miles to Cumberland House and then traveled on another 600 miles to the Red River settlement. He was back at York Factory in July 1822. After the meeting, he went by water to Lac Île-à-la-Crosse and harnessed dog sleds for the run up to Fort Chipewyan and Fort Resolution on the Great Slave Lake. He then returned south to Fort Dunvegan on the Peace River and then shot out to Fort Edmonton, and after the ice broke up, he returned to York Factory. He would remain on the move for the next forty years, meeting the men, learning the tribes, lakes, rivers, and the fur business.

Simpson had a number of native and Métis women in his life. He helped assign his rejected "partners" to new mates but often treated his mixed-blood partners poorly. He did not have much contact with his children. Two of his many sons had careers in the HBC after Simpson farmed them out to be raised by other fur trade families. Simpson did not favor permanent marriages between fur traders and native or mixed-blood women, and he discouraged the practice of taking them to new postings. He felt that too many employees were more concerned with family affairs than with the goings-on of the HBC. However, later in his career he placed financial responsibility, if not parental responsibility, squarely on the fathers; employees were not allowed to leave or retire from service without making adequate provision for their offspring. His own country wives and children would be kept at a distance from him and his life with his "legitimate wife" Frances.

In 1824, Simpson "married[45]" Jane Klyne, the daughter of French-Canadians Michel Klyne and Suzanne Lafrance. She accompanied Simpson to Fort Vancouver, and his son James Keith Simpson was born there. They had gone west using the Nelson River via the Burntwood River route, up the Churchill River and Athabasca Rivers to Jasper House. They caught up with McLoughlin's party in just six weeks, despite its twenty-day head start. He then crossed Athabasca Pass, and after reaching the boat encampment he headed down the Columbia River. His eighty-day journey to Fort George was twenty days faster than the previous record.

He and McLoughlin planned the Snake River Country expeditions and revised allocations to different outposts. Simpson also initiated the move from Fort George to Fort Vancouver after first trying for a site on the Fraser River. He replaced canoes with boats in areas where it would reduce transportation and labor cost.

In 1825, when, according to the HBC promotion rules, apprentice clerks with the same length of service were receiving £50 per annum, and full-fledged clerks were paid £75, Simpson wrote to the directors, thanking them for his £500 bonus and the £200 a year increase in salary. He may, in fact, have been an inside inspector/investigator with wide powers of discretion. Although he had started with no fur trade experience, he learned quickly. While the clerks, traders, and factors knew the fur trade, he had the business management acumen, accounting skills, and an eye for efficiency.

He arranged for Jane, who stayed at Fort Vancouver, to "marry" Archibald MacDonald when he headed east in 1825. He crossed snow-covered Athabasca Pass, and from Fort Assiniboine he went on to Fort Edmonton. He ordered the building of a new portage route that provided many benefits over the old Methye Portage route. He then rode 500 miles from Fort Carlton to the Red River settlements and then took to canoes to reach York Factory.

He returned to England for a visit before sailing back to Montreal and making it to the Rock Depot for the annual meeting of the Northern Council that summer (usually in July). His former boss had retired and he was given the eastern area to administer as well. He inspected his new area of responsibility and then returned to Montreal. He returned to England in 1826 to find a proper English wife so he could start a family with sons to inherit his name and wealth, but to no avail.

When he returned to Rupert's Land in the spring of 1826, he "married" Margaret Taylor, the daughter of sloop master George Taylor. Their son George Stewart Simpson was born in 1827, and he and Margaret remained together for four years. These informal partners were critical for their husbands, providing comfort, helping with food and shelter, and caring for them when they were injured or sick. When Simpson returned to Lachine for the winter of 1827–28, she probably went with him. She travelled with him to Rupert's Land in 1828, and on to the Columbia. The need for her companionship was great, and he could report that she "...*has been a great consolation to me.*"

While at Fort Vancouver, Margaret became pregnant with her second child and travelled back to Rupert's Land with George in the spring, crossing Athabasca Pass on snowshoes and continuing on to

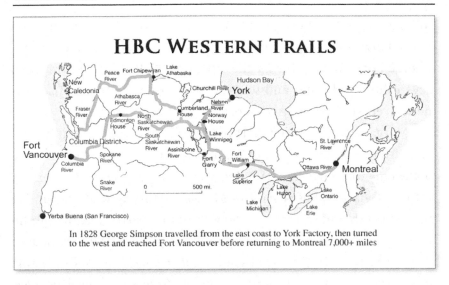

HBC WESTERN TRAILS

In 1828 George Simpson travelled from the east coast to York Factory, then turned to the west and reached Fort Vancouver before returning to Montreal 7,000+ miles

Fort Edmonton. It was here that George decided her advanced pregnancy would slow her down too much, so she was left behind, under the care of the chief factor. She went on to Fort Alexander on the Winnipeg River at a more modest pace, where her second child was born on August 29, 1829, later baptized as John Mackenzie Simpson. For good reason, Simpson was more enamored by her than by any other woman in his life, but his prejudice against natives kept him from making her an official wife with a church wedding.

In May 1828, Simpson started his second trip to the Pacific along with Margaret (the children?), his dog, and a bagpiper (later he would add buglers) to add color, dash, and éclat to each arrival. Simpson always traveled with the best men—voyageurs picked for appearance, endurance, and speed. His canoe or boat would stop at the last bend so the crew could change from worn, dirty clothes to regalia, and Simpson could put on his dark suit, black stock, white collar, and beaver hat.

He first raced out to York Factory and then used the Peace River route to the west. They went over the Rockies and to the headwaters of the Fraser. Simpson went overland to Fort Kamloops but most of the party, including Margaret and the children, apparently went down the river. One of the goals was to evaluate the Fraser River route and it was deemed unusable. The party reunited and traveled to Puget Sound and overland to Fort Vancouver. This remains one of the longest canoe journeys on record to be made in one season. George boasted that during the summer of 1828 he had travelled seven thousand miles and was the first to complete a transcontinental return trip in one season.

Margaret may have covered the same distance. She certainly travelled from York Factory to the Columbia in 1828 and is probably one of the only women to have run the Fraser Canyon by canoe. Simpson returned via Athabasca Pass to Moose Factory and Montreal. He turned south and sailed from New York to Liverpool. Although he was not ill, his constant traveling took its toll: *"Exertions which were formerly but exercise for me are now fatiguing, indeed my snowshoe walk across the Mountains and overland journey from Saskatchawaine have wrought me a good deal."*

Never one to dilly-dally, he quickly courted and married his first cousin, 18-year-old Francis Ramsay Simpson, in 1830 in St. Leonards Church, Bromley on Stratford. He returned with his official bride to New York and then moved quickly on to Montreal and Michipicoten, Ontario for the annual meeting. She would quickly learn about her workaholic husband. Her journals reveal the pace: *"Mr. Simpson being anxious to get to Fort Garry (about 100 miles distant) today, gave his usual Leve at 12 P.M. [midnight] and although it blew very hard, occasioning a heavy swell on Lake Winnipeg when we embarked, we got to the mouth of Red River at 11 A.M. The beauty of this Stream surpasses that of every other I have yet seen in the Interior."* They then went on to York Factory and Red River where she gave birth to his first legitimate child. Sadly, the child died young and his wife never fully recovered from the birth; she remained an invalid for most of her life and was very unhappy during their three years at Red River. This was a far cry from London, even though he had arranged for a piano to be shipped from England to the remote site for her.

The Company bought him a house in Lachine in 1833. He apparently suffered a mild stroke in May 1833. The family returned to England, where Francis would remain for the next five years. His wife was in poor health and contracted tuberculosis in 1846. She had difficulties with her pregnancies with three daughters and then died soon after John Henry Pelly Simpson was born in 1850. Simpson returned to Canada the following spring and attended the Council Meetings at Moose and York Factory. He inspected posts on the Saint Lawrence and arrived in England in October 1835. Between 1835 and 1840, annual returns on capital for the HBC ranged from 10–25% and the shareholders were quite happy.

He foresaw the way to beat the Americans on the coast and commissioned the HBC vessel the *S.S. Beaver* in 1836 for the coastal trade. The steamship was better in the tight passages and bays and big tidal flows than the sailing ships were. The *Beaver* also went down to Yerba Buena (San Francisco) and out to Hawaii, making it the first steamship used in the Pacific Northwest. He also helped establish the Puget Sound Agricultural Company to grow food for the HBC and provide food for negotiations with the RAC.

Simpson took the steamship *Britannia* from England to Saint Petersburg in 1838 and he negotiated a deal with Ferdinand von Wrangel of the Russian-America Company, where the RAC would recognize the HBC posts on the coast, and the HBC would essentially lease the Alaskan Panhandle in return for the provision of fresh foodstuffs and other supplies for Sitka. Simpson then returned to London and traveled back to Montreal, Red River, Moose Factory, the Saint Lawrence posts, then back to Montreal and down the Hudson River to New York and continued on again to England. There he received the non-hereditary title of Sir George Simpson from the young Queen Victoria in January 1841.

Leaving London in March 1841, Simpson sailed to Boston, then went on by carriage and sleigh to Montreal under horrible conditions. In early March he left by canoe for Fort Garry (now Winnipeg) and then by horse to Fort Edmonton. On the way, he caught up with a wagon train of over 100 settlers heading for the Oregon country. Instead of taking the usual route, he went by what is now Banff, and made the first recorded passage of Simpson Pass.

On his arrival at Fort Colvile, he recorded that he had *"performed a land journey of about 1,900 miles in 47 days out of which we had travelled but 41, having been detained 6 en route."* He and his party had ridden eleven hours a day. They proceeded on to Fort Vancouver, arriving at the end of August, having covered almost 60 miles a day for four months in crossing the continent. He wisely started the move of the HBC headquarters to Vancouver Island even though Dr. John McLoughlin was not happy about it after his many years of work developing the Columbia District.

On September 1st, Simpson left aboard the *S.S. Beaver* to tour posts along the Northwest Coast. After short visits to California and Hawaii, he left Honolulu in February 1842 on the last leg of his journey and sailed back to Sitka. Finding that the vessel in which he was to proceed to Okhotsk would not sail until much later than he had expected, Simpson visited the HBC post established at Stikine on land leased from the Russians. Returning to Sitka, he counted thirteen ships, steamers, barques, brigs, and schooners and wondered about new business prospects. He then sailed on a Russian ship to Okhotsk. He then made the very difficult trip overland to Yakutsk, then up the Lena River by horse-drawn boat. He visited Lake Baikal and then traveled on by horse and carriage to Saint Petersburg to meet with the RAC. By horseback, carriage, and boat, his route covered about 7,000 miles in just 91 days.

He finally reached London by ship at the end of October 1842 after an incredible 19-month voyage around the world. Lieutenant Henry Lefroy met him in 1843 and described him as *"the toughest looking old fellow I ever saw, built upon the Egyptian model, height two diameters, or like one of those short, square, massy pillars one sees in our old country church. He is a fellow whom nothing will kill."*

Simpson and his wife had a grand house in Montreal on the Lachine Canal across from the HBC Fur Depot. As a wealthy business leader, Simpson played a major role in Montreal society and became one of the leading figures in the Anglo-Scottish community. He refrained from expressing his political opinions publicly due to his position as governor of the HBC. He also invested in railroads and canals.

Simpson traveled to Washington, DC in 1845 for further discussions on the Oregon boundary issue, but in 1846 the Oregon Treaty established the current border, much to the disappointment of the HBC. His decision to move operations to Vancouver Island was validated. He continued to travel and manage his large empire. He was in Washington, DC again in 1855 discussing Oregon affairs. In 1857, he had to return to London to defend the HBC monopoly. He then returned to Lachine, and in the spring of 1859, he brought up the question of retirement in a letter to the London governor, H. H. Berens.

In May 1859 Simpson started west once again but realized that at 72 he was no longer up to the stress and he returned to Lachine. In August of that same year he entertained the Prince of Wales with the city elite, earls, dukes, bishops, generals, admirals, and dignitaries of lesser rank gathering to admire the canoe fleet as it paddled around the island to the music of the Royal Canadian Rifles' band. The prince then went for a ride in the lead canoe bearing the royal standard.

Soon after this royal visit Simpson suffered a massive stroke and died at age 76. He left an estate worth well over £100,000 (about $10 million today). He owned part of the estate of Sir Alexander Mackenzie in Montreal and a lovely 15-acre site on Mount Royal. The bulk of his estate, including £75,000, was bequeathed to his son, John Henry Pelly Simpson, with each of his three legitimate daughters getting £15,000 with stipulations about who they might marry, and £100 for his illegitimate daughter Maria Taylor, who had been sent away and raised in Scotland.

Simpson was the effective ruler of much of North America for more than 40 years. He made at least one major journey every year, with the exception of three years when he traveled to London. In his later years he noted, *"It is strange that all my ailments vanish as soon as I seat myself in a canoe."*

WILLIAM HENRY ASHLEY, ENTREPRENEUR PUSHING WEST

William Ashley was born about 1778 in Powhatan County, Virginia. He received a good education for the time. He was a slender, energetic man of medium height with a narrow face, prominent nose, and jutting chin. By 1805 he was in the area around St. Genevieve, Missouri and running a plantation. In 1808[46] he was working around Saint Louis. In 1811, he and Andrew Henry moved to Washington County where Henry worked a lead mine and Ashley processed saltpeter and manufactured gunpowder.

William Henry Ashley

He was a successful businessman and speculator with interests in real estate, gunpowder, mining, banking, and furs. He served in the War of 1812 as a captain, rising to colonel in 1813 and ending up as Brigadier General of the Missouri Militia in 1821. He was often referred to as General Ashley. He was the first Lieutenant Governor of Missouri, serving from 1820–1824 while taking time out for his speculations in fur trading.

In 1822 he and bullet manufacturer Andrew Henry set up the Henry and Ashley Company, later to be the Rocky Mountain Fur Company. He made four successful trips to the mountains for beaver and he helped create the rendezvous system before selling out to Jedidiah Smith in 1827. In just four years Ashley had reshaped the fur business and helped drive the fur trade west. His companies also provided training and opportunity for many of the men who would lead the advancing Americans. "Ashley beaver" was noted as being of the highest grade.

In 1822 he posted the now famous advertisement (shown below) for 100 enterprising men to go west in the fur trade for one, two, or three years. Ashley and Henry contracted their fur trappers to be paid "on halves." The company outfitted the trappers with a horse, saddle and tack, a rifle, six traps, and a camp axe. In return, each trapper would receive the value of half of the fur taken at a contracted price per pound. He would also be required to purchase all his supplies from his employer.

The first year was not a success. Even though the company made a good start at the junction of the Yellowstone and Missouri, they lost $10,000 worth of furs in a boat wreck on the river on the way home. In 1823, on the way upriver, the party of 70 men was attacked by several hundred Arikara warriors and fifteen[47] of his men were killed with many more wounded. The Arikara were angry because a group of trappers had rescued several Sioux warriors the Arikara had been hunting and killed several warriors. His two boats of supplies were held up and 1823 was another bust.

For the Rocky Mountains.

THE subscribers wish to engage. One Hundred MEN, to ascend the Missouri, to the

Rocky Mountains.

There to employed as hunters.   At a compensation to each man fit for such business,

$200 Per Annum,

will be given for his services, as aforesaid,— For particulars, apply to J.V. Gartner, or W. Ashley, at St. Louis. The expedition will set out from this place, on or before the first of March.

Ashley & Henry.

jan 18. 1823

The Rocky Mountain Fur Company would be competing head to head with Manuel Lisa's Missouri Fur Company (1808–1830), Astor's American Fur Company (1808–1842), independent traders, and the HBC. Ashley needed to find new beaver trapping areas, so he sent two trapping parties out, one with Andrew Henry and the other with Jedediah Smith. During the winter of 1823–1824, they found an abundance of beaver further west. When they returned in the summer of 1824, the trappers also reported that they had found a route that a wagon could cross. Andrew Henry had had enough and quit. Ashley took on Jedidiah Smith as a partner and the new Ashley-Smith firm took to the mountains.

Trappers were told that there would be a rendezvous on the Yellowstone with the Rocky Mountain Fur Company supplying trade goods in the summer of 1825. Ashley had seen the value of the Ashley-Henry partnership taking trade goods overland to a predetermined meeting place where trappers could bring their furs to trade for a variety of goods. Ashley and his men set out from Fort Atkinson in the fall of 1824. They covered parts of present-day Colorado, Wyoming, Idaho, and Utah in reaching the site of the highly successful 1825 rendezvous on Henry's Fork.

Ashley's Inventory of Goods from caches and other sources available at the 1825 rendezvous on Henry's Fork suggests what the trapper's beaver could buy. The duplicated items were from separate caches.

Ashley's Inventory

- 2 bags coffee
- 1 ham goods
- 3 pack powder 1 1s qt (unclear? powder was around $1.50 pound)
- 2 tobacco
- 3 B. Lead (bars?)
- horseshoes
- beads, large & small
- 2 packs sugar
- 1 pack cloth with some knives therein
- 7 dozen knives
- 2.5 kegs tobacco (150 lbs.)
- 14 dozen knives
- 2 pieces of scarlett cloth
- 2 ditto Blue Stroud (a wool fabric)
- 3 bags coffee (200 lbs.)
- bale & bag sugar (130 lbs.)
- pack beads, assorted
- & vermillion
- assortment of Indian trinkets, mockerson alls (awls) do.
- 2 bags gun powder (150 lbs.)
- 3 bars lead (120 lbs.)
- bag flints 1000
- bag salt 10 lbs.
- pack cloths
- blankets
- buttons
- pack containing a variety of Indian trinketts
- ribbons, binding & c (etc)
- axes, hoes & c (etc)

From Ashley's journal (July 1825) we can also see what Johnston Gardiner bought, preparing for another season. Gardiner also purchased more as listed in Ashley's memorandum of goods for Mess. Gardner & Williams, presumably pounds for many items.

J Gardner	Dollars
28 tobacco	84
35 coffee	70
9 sugar	18
6 fire steels	?
3 doz. knives	75
3 gross buttons	24
3 doz. fish hooks @ $1.50	4.50
5 doz. alls (awls)	5
9 doz. rings @ $1	9
2 peaces binding	6
3 peaces ribband	9
7 pr scissors @ $2	14
2 doz. combs	3
1 1/2 gr. thread @ $3	4.50
7 doz. flints	3.50
7 1/2 yds. scarlett @ $6	45
5 1/8 do	30.70
6 yd Stroud @ $5	30
32 powder	?
43 coffee	?
6 beads	18
62 lead	62
2 doz Sersingles (surcingles)	42
pads marto	90 (soft saddles, saddle pads?)

Beaver pelts would bring from $3 to $7 each, depending on size, quality, and the terms of the contract between the trapper and the company.

After the rendezvous they loaded the fur packs and headed for the Bighorn River by way of South Pass. Ashley took twenty of the men to dig up a cache of 45 packs, most likely left by Jedediah Smith in 1824. Ashley and his men were attacked by Blackfeet but managed to send for help from the main group and were able to escape. Ashley's party arrived at Grapevine Creek on August 7, constructed bull boats,[48] and floated the Bighorn River down to the Missouri. William Sublette returned to continue trapping around Green River. The rest of the run down the Missouri was uneventful and they reached St. Louis in October with 100 packs of beaver pelts valued at $50,000.

The first rendezvous set the pattern for the next fifteen years as traders brought goods and supplies to the mountain men at the height of the summer when fur quality was low and there was little point in trapping. The trade goods were brought out West overland, allowing the mountain men at the rendezvous to sell their furs to Ashley's company at a mountain price. But most agreed it was worth it to avoid the time and risk of a long journey back to St. Louis. The rendezvous enabled smaller groups to survive and they could stay out in the field longer. The trading company could make good profits and offer higher prices for furs than the HBC. This attracted the freemen and even some contracted workers to switch to the American side. In 1825, more than twenty of Peter Skene Ogden's men deserted to get higher prices and to pay lower costs for essentials.

The 1826 rendezvous was also a success, but Ashley sold his remaining interest in the company to Jedediah Smith, David Jackson, and William Sublette. Ashley would market all of the new firm's fur and supply all of their trade goods and supplies under a new contract. Ashley could make money with much less risk by brokering furs and supplies. Over the years, he probably brought in more than 500 packs of beaver at 90 lbs., worth about $250,000 in St. Louis (about $6 million today).

The rendezvous provided a place to trade but was also an important social event. Trappers would eat, drink, gamble, race horses, wrestle, shoot, and tell stories. These meetings became a way of life, with attendance rising from 120 in 1825 to a peak of more than 1,000,[49] including many natives. Thousands of horses, hundreds of teepees and tents, and a remarkable variety of women and men created a rollicking temporary village.

Ashley's life outside the fur trade is not well known, but he married at least three times. We do know that he married Mary Able in St. Genevieve, Missouri in November 1806.[50] She died in 1825. He then married Elizabeth Christy in 1825 and she died in 1830. His third wife was Elizabeth Wilcox Moss, married in 1832. She would outlive him, remarrying and making it to 1873. It is believed that his son William Henry Ashley may have served in the Mexican War and Civil War.

Ashley returned to business in 1827, had a very nice home, and participated in the local community. He was a member of the Board of Directors of the Bank of the United States in 1829. He also bought 25,000 acres of land that included a mineral spring in Cooper County. He ran for governor of Missouri in 1824 but lost. He was elected to the U.S. House of Representatives in 1831 after the incumbent was killed in a duel in which both men died. Ashley served from October 31, 1831 to March 3, 1837. In 1832, he supported the creation of the Bureau of Indian Affairs. He lost a run for governor in the election of 1836; he won Boone County with 827 votes to 444 for Lilburn Boggs but lost the state for being too pro-business. He died of pneumonia in 1838 and was buried on an old Indian mound near the Lamine River.

PSYCHOPATHS

IVAN MAKSIMOVICH SOLOV'EV, THE DEADLY NIGHTINGALE

Little is known about the full life of Ivan Solov'ev.[51] He was from Tobolsk and began working in the fur trade at an early age. He learned navigation and seamanship as a *promyshlenniki* and was a merchant leader and captain of early fur hunting trips to the Aleutians. He was as ruthless as they come.

Ivan first appears on record as foreman for Stepan Glotov on the *Julian* at the southern tip of Umnak Island on September 1, 1759. The vessel was greeted by spears hurled from atlatls.[52] The anger was not surprising because the Russians who came before them had followed the brutal practices refined in Siberia and Kamchatka. The *promyshlenniki* would surprise and storm a village and kill any people who resisted. They would then hold the women and children for ransom, while releasing the men to fill a large quota of furs (this could take months). The Russians exploited the women as sex slaves while they waited

Ivan Maksimovich Solov'ev

for "their" furs. With the furs delivered, they might release most or all of the hostages, or not. They left behind venereal diseases, a few babies, and a token payment of trade goods for the sea otter pelts. The spear throwers managed to kill two of the crew and wounded Savin Ponomarev (the government representative) and the skipper Glotov. Glotov did not retaliate, probably because Ponomarev was on board. They then explored and hunted around Umnak and the southern tip of Unalaska Island.

Near Kashega Bay in 1761, Ivan Solov'ev was given a small amount of *"silver dye with sparkles used for coloring faces."* Captains Glotov and Solov'ev offered friendship and succeeded, they thought, in bringing the natives under the rule of Her Most Powerful Majesty Catherine and inducing them to pay fur tribute. When they left the islands in late 1762 with over a thousand fox pelts and a good collection of sea otter skins, they thought they had established good relations with two chiefs on Umnak and three on Unalaska. How little they actually understood would soon become clear.

Also in 1762, the Fox Island Aleuts staged a coordinated attack on four vessels and several shore parties in the islands, killing more than three hundred Russians. The attack on Korovin's men included a large number of natives in forty *baydars* (perhaps 600 men). The massacre of the Russians had come in response to unspeakable acts committed by Sergeant Pushkareff and others of the Becherin[53] Company in 1761–1762 and other abuses by *promyshlenniki*. The Russians would exact a severe revenge for the 1762 attacks.

Ivan Solov'ev, on the *Petr i Pavel* (Peter and Paul), returned to Unalaska in 1764. This was a well populated island at the time, with many communities composed of fifty, up to two or even three hundred people. They lived in large earth-sheltered houses from 120 to 240 feet long, 18–21 feet wide, and 12–15 feet tall. The roof was a complex wooden framework of driftwood covered first with a layer of grass and then earth. These *barabaras* provided good protection from the brutal cold of winter.

Solov'ev explored the area and learned more about the recent killing of the Russians. Chief Siida was apprehended by Solov'ev after a brief skirmish in which four Unangax̂ were killed. The chief's men then attempted to free him and six more were killed. In October, Solov'ev released Siida on the condition that he leave his son as hostage. In November 1764, Solov'ev explored Makushin Bay and found 180 villagers hunting fur seals. Two chiefs escorted the Russians to Makushin Village which had a *"hot spring below the sea mark, which is only to be seen at ebb tide."* Solov'ev was later led to another village at Reese Bay where people fled at their approach. The Russians summarily appropriated this settlement, set up camp, and destroyed three hundred hunting spears and ten rare bows and arrows. The village *toion* (chief) led over two hundred villagers in an attack and nineteen more Unangax̂ were killed, including the chief. The secondary chief Agaladok was captured and his release was made conditional upon the surrendering of his son as a hostage. Solov'ev was able to collect a couple dozen hostages altogether.

He described the value of hostages: *"And I, seeing their lack of inclination by sufficient admonition, decided to take from them for myself amanaty* (hostages), *since the above-mentioned were treacherous, in order that they did not rise up and attack me, as they rose up against the other companies."* Even this was no guarantee of safety. In the spring of 1765, scurvy appeared among Solov'ev's crew, and twenty Russians and one Kamchadal died. The hostages held by Solov'ev were able to visit with their relatives and let them know that the Russians were weak. An informer told him that the men of Makushinskoe village were planning an attack. Solov'ev seized the *toion* of Makushinskoe village when he came to visit *amanaty* relatives. Under harsh interrogation he acknowledged he had planned an attack.

Solve'ev continued to attack various groups of Unangax̂ from Umnak to Akutan Pass. A chief watched the Russian camp from his *baidarka* offshore but stayed far enough away to avoid a direct confrontation. It was clear that he was assessing the strength of the Russian party. On May 27, 1765 he was captured; and although Solov'ev suspected he had planned to surprise his guards and burn his vessel, he set him free after a week with the exhortation "to desist from hostilities." Solov'ev then destroyed all spears, bows and arrows, and skin boats he could find. Solov'ev saved one bow to send to St. Petersburg.

Solov'ev explored more of Unalaska Bay in the summer and continued his preemptive destruction of weapons and boats. The Unangax̂ continued to attack and suffer severe losses. Following the burning of one fortified village, he had two hundred bodies tossed into the sea. He also sank two *baydars* of people traveling to visit relatives. Solov'ev, or more likely his foreman, Gregorii Korenev, committed a general slaughter on Egg Island. By destroying Unangax̂ *baydars, baidarkas,* hunting equipment, stored food, and war weapons, he forced the Umnak/Unalaska people to starve, suffer terrible losses, and to sue for peace.

With minimal casualties to his own force, Solov'ev is believed to have killed more than 200 men; but other accounts suggest he killed 3,000 men, women, and children. As so often happened on the fur coast, most of those killed were probably innocent in the deaths of the Russians. The larger totals of dead may reflect the killings of all the Unangax in the area (not just due to Solov'ev and the impact of diseases and starvation). The loss of hunting equipment and boats and the death of so many men would have led to the death by starvation of many women and children.

Solov'ev sailed on the vessel *Petr i Pavel* in 1764 to Unalaska Island for owner Jacob Ulednikoff, a merchant of Irkutsk. They were attacked while building their winter camp but they repulsed the natives and killed more than one hundred. He then started sending companies of Russians out on punitive expeditions. Solov'ev became known among the *promyshlenniki* as the "deadly nightingale"[54] for his harsh measures. He was said to have lined up a number of Unagax men and fired a musket into the chest of the first to see how many others it would penetrate. The severe punishment of Solov'ev and others after the Fox Island revolt effectively ended Aleut resistance to the Russians. He was the first Russian to visit Reese Bay and he stayed a couple of weeks in 1765.

In 1767, Ivan Solov'ev was recruited to be a pilot for the Imperial Naval Expedition under Captains Krenitsyn and Levashev in the Aleutians and Bristol Bay. This group left Kamchatka in Spring 1768; Solov'ev's Unangax godson Alexey went along as interpreter since he was literate in Russian. Krenitsyn wintered on Unimak, where half of his crew died of scurvy because he refused to trade for fresh meat and kept his men from hunting to "keep them safe." Ivan's godson died on the way to St. Petersburg in 1770.

Vasilii Shilov, Ivan Lapin, and Afanasii Oryekhov selected Solov'ev to command the ship *Sv. Pavel*, which sailed from Okhotsk in July 1770. During his last voyage to the Aleutians, beginning in 1771, he visited Unalaska, Umnak, and neighboring islands. In his journal, Solov'ev remained largely silent about his thirty-five months cruising the area. There was "nothing worthy of notice" in the journal, declared the Russian Senate, which ordered future voyagers to keep better records. Solov'ev's reticence may have been grounded in knowledge of the fate of Ivan Bechevin, a wealthy Irkutsk merchant who was put on trial in 1764 for the actions of his company. The official investigation concluded that Bechevin's *promyshlenniki* kidnapped, raped, and murdered a number of Aleut women and committed *"indescribable abuses, ruin, and murder upon the natives."*

Solov'ev set up headquarters at the deep, protected harbor on the north side of Unalaska Island where Druzhinin had camped. Hostilities continued and shortly after Solov'ev set up camp he sent out two hunting parties. A detachment from the first became stranded in a cove surrounded by high cliffs and all were killed by the natives. The Unangax̂ boasted, *"We will kill all of you too, as we have already killed many Russians in the past."* The remainder of the first party went west to hunt on Umnak and other western islands where the natives cooperated and paid their tax. They may certainly have remembered the 1760s when, according to one report, *promyshlenniki* had virtually "exterminated the disobedient" populations. However, the outpost attracted more Russians and became consolidated.

The second party went east to Akutan, Akun, Avatanak, and Tigalda, now known as part of the Krenitzin Islands. In October 1772, Natrubin's party encountered heavy blizzards on the Akutan island. By "invitation" they took refuge in the Unagax̂'s *barabara* but were soon driven out when the residents attacked them with knives. They moved on to Avatanak Island and for a few weeks the *promyshlenniki* and Unangax̂ lived uneasily at opposite ends of the house. In early December, the Avatanak stormed the *barabara* to kill the sleeping Russians. Natrubin survived and killed many natives. In 1833 an elder woman said that after Natrubin cast the bodies of the murdered Unagax̂ into the river, the fish never came back.

The natives took refuge on a small rock pillar that lay just off the northwest coast. In the past the vertical walls had offered protection from native marauders, but this time they were shot to pieces by the hunters' five-foot-long rifles.

After the subjugation of Unangax on Unalaska, Soloviev established the village of Iliuliuk on Unalaska Island as a Russian trading station. The Russians called this village *Dobroye Soglasiye* (The Harbor of Good Accord). Despite the peaceful appellation, however, the settlement became a point of embarkation for several notorious trading/raiding expeditions, including Soloviev's expeditions to the Peninsula and Sanak Islands.

One of Ivan Solov'ev's crews was the first to visit Sanak island, where they found a few hundred Unangax living on a tense frontier with the Koniag of Kodiak Island and Prince William Sound to the east. Solov'ev confirmed his violent reputation yet again, and after a short stay on the island the Russians fled in 1772.

Solov'ev returned to Russia in 1775 with a good catch of furs. Seven Unangax crossed the Bering Sea with Solov'ev but only four made it to Irkutsk. These men were awaiting a smallpox inoculation[55] before they left for St. Petersburg to have an audience with Catherine II. Sadly, all of them died before making it there. Solov'ev became an investor in ships and traders, and in 1778 the *Barfolomei i Varnava* (Bartholomew and Barnabas) sailed under command of Afanasii Ocheredin to the island of Kodiak, arriving in 1779. Here his trail is lost.

A commission arrived in Unalaska in 1791 to investigate charges of misconduct by the Russian traders. The local chiefs testified that some of the traders had abducted natives of both sexes, withheld payment for delivered furs, and robbed natives of their food stores and other provisions.

Perhaps his trail continued, as Alaska records show that Nicolas Solovief had a male child named Sabba born in Sitka in 1817. Mariner Nikifor Matfeef Solovief then had a son named Loubof in 1853, also in Sitka. Church records include a financial contribution by Vasilli

Soloviev in 1844. Kenai Peninsula teacher Ivan Soloviev was listed in 1896 and Sitka student Ioann Soloviev, from 1893–96. The Solov'ev family may have continued in the Aleutians as well with an elder named Isidor Solovyov (1849–1912), a Unangax from Akutan.

CAPTAIN SAMUEL HILL, DEVIL ON THE DEEP BLUE SEA

Sam Hill was born in Machias,[56] Massachusetts on February 20, 1777 into the large family of Obediah and Sarah Hill. He ran away from home at the age of 13 after a savage beating by his soldier/farmer father. Hill was not very competent as a skipper and was unable to command the loyalty of his officers and men. When they did not respect him "properly" he treated them savagely. Contemporaries noted that he beat his men mercilessly, abused them with foul language, and threatened them with abandonment, starvation, and even shipwreck. He was said to be poor at celestial navigation. He was also a terrible businessman who often misjudged business opportunities. He did have an uncanny knack for appearing at important historical intersections and taking the wrong turn. His violent behavior helped poison relationships with the many people and tribes he encountered on his voyages to the Pacific Northwest. True sociopaths are rare, but Sam Hill may have met the criteria.

He was among the first Americans to spend time in Japan. He spent four months on the traders' island of Deshima in Nagasaki while serving on an American ship under a Dutch flag. After fifteen voyages in 14 years, he had climbed the ranks and was appointed captain of the *Lydia*,[57] a small brig. He was a violent and unstable tyrant, subject to fits and seizures. He developed a hatred for his supercargo, Isaac Hurd, who was not only seven years younger, but smarter and more able. When the mate began turning to Hurd for guidance, Captain Hill was furious. He threw the mate off the ship in Hawaii and picked up a 15-year-old Hawaiian girl who would be his sex partner for 18 months. He often neglected his duty to spend time with her. He later replaced her with a Chinook woman and returned the Hawaiian girl to her home. He plotted against other

captains, refused owners' instructions, cheated his American owners and native trading partners, and stole furs when he could not
buy them at a good price.

In conflict with his supercargo and enjoying excursions on the
ship's boat with his "wife," Hill missed several key trading opportunities. This ratcheted up tensions on board the small stage of the

Captain Samuel Hill

Lydia as the supercargo could
see more and more money
being lost. Disputes between
Hill and Hurd grew worse as
trading and shipping decisions
were being negotiated between
several Lyman ships. Hurd saw
no point in continuing and left
the ship. The owners would
hear from their representative
and Hill would never work for
the Lymans again.

Hill then proceeded to trade on the coast. He rescued the captives John Jewitt and John Thompson, but Jewitt found conditions
so evil on Hill's ship that he soon wished he hadn't been rescued.
Shortly afterwards Hill ran the ship onto a reef by failing to heed the
mate's call. The rudder was torn off but fortunately the ship floated
free. The repair was made and a partial crew swap with other ships
enabled the *Lydia* to continue. Hill was in the Columbia River at the
same time Lewis and Clark were wintering nearby at Fort Clatsop.
Although he received a letter from them carried by a native, he did
not bother to go visit them.

The crew refused to work when the rum ration was cut in
December. Hill savagely beat one sailor and threatened to kill the
rescued Thompson when he intervened to stop the beating. Hill got
worse and began treating the natives with savage malice. When one
party arrived to trade he told them all to "go to hell." In early 1806,
his new mate jumped ship to escape the evil captain. Hill began to

more actively cheat his native customers by adding sea water to the molasses and putting old ropes in the bottom of the gun powder kegs. This infuriated the natives. He also started taking hostages to trade for furs. His abuse on this trip led directly to the native attacks on other ships later on. The clerk in charge of recording accounts noted that the captain was undercounting the furs, most likely to create a fur trade of his own rather than for the owners, when the ship reached China.

The crew members were delighted to escape the coast alive. The ship spent some time in Hawaii and then went on to China. Hill wrote a remarkably effective letter detailing his supposed heroics in the rescue of the captives and sent it back for the newspapers. Although he left school at an early age, he was an avid reader and learned to write well. His manuscripts often read like fantasies of what he might have done but had failed to do; nevertheless, they helped prop up his endangered reputation.

Hill married Elizabeth Bray in 1800 and would have several children (Elizabeth, Frederick, Charles, and Charlotte(?)) with her during his infrequent stays at home. Hurd thought it odd that while sharing a cabin for almost a year, Hill had never mentioned his wife or children. In his autobiography (which is quite fantastical) he mentions her only three times and never by name. The shipping embargo kept Hill ashore for two years and when he ran out of money he sued Lyman for additional payment. This messy court case revealed much of Hill's sexual escapades but downplayed his toxic command climate.

His glowing article about his rescue of the captives got him another ship to the NW Coast. His pattern of violence and bad judgement continued. On the cruise of the *Otter* he would massacre dozens of Tlingit people and lose five members of his 26-man crew to death, with two murdered. Three crew members kept journals and these lay out the horrific details of Captain Hill's behavior. By 1810 the sailors were terrified of the captain and suffering from the cold weather. All were frustrated by the slow trading as the plentiful sea otter skins were gone. The *Otter* met O'Cain's ship, along with many *baidarkas* and Russian Aleut hunters, and Hill realized bitterly that there would be few furs left anywhere. The Russians suspected Hill of encouraging the Haida to attack the Aleut hunters. The Hawaiians Hill had added to the crew began to die of cold and scurvy, but he eventually made his way back to Hawaii, China, and then home.

The War of 1812 kept Sam Hill on shore for a while, but he then sailed as captain on the *Ulysses,* a ship he co-owned. He described it as a letter of marque brig, so he had his privateer's papers. His ship was captured by the British ship of war, the *Majestic.* Hill was captured and kept for six months in Halifax. While his crew rotted in prison he was able to live modestly ashore before being exchanged. In his later years, he would go on other cruises and spend three fruitless years trying to start a business in Chile during the revolution.

By 1822 it was clear Hill would not get another ship; he was involved in further litigation with owners and partners. He effectively manipulated the books and courts in order to retire with considerable money and buy properties in Boston. He lived with his wife and children for a few years but then left them. Sam Hill died alone and in obscurity in Boston in 1825 at the age of 49. His wife Elizabeth would die in 1863 at age 83.

A complex, sometimes tortured man, Hill had undergone a religious conversion on his final voyage, but even then he could not admit to the full extent of his evil doings. His violent abuse in childhood may have led to his subsequent behavior, and perhaps he inherited mental illness from his father. He could appear civilized and sensible at home and he had been able to fool some ship owners for a while. Once he sailed out of the harbor in Boston the mask slipped away to reveal his insecurity, sadism, recklessness, ambition, braggadocio, and violence. As his biographer noted, he was "the devil on the deep blue sea."

Captain Jonathan Thorn: hero, martinet, and master of disaster

Jonathan Thorn was born in Schenectady, New York on January 8, 1779, while the Revolutionary War was raging. He was the first of fifteen children born to Samuel Thorn and Helena Van Slyck. He was appointed midshipman in the U.S. Navy at age 21. One of his first assignments sent him to the Mediterranean to join the fight against the Barbary pirates. His time on the frigate *John Adams* was followed by service on the *Enterprise* and *Constitution*, both part of a blockade off the coast of Tripoli. He must have impressed Lt. Decateur as he was selected for a raid. The raid was a success and he

Captain Jonathan Thorn

was commended for bravery and given command of a captured gunboat. He then served as the first commandant of the New York Navy Yard at age 27. He was promoted to full lieutenant in 1807.

In 1810, he was granted a two-year leave to command the Pacific Fur Company's 290-ton sailing ship *Tonquin*. This effort was part of John Jacob Astor's two-pronged approach (by land and by sea) to gather the fur riches of the Northwest coast. The *Tonquin* was to sail to the Pacific Northwest to establish a fur trading post, trade furs on the NW coast, and support the overland party.

Friction between the easygoing French-Canadian voyageurs, the clannish Scottish fur traders, and the strict disciplinarian (some would say martinet) began almost immediately and increased during the voyage. Thorn wished to be treated as the absolute master of his ship as he would have been in the navy. This imperious behavior grated on the talkative, free-spirited, and unpretentious fur men. Thorn raged against them all in letters to Astor.

Thorn tried to leave nine of the fur party behind at the Falkland Islands; he sailed away leaving them with only a 20-foot boat. They tried to catch the ship by rowing furiously in dangerous seas, but eventually realized they could not catch up. Thorn returned to pick them up only after Robert Stuart, one of the other Canadians, pulled his pistols on the captain. *"Turn back or I will blow your brains out,"* he said.

The *Tonquin* rounded Cape Horn on Christmas Day and stopped in the Sandwich Islands (now Hawaii) for additional men (24 *kanakas*), food, and resources. Prophetically, several men visited the site where Captain Cook had been killed in 1779. The bosun, like many other officers, was unhappy with Thorn's leadership and left the ship. A sailor late getting onboard was beaten almost senseless by Thorn and then thrown overboard. He managed to make it to shore and joined the bosun in staying in Hawaii, thus saving his life.

On March 11, 1811, the *Tonquin* arrived at the mouth of the Columbia River. Horrible breakers at the river mouth suggested patience was needed, but Thorn sent five men to their doom (including the first mate, who had become "too friendly" with the fur traders; three voyageurs, and an aging sailor). Two days later Thorn refused to pick up the second ship's boat after it had found the channel and condemned the sailmaker, armorer, rigger, and two *kanakas* to almost certain death. The armorer and one *kanaka* survived after overturning in the high waves. The *kanakas* helped right the boat and after spending a desperate night offshore in the waves, the armorer and *kanakas* surfed in through the breakers. One of the *kanakas* then died of exposure. At the unnecessary cost of eight lives, the *Tonquin* had crossed the bar, leaving the ship without critical crew members (the bosun, first mate, sailmaker, and rigger).

The *Tonquin* spent more than two months near the river mouth as the Astor party started building Fort Astoria. In June, the ship successfully crossed the bar and headed north along the coast to trade for furs. In mid-June they traded near the village of Newity or Echatchet in Clayoquot Sound (or Woody-point, sometimes called Wickaninnishes, after their chief). The Nawity (now *Kwakwaka'wakw*) had heard many stories of the bad behavior of the fur traders and bitterness had developed in the area. Among the worst grievances was the burning of the village of Opitsaht by Captain Gray in 1792 because a chisel had been stolen and there were rumors of an attack. Captain Smith of the *Albatross* noted that animosity had also increased because Captain Eayres had abandoned a group of Newity hunters on an island off the coast of California, and only two had made it home.

Unaware of the historical wrongs done to the local people and contemptuous of their fighting ability, Thorn ensured his doom by being careless in managing access to the ship and further insulting the native people. What really happened is unclear but the most likely story is that the old chief Nookamis was especially persistent in his bargaining for a better price and followed Captain Thorn back and forth on the deck, thrusting a roll of skins in front of him. The irascible captain lost his temper and grabbed the skins, rubbed them in the face of the indignant chief, and then took him by the scruff of the neck and threw him overboard.

Outraged, the local people planned an attack and took the ship; they killed the captain and most of the crew. Four men escaped from the ship, but were later found, tortured, and killed. Seventeen white men and twelve *Kanakas* were killed; only the interpreter Lamayzie from Gray's Harbor survived. He jumped overboard and acknowledged he would willingly be a slave—so his life was spared.[58] After two years he was released and he told the story of the taking of the *Tonquin*.

Four or five hundred natives had gathered to plunder the ship (either the same day or the next day). The gunpowder magazine exploded and it blew the back out of the ship, killing as many as 100 or 200 people. The four who fled might have set a slow fuse, the natives may have been careless, or the wounded armorer may have survived long enough to touch off the gunpowder. Thus died a cruel and violent man, while sowing the seeds for future catastrophes.

YAKOV BABIN — UNABLE TO SAVE THE NICOLEÑOS

Yakov Babin was a native of Tobolsk, Russia, and was born about

1790. He was taken on as a worker at the Russian-American Fur Company about 1805 and assigned to Fort Ross. Khlebnikov notes, *"The cooper Chechul'ka and Iakov Babin live on a hill near the Aleuts' huts in neat and tidy little dwellings made of redwood planking."* He was a fur laborer, carpenter, and hunt

Yakov Babin

supervisor at different times during his career.

Natives had lived on San Nicolas Island for 5000 years with almost 600 sites known today and others no doubt lost to erosion. The Nicoleño lived reasonably well from the sea, and despite the distance to the coast, they traded there and with other islands. They manufactured beads for native trade. The study of bone remains found two types of dogs: early on there was a larger dog and later a smaller one with a short nose. The small dog was about the size of a Jack Russell terrier, much like the natives' Plains dog. The dog bones showed arthritis consistent with hard work in hauling, hunting sea lions, etc. Healed injuries and special burials suggest natives took very good care of the dogs and valued them.

San Nicolas Island was visited by many ships over the years, from early Spanish and English explorers to sea otter hunters. The *Albatross, Amethyst, Catherine,* and *Isabella,* along with other contrabandistas, may have hunted around San Nicolas in 1811–12. In 1812, Captain Whittemore of the *Charon* dropped off Koniag sea otter hunters for the RAC. The *Charon* returned from the California coast with 1,792 (1,596 grown, 136 yearlings, 60 pups) sea otter pelts. They may have also introduced diseases that adversely affected the island people.

Worse was yet to come. In fall of 1813, the *Lydia* was sold to the RAC and renamed the *Il'mena*. Captain Wadsworth left Sitka on the *Il'mena* in January 1814 headed for California with 50 Aleuts and *kreols*; 25 *baidarkas*; commander of hunters, Timofei Tarakanov; assistant hunt leader, Yakov Babin, and Alexander Baranov's son Antipater. Tarakanov, born about 1774, was an experienced fur hunt manager who was probably expected to teach his assistant the trade.

By some accounts Timofei had orders to clear the island by moving the people to Fort Ross (to be agricultural workers) or perhaps to a larger island where they could be more useful to the RAC. In 1814, the *Il'mena* arrived at San Nicolas Island with the Aleut hunters. Babin was originally to stay with the Tarakanov hunting party but Timofei ordered him to stay behind on San Nicolas Island with some *baidarkas* and hunters while the rest of the party went on to San Clemente Island in hopes of finding more sea otters.

The hunters would often make camp on the islands and hunt from shore with *baidarkas*. The well-armed hunters would also take what they wanted from the natives—furs, women, and food. The local men were unable to resist the well-armed, fierce Aleut and Koniag warriors. Yakov Babin was too young and inexperienced to oversee and manage the older, tougher Aleuts. After they went to work, a dispute with natives (over women or furs) erupted, tempers flared, and the Nicoleño natives killed an Aleut hunter. In return, the well-armed warriors killed all or almost all of the men on the island, perhaps as many as 200. Only one old man survived his wounds. The Aleuts then could have any of the women they wanted. It was rumored that many of the women were taken by the Koniags as slaves. The *Il'mena* retrieved the remainder of the otter hunting group on October 1, 1815.

When the Aleuts involved returned to Sitka, Chief Manager A. A. Baranov took statements from them, perhaps at the urging of his son. Baranov wrote to Kuskov in 1815: *"...in regards to Tarakanov and Babin, remind them about their bad behavior and tell them that this comes from me, that Tarakanov [is] to stay within the limits of his service, and reprimand Babin for his act of madness, as Tarakanov was ordered to remove the islanders without causing them any harm."* The *Il'mena* returned to Sitka with 392 (322 grown, 50 yearlings, 20 pups) sea otter pelts. The RAC hunters returned again in 1815. When Boris Tarasov (RAC) was arrested by the Spaniards for hunting sea otter in Spanish waters, he said that he had been left in charge of Aleuts on the Channel Islands. He and his men had been on San Nicolas for seven months and obtained another 955 sea otter skins.

At Fort Ross in 1818, Ivan Kuskov reported the incident to Baranov's successor, L.A. Hagemeister and was reprimanded for his failure to report this violence sooner. Babin was ordered to be brought on the *Kutuzov* to Sitka for further questioning and put under guard. From there, he was to be sent to St. Petersburg for inquiry by the main office. He may (or may not) have been sent to St. Petersburg for investigation and trial for allowing the sea otter hunters under his command to slaughter the natives. In any case, Babin was back at Fort Ross in 1822. In 1825, stating that he had received nothing from the company since 1805, he requested permission to leave the colonies. His request was denied. On January 30, 1827 he married Anisia, *"a baptized Indian of the people of Albion (California)."* Their daughter Matrona was baptized at Kodiak in 1827. In 1830, when a son named Paul was born in Sitka, Yakov was listed as a laborer. His first wife died, possibly in 1833, and on February 6, 1838 he married Elisaveta Unali at Kodiak. He died about 1841 on Kodiak Island.

Hagemeister took steps to reduce the likelihood of future abuses. He made personnel changes at outpost manager level, and ships' commanders were changed. Regulations, old and new, were to be strictly observed. Men who were without passports or held expired documents were required to apply for renewals. Accusations of crime were immediately dealt with.

A few people survived on San Nicolas Island, and a child was born about 1815, perhaps the offspring of a Nicoleño woman and Koniag sea otter hunter (or an Aleut woman and otter hunter). By the 1830s only about twenty people remained; by other accounts just seven (six women and an old man named Black Hawk) remained. Black Hawk had suffered a head injury during the massacre but survived. The Santa Barbara Mission sponsored a rescue mission, and in late 1835, Captain Charles Hubbard sailed out to the Channel Islands aboard the schooner *Peor es Nada* and took most of the tribe on board. A lone woman later known as Juana Maria remained. In 1843 the brig *Oajaca* (formerly *Bolivar*) set to work around San Nicolas and San Clemente and within a few days they took twenty-one otter skins. The *baidarkas* set out down the coast while the big ship sailed down to Todos Santos. Juana Maria was picked up by George Nidever in 1853. She was a cheerful woman who liked to sing, but she quickly succumbed to disease.

Yakov Babin, through inexperience and weakness had condemned the Nicolenos to disaster. His boss Timofei Tarakanov was also culpable, but Babin was on the ground. He was punished but that did little good for the people who had suffered the atrocity.

SURVIVORS

FRANCOIS RIVET, INTERPRETER FOR LEWIS AND CLARK

Francois Rivet was the son of Pierre-Nicolaus Rivet and Madeleine Landréville-Gauthier. He was born in 1754 and baptized at St. Suplice, Quebec. This was a prime area for fur trade recruiting and he followed his father into the trade. He probably started work as a fur trade employee about 1770. Records in the archives of Quebec show that he signed at least three legal voyageur contracts in the 1790s. Chances are good that he also worked as a *coureur de bois*[59] during the 1780s as well. Records indicate he was a voyageur in a contract to go anywhere as needed for Jacques Giassson in 1791. He then must have shifted to the Missouri River trade.

In 1804 Francois signed up with Lewis and Clark in St. Louis; he would work on the river and stay near the Mandan villages. He and several other French traders built their own shelter and waited for the winter to pass. The dull winter was enlivened during Christmas week by extra rations of grog and tobacco, and dancing to the music of Pierre Cruzatte's fiddle. The astonished Mandans saw Rivet "dance on his head" (break dancing), a sign of his fitness. In the spring, he helped take Lewis and Clark's keelboat back to St. Louis[60] and was paid $87.50 for his work.

Rivet, Grenier, and an unnamed young man then made a hunt up the Missouri. Returning downstream in the spring of 1806, they left their traps at the Mandan villages before going on to the Arikara towns. Low on powder by midsummer, they headed back to

Francois Rivet

the Mandans to recover their gear before returning to St. Louis. The hunters were not entirely surprised to meet the returning Corps of Discovery on August 22nd.

He was often called "Old Revay" in the records of the fur trade, because he was already 50 years old by the time he worked for Lewis and Clark. He remained out west and worked for the Pacific Fur Company as an interpreter and hunter. He entered into a country marriage with a Salish woman, Therese Tete Platte, a widow with a daughter Julie (to become Peter S. Ogden's wife). Their first child was François, a son who died young; followed by Antoine, born about 1809 in Montana, and Joseph.

By 1813 Rivet was a freeman engaged by the NWC as an interpreter for Flathead House. He worked in the interior for many years—a decade in Montana and Idaho for the NWC and HBC. He was listed as interpreter for Alexander Ross in 1824 on the Snake

River. His wife and family were traveling with him. The 1824 expedition was perhaps typical of his years in the mountains. Rivet had two guns, six traps, fifteen horses, and a lodge. His wife[61] and sons Antoine and Joseph, now fifteen and thirteen years old, were probably also with him. They started from Flathead House in February and spent ten months in the valleys of the Bitterroot and Snake rivers. The winter weather was particularly severe and they were plagued by threats of desertion by their Iroquois trappers. There were also attacks from hostile natives.

In March 1826, Rivet helped take 62 pack horses to meet the boats at the mouth of the Spokane River. In 1827, at a reported age of 60 but actual age of 73, his salary as an interpreter in the Columbia District was £50 a year. He continued with Ross at the Flathead Post as an interpreter until 1829 and then transferred to work with John Work at Fort Colville. He was an interpreter and handyman, working on the river boats and blacksmithing. After Work left the fort, Francois was engaged for three years with an advance of £15. At the age of 75, Rivet was able to work for nine more years.

In 1838, at the age of 84, François retired and settled on French Prairie. He officially married Therese[62] in 1839 in the St. Paul Catholic Church, on the same day his two sons were married. In 1842, Frances (Francois) and Antonio Rivet were enumerated together in Elijah White's Oregon census. The household consisted of two males over eighteen, two females over eighteen, and three children, with seventy acres under improvement. In 1842, they harvested 400 bushels of wheat and 180 bushels of grain. They had fifty-one horses, fifteen cattle, and thirty-eight hogs.

At the fall 1841 auction and sale of Ewing Young's estate, "F. and A. Reavy" purchased a cow without a calf for $22. François also purchased a sieve for $2, five files for $1, a froe for $1, sundry items for $.80, one auger for $1.16, one kettle for $.70, and one hammer for $.16.

In 1844, Joseph L. Meek collected a poll tax of $2.92 from "Anturye Revit and Joseph Revi." In the 1845 census, Francois,

Joseph, and Antoine Rivet were all enumerated as heads of households. That census named the head of the household and then listed the rest of the household categorically by age. In 1845, François and his son Antoine claimed 1,280 acres about three miles southeast of the Catholic church in Champoeg District. François Reveate, Senr. of Champoeg County, claimed 205 acres of the Catholic Mission Prairie in 1848.

In 1851, the *Spectator* newspaper (Oregon City) noted, "*The oldest resident*[63] *of Oregon, Monsieur Rivet, was in town yesterday.*" Francois died in September of 1852 at the age of 98, and was buried at St. Paul, Oregon. Therese died later that year at age 97. They had enjoyed a marriage of more than 40 years and had seen most of the interior Northwest. Francois had helped Lewis and Clark open the West and was then among the first to settle in Oregon.

NAUKANE: HAWAIIAN ADVENTURER, SAILOR, TRAPPER, INTERPRETER, FARMER

Naukane was apparently one of the sons of high chief Kamanawa on the island of Oahu, born about 1770. He claimed he had witnessed the death of Captain Cook in 1779 when he was a child. *Kanakas* (as the Hawaiians were known in the Northwest) played a major role in the fur trade; they were praised for their hard work, skills as paddlers, swimmers and sailors, and fearlessness in dealing with native people. Their skill as divers was remarkable. After the *Iphigenia's* anchor line was cut, *kanakas* dove to a depth of 120 feet and reattached a rope to the anchor. In another case, before the *Tonquin* left Hawaii in 1811, two *kanakas* volunteered to dive for some pulleys that had been dropped overboard. Captain Thorn promised to pay four yards of cloth if they succeeded in retrieving them. They were timed under water for four minutes on one dive as they collected the pulleys. *Kanakas* in the interior fur trade often recovered goods spilled from canoes in the rapids.

In 1811, twenty young Hawaiian men were enlisted to help with the construction of Fort Astoria, trading operations, and sailing ships in the Northwest. The higher status Naukane was sent to oversee the younger commoners. On the voyage to Fort Astoria on the Columbia River, Naukane was given the name John Coxe, for his resemblance to a shipmate. Fortunately, Naukane stayed in Astoria after reaching the Columbia River and avoided death at the *Tonquin* massacre. He worked on the new fur trading site of Astoria for a while, but began a new voyage in July with David Thompson of the Montreal-based NWC. Thompson had arrived from the east by land soon after Naukane arrived on the *Tonquin*. The NWC party and competing Astorians headed up the Columbia River together to

Naukane

establish trading posts. They traveled together until they reached the Columbia Gorge. Thompson then forged ahead after an exchange of workers. An older voyageur, Michel Boulard, was traded to the PFC for Naukane (Thompson referred to him as Coxe). According to Astorian clerk Alexander Ross, "*On Mr. Thompson's departure, Mr. Stuart gave him one of our Sandwich Islanders, a bold and trustworthy fellow, named Cox, for one of his men, a Canadian ...*"

Mr. Thompson was impressed with Naukane's wit and humor, intelligence, skills, and strength. Thompson later also recalled Naukane's desire to master English. Naukane first traveled with Thompson to Spokane House where they rested for a few days before returning to the Columbia at Kettle Falls. They then made a quick roundtrip to the mouth of the Canoe River to pick up a shipment of trade goods coming across Athabasca Pass. He stayed with "Jaco" Jacques-Raphaël Finlay that winter while David Thompson continued on to the east.

King George IV's Royal Box, Theater Royal, Drury Street June 4. 1824
Standing: Naukane, unknown, Chief Boki, Frederick C. Byng
Seated: King Kamehameha, Queen Kamamalu, Liliha

Naukane was soon traveling east as well, crossing the continent by foot, horse, and canoe to Montreal. He created a sensation with his stories of Hawaii and his Polynesian dancing demonstrations. In 1812 he sailed to England on the NWC's ship *Isaac Todd*. In early 1813, still during the War of 1812, he sailed from Portsmouth to Rio de Janeiro, Brazil. There, John McDonald took him aboard *HMS Phoebe* to Juan Fernandez Island (Robinson Crusoe's island) where they transferred to the warship *HMS Raccoon*. In December, he arrived at Astoria for the second time to find that the fort had already been purchased by the NWC; this meant there was to be no warfare or seized goods, much to the disappointment of the captain of the *Raccoon*.

After the collapse of John Astor's Pacific Fur Company, Naukane and the other *kanakas* returned to Hawaii. Naukane became one of the bodyguards of King Kamehameha and a member of Liholiho's entourage. When Kamehameha I. died in 1819, Naukane rose in stature as Liholiho ascended the throne as Kamehameha II. In 1823, Naukane travelled to London with the Hawaiian king and queen on the *L'Aigle* to help with translations, cultural explanations, and negotiations. Sadly, both the royals died of measles, but Naukane and Chief Boki met with King George IV., who had ascended to the throne when George III. became mentally incompetent. One story says that Coxe was caught by a patrol while rowing around the harbor and needed all his English and diplomatic skills to escape being press-ganged and sent out on a ship as crew. The Hawaiians returned to Hawaii with the bodies of the king and queen on the *HMS Blonde.*

Naukane returned to the Pacific Northwest to work for the NWC. After the merger of the fur companies in 1821 he worked for the HBC for more than twenty years. After the merger, the *kanakas* were receiving subsistence plus £17 a year as salary. Naukane was a skilled worker and probably earned more. He lived at Kanaka Village, the multicultural village near Fort Vancouver, in his later years. Naukane married a young native woman (tribe not known) and may have inherited a female slave from her named Marie. He may also have fathered a child in Hawaii (1813) who later came to the Northwest and was known as William Naukana.

Naukane was the first Hawaiian to penetrate the interior, the first to cross the continent by canoe, and one of the first to England. He was also one of the first settlers in Oregon Territory. The vast meadows between Fort Vancouver and the Columbia became his memorial, known as Coxe's Plain. In his later years, he was the chief swineherd for the HBC's large pig farm.

His home was among the oaks that dotted the edge of the plain. By the time he retired, about 1843, there were 100 *kanakas* working at Fort Vancouver and perhaps 300–400 in the NW fur trade. Paul Kane painted his portrait in 1847, and although in his seventies at the time, he appears vigorous. Many of the *kanakas* joined the California Gold Rush, and in 1850 a Hawaiian named Captain Coxe tried to mine a legally purchased claim along the American River. He was denied by the growing racism that prohibited Chinese or *kanaka* miners from working mines, even if they owned the claim. This might well have been Naukane. Increasing prejudice and the transfer of HBC operations led many *kanakas* to move to Victoria, BC. Naukane died of TB at Fort Vancouver in 1850 and was laid to rest with a reading by Dr. John McLoughlin.

MARIE DORION: WALKS FAR WOMAN

Marie Dorion[64] was a Métis woman born in northern Iowa or Illinois about 1786. She had a fur trader father and Báxoje[65] tribe mother. Little is known about her early years but many of them were probably spent in fur camps, around trading posts and the town of St. Louis. In about 1806 she became the common-law wife of Pierre Dorion Jr.[66] "through barter or wager." Perhaps her husband had gambled her away. Like Sacajawea, who she probably knew,[67] she would travel more than 2,000 miles to the West Coast, traveling with a party of John Jacob Astor's employees sent to establish an American trading post on the Columbia River. Her husband Pierre was hired as interpreter for the overland party. He had worked for other traders on the Missouri and was considered the best qualified Sioux speaker in St. Louis that year. Along with her came her two children, Jean Baptiste, age about 5, and Jean, age 2. They left St. Louis on October 21, 1810.

Pierre had been in some trouble with an unpaid liquor bill due Manuel Lisa, and was afraid of being detained in St. Charles as the party went upriver, so he left and rejoined it past St. Charles. He insisted that his family must come as well. Sadly, Pierre had beaten Marie and she was hiding in the woods. Hunt's men

Marie Dorion

helped search for her but the group finally left without her. The following morning, she and her children rejoined the party. Another argument with Marie led to violence at Fort Osage when she wanted to stay there with newfound friends. Pierre restrained her and took her in the boat. There are no other records indicating that she tried to leave again, and the couple remained together until his death. She gave birth on December 30, 1811 under difficult circumstances, with the baby dying just a week later.

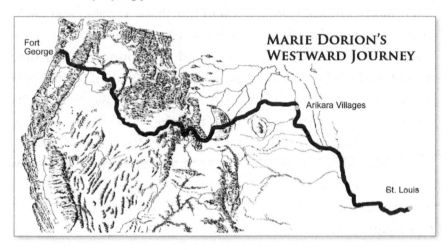

MARIE DORION'S WESTWARD JOURNEY

Fort George

Arikara Villages

St. Louis

After an extremely difficult crossing of the wilderness to Astoria in February 1812, Marie, her children, and her husband could finally recover. Her husband helped build canoes and hunted to provide meat for the fort; one of their sons died. With Marie pregnant again, the family returned to the rich beaver country along the Snake River in 1813 and set up a base camp at the mouth of the Boise River. Working in a smaller party, Pierre, Giles Le Clerc, and Jacob Reznor trapped north along the Boise River. Marie stayed at the larger camp where, in January 1814, she heard rumors of a plan by the Bannock tribe to attack her husband's trapping party. By the time she reached them to pass along the warning, only one man was alive but mortally wounded, and he died despite her attempt to help. She corralled two horses and then left for the larger outpost with her young child and infant only to find everyone there was dead or gone as well.

Marie headed west toward the larger trading posts. To avoid the impossible Hells Canyon of the Snake River, she turned northwest to cross the Blue Mountains. She had seen parts of this country before and probably had a good idea of where she was going, but winter weather and deep snow were too much for the horses and children. After nine days of struggling along and covering more than 100 miles, she decided she had to make camp and wait for spring. Smoking the horse flesh provided an initial viable food source, and using her lifetime of wilderness skills she built a shelter and made snares to trap mice and rabbits while also gathering edible bark and plants. Fifty-three days later, conditions improved and they set out again. When the children could go no further, Marie made a snow hut, lined it with furs, stashed Paul and Baptiste inside, and went for help. Partially snow-blind, she was found wandering by Walla Walla hunters and taken to their village. Her sons were picked up and returned to her. In April 1815, she started out again for Fort Vancouver. She was spotted on the riverbank by Stuart's party on their way back to St. Louis and she was helped back to Fort Okanogan.[68]

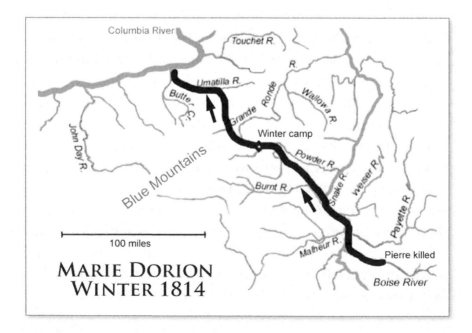

MARIE DORION
WINTER 1814

Marie lived there for several years with Louis Joseph Venier[69] (NWC), married him *à la façon du pays* in 1817, and had a daughter. It can be assumed that she probably accompanied him on several fur brigades in the Snake River country. After he was killed by the Shoshone in 1821, she married Jean Baptiste Toupin (HBC) in 1824 and had two more children. She and Jean may have met earlier when Hunt's party went by the trading post. Toupin was a translator at Fort Nez Perce at times from 1821–1841, a cook at Spokane House, worked at Fort Colville (1827–1830), travelled on fur brigades, and may have spent time in Hawaii and on the Willamette River.

In 1832–33 Marie was with her husband on John Work's HBC Brigade to California. The brigade left for California on August 17 with 26 men, 22 women (including Work's wife Josette), 44 children including his three young girls and Marie's three children (possibly ages 13, 7, 5), and six natives. One of the natives was with the Toupin family, perhaps as a slave. The women played a critical role in preparing food, sewing and repairing clothing, setting up camp, and processing furs, enabling the men to devote their time to trapping.

Sadly, Marie's husband took sick with the intermittent fever that would decimate the native tribes that year. She must have had her hands full with a sick husband and three children on this epic journey. Work notes, "*Sept. 1, 1832, J. Toupin who had recovered a little relapsed & is very ill. Friday 14th. Continued our route across the mountains 4 hours 12 miles S.S.E. ... J. Toupin had a relapse of the fever and nearly died of thirst on the road, no water to be found near. This man had recovered but has been ahead and imprudently went in the water which has caused him to fall ill again. October 2, Raw cold weather. Rained during the afternoon. Did not raise camp on account of the sick people. F. Champaign & Rondeau's wife are a little better, but another of the men, J. Toupin, was again taken with the fever and had a shaking fit this is the third time this man has relapsed, if ever those who have been ill wet themselves they fall ill again. October 8, L. Rondeau's wife has again fallen ill with the fever & could with difficulty be got up to the encampment. Two of the men A. Longtain & J. Toupin are recovering but very slowly.*"

The Work party traveled down to the San Joaquin Valley by the eastern route, reaching French Camp (near what is now Stockton) and returned by the western trail, perhaps visiting Fort Ross. Remarkably, Toupin survived and would go on to outlive his wife.

Toupin later acted as translator for missionary Samuel Parker in discussions with the Nez Perce. Marie was baptized as Marie Lauivoise in 1841, and she and Jean were formally married in the

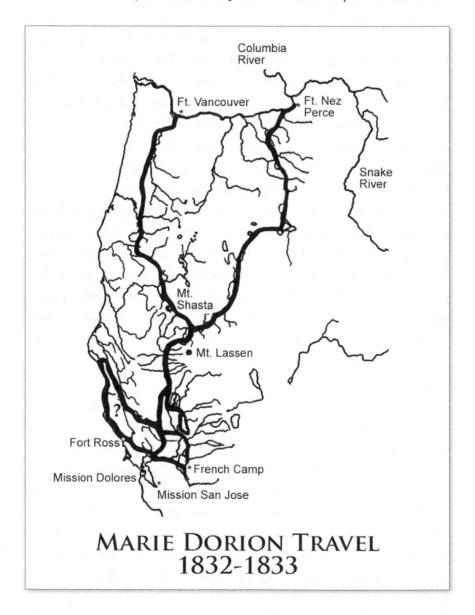

Marie Dorion Travel
1832-1833

Catholic church in August of 1841. They settled in French Prairie and she was given the honorific title of "Madame" or "Madame Iowa." Dr. Elijah Woods commented on her "noble and commanding presence." She was said to speak "pretty good English" and was quite polite in her address. In 1842 the "John B. Toupan" household included four males over 18, three females over 18, and five children, with 70 acres producing 400 bushels of wheat. Marie died in 1850 and was buried inside the original log Catholic church in St. Louis (Oregon)--a testament to her popularity.

Marie was a remarkably strong and capable mother and adventurer. She was the first woman to cross overland to the west and settle. She was one of the first women from the east to see California, and the first to reach it over land. She survived an abusive husband and was married to men who worked for the three most important fur companies. Of significant note, her first husband had known Lewis and Clark. However, she became famous in her own right for her survival journey after her first husband was killed.

Timofei Nikitich Tarakanov, skilled survivor

Timofei Tarakanov[70] was born a serf in Kursk about 1774. His father was Nikita Tarakanov. Kursk is located at the junction of the Kur, Tuskar, and Seym Rivers and was a good location to train for the fur trade. Timofei was an important worker for the RAC during the

early years. Although he had received a rudimentary education, judging by his letters he was literate and able to keep accounts. He developed a reputation for trustworthiness, sobriety, and resourcefulness that earned him the respect of Baranov and other

Timofei Nikitich Tarakanov

RAC officials. He was freed in 1818, at which time he went from being a serf to a citizen.

Timofei's owner was a merchant in Kursk and may have sold him to the RAC. Or, like his grandparents, he may have run away from his owner and made his way to Siberia. He was recruited by the RAC and brought to America between 1799, when the Company was chartered, and 1803, when he finally entered the written record. In 1803, Timofei sailed to California for the first time with Joseph O'Cain on the *O'Cain* to help manage the sea otter hunt with a crew of native hunters and 20 *baidarkas*. This was a successful trip, yielding 1,100 sea otter pelts on the first Russian/American California sea otter raid.

In October 1805, he was a captain[71] at Karluk[72] and considered to be essential for managing hunting expeditions. In October 1806, he left Kodiak with 12 *baidarkas* and a crew of Aleuts[73] to hunt the California Coast on the *Peacock*; they returned in 1807 with more than 1,200 furs. The same year, the *O'Cain,* with more *baidarkas* under Captain Winship, brought in 4,864 sea otters.

Tlingit opposition helped persuade Baranov to move RAC operations further south. He could bypass the Tlingit warriors and defend and advance Russia's imperial frontier against the Spanish, British, and Americans. He could also grow essential food. Baranov outfitted the *Nikolai* in the fall of 1808 for a voyage down the coast to trade and explore. Tarakanov sailed as the supercargo (*prekashchik*) managing the goods, conducting trades with the natives, and directing the fur hunters. Nikolai Isaakovich Bulygin, the captain, was the only person who out-ranked him.

Five weeks later, in November, the *Nikolai* was wrecked in a storm on the Washington coast just north of the mouth of the Quillayute River.[74] The *Nikolai* was becalmed near Destruction Island and the tide plus heavy swells drove the ship toward shore. Captain Bulygin had the anchors set but the hawsers failed and the ship crashed onto the beach at high tide. Twenty-two Russians and the Aleuts (5 men, 2 women) survived the initial disaster. After salvaging part of the cargo, the Russians clashed with the Quileute, abandoned most of their supplies, and fled south into Hoh tribal territory. Tarakanov described their encounter with the Quileute this way: *"We killed three of the enemy, one of who they dragged away. How many we wounded I do not know. As spoils we acquired a large number of spears, raincoats, hats, and other things left at the scene of the battle."*

Their initial encounter with the Hoh was friendlier but it became clear the Hoh wanted to capture the group to sell as slaves. Two men and two women, including Bulygin's wife, were captured. The rest of the Russians and Aleuts fled toward the interior; they spent a miserable winter struggling to avoid starvation, and they survived only by stealing from the native people. Tarakanov justified it by necessity: *"We had every right not only to take from their countrymen by force what we needed for our lives... we showed a spirit of magnanimity by not wanting to inflict on them any great physical harm."* Natives were forced to accept trades of food for glass and metal beads. When this was not sufficient they took the son of a noble captive and demanded 400 salmon and 10 bags of roe for his release. The ransom was paid, along with a canoe, and in return, the Russians gave the leader several trinkets and clothing as a measure of goodwill.

They returned to the coast the following year, hoping for rescue. Bulygin's wife had been sold by the Hoh to the Makah and when they made contact with her, they found to their surprise that she was fairly comfortable and content. She urged the rest to surrender. A few surrendered to the Makah and the rest were captured by the Hoh and the Quileute. Tarakanov ended up north at Cape Flattery, the property of Utramaka of the Makah tribe. He was treated well, thanks to his skill with tools and his entertainment value (he built a kite). It seems he was also proficient in learning new languages.

Tarakanov kept a rough manuscript journal of the shipwreck of the *Nikolai*, their flight, captivity, and eventual return to New Archangel. After the expedition shipwrecked, he assumed leadership when Bulygin had a breakdown. His good sense, the force of his personality, and his strong will enabled many to survive the ordeal.

On his return, Timofei turned his journal over to Baranov who interested Pavel Golovin in the story. Golovin interviewed Tarakanov and a number of his shipmates in New Archangel and wrote up his remarkable story of survival on the rugged Washington Coast.

On May 6, 1810, Tarakanov and the Englishman John Williams were ransomed by Captain Brown of the *Lydia*. Many of the other Russians were also purchased. Another American captain ransomed one or two more survivors from natives in the Columbia River area. Both the Bulygins had died before they could be ransomed, and at least one Russian is reported to have gone native.

Although he must have gained some renown after his return, he was off in June 1810. This time he was on the *Isabella*, Captain Davis, for another sea otter raid on California's coast. There he remained until summer of 1811. He conducted the negotiations for the purchase of land for Fort Ross and the Miwok[75] thought he was the captain of the Russians. Two separate transactions were completed, one with the Kashaya Pomo chief at Fort Ross, Pánac-úccux, for an actual transfer of property, and a use permit from Ióllo, chief of the Bodega Bay Miwok. Timofei returned to California again in January 1814 aboard the *Il'men* and stayed behind at Fort Ross. He may have led a crew of sea otter hunters from Fort Ross traveling northward in *baidarkas* to Humboldt Bay during the summer of 1814.

In August 1814 he was in charge of the sea otter hunt in California. His underling, Yakov Babin, and hunters were left on San Nicolas Island. A sea otter hunter was killed and this resulted in a massacre of all the male islanders except one old man. Babin was reprimanded for this incident and a chain of letters were written and actions taken. Timofei was reprimanded, and in 1815 he was demoted; in turn, he fired Yakov Babin over the massacre. The correspondence suggests that Timofei was under instruction to transport the Nicoleño people off of the island to a place that would provide more benefits to the RAC— perhaps Fort Ross, then facing a shortage of agricultural labor. The Russians viewed the island as being in international waters and may have planned to establish a permanent trading post there.

Tarakanov is known to be at Ross Colony through April 1816 when he boarded the *Il'men* and was expected to return to New Archangel. However, Bodega Bay had a challenging bar, the ship grounded and lost its false keel. The captain decided to take the damaged ship on the much easier leg to the Hawaiian Islands. On the way, the servant Balashov came in asking for a candle. Because there were none in the cabin, Captain Wadsworth went down into the hold to get the candles. He called up for a light. Timofei told him that it would be dangerous to have anything burning because the gunpowder stores were there. Wadsworth called up to say there was no danger of that because the gunpowder was already under water. The captain immediately ordered both pumps put into operation, which pumped out the water but also carried away the wheat loaded in the hold. The whole crew took turns pumping water and they made it to Hawaii in twenty days.

In Hawaii, Timofei was tormented by Dr. Georg Schaeffer, a German adventurer engaged by Baranov to establish a Russian claim to the islands. Schaeffer gave confusing and contradictory commands and Timofei finally gave up. In January 1817, a schooner arrived at Kauai and dropped anchor. Captain Brown, who had rescued Timofei from captivity, brought in letters from Baranov. Doctor Schaeffer had a letter from His Honor Alexander Baranov who told Timofei, "It is better for you to hunt beavers than to till the soil; report with all [your] Aleuts to Sitka." Also in 1817, it is suggested that he had a wife and children in Hawaii.

When Timofei showed the letter to Schaeffer, he gave it back and said with contempt: *"Go on foot, if you wish. I will not give you a ship and I will keep all the Aleuts."* This was the final straw and Timofei retreated to his room where he got drunk and stayed that way for several days. He saw no way out of this mess. Whatever he did, one of his superiors would see it as insubordination. People later started to wonder about the excessive drinking because Timofei had always considered drunkenness as one of the worst possible vices. He was lost, feeling everything he undertook for the Company had been in vain. Schaeffer was eventually deposed and fled. Timofei was left in charge and arranged with an American shipmaster named Johnson (or Davis) to take two Russians and forty-one Aleuts, then on Oahu, back to Sitka. The Aleuts would pay their passage home by hunting on the California coast.

Timofei was back in New Archangel in February 1818 and married Thekla[76] Stepanof from the Aleutian Islands. He journeyed to St. Petersburg to report on the Hawaii affair. He then returned to his family in Sitka. A son named Alexis was born in 1819. The somewhat confused record suggests Timofei was then sent to Okhotsk in 1820. He eventually returned to his home in Kursk. Thekla died in Kursk, presumably of a disease she had no resistance to. Timofei was 60 years old in the Kursk census of 1834, his son Alexis was 15, his new wife Alexandra was 45. He was still alive in 1858, in his eighties, but no longer living in Kursk, after a life of remarkable adventures and survival stories.

GEORGE NIDEVER: TRAPPER, SEA OTTER HUNTER, SAILOR, RANCHER

George Nidever was born December 20, 1802, near Sullivan, Tennessee to George and Christina Neidhoefer. He was the third child of six sons and three daughters. When he was five years old the family moved to Buncombe County, North Carolina, and nine years later on to the Moreau River area of Missouri. When he was 18, he joined a party scouting farm locations in the Six Bull River area north of the Arkansas River. Finding the area was occupied by Cherokee and other Indians, they went on to the vicinity of Fort Smith.

In 1828, George Nidever and Alexander Sinclair joined in a venture to raft cedar logs down the Canadian Fork and Arkansas River to the Mississippi and on to New Orleans. The partners, plus some hired men, spent nearly a year cutting trees and assembling a raft of logs, but it soon ran aground on a bar and broke up.

In 1830, he joined a hunting and trapping party at Fort Smith, Arkansas that was being promoted by John Rogers, a merchant[77] at Fort Smith. This never really took shape but a small party headed west anyway. As they moved up the Canadian Fork and passed the Cross Timbers, they had their first skirmish with Comanches. After

a fight with Pawnees, half of the men turned back, but the remaining fifteen continued on up the Arkansas River and northward into South Park. There were plenty of beaver, but hostile natives as well. Two men were killed and winter snows began to fall, so the surviving trappers decided to seek refuge in Taos, Mexico.

George Nidever

In 1831, he trapped on the North Platte River starting in March and returned to Arroyo Seco in July. In September they set off again, planning to go first to the headwaters of the Arkansas River. A few Mexicans and a number of French trappers accompanied them, but they separated after they hit the Platte. They wintered along the Green River at Brown's Hole. In 1832, they trapped on the Green and made it to the rendezvous. Here, Nidever took part in the battle of Pierre's Hole. The remnants of the original Fort Smith group broke up in July 1832. At the 1833 rendezvous, Nidever joined up with Bonneville's company and became part of Walker's brigade.

Nidever decided to leave Walker's party and stay in California. He began his new hunting career around San Francisco Bay. He then made his way south and boarded a vessel at Monterey and arrived in Santa Barbara in 1834. This would be his home for the next 50 years. He, Allen Light "the black steward," and George C. Yount hunted sea otters with some success. At first, they hunted under a license granted to Captain William Goodwin Dana, formerly of Boston, who had settled in Santa Barbara and become a Mexican citizen. Dana also furnished Light and Nidever with provisions. In return, they paid him forty percent of their catch for using his license and supplies. While working for Dana the men visited the Channel Islands and hunted along the coast.

In January 1836, a rival hunting party composed of Northwest Coast hunters suddenly attacked Nidever and his group on a foggy morning near Santa Rosa Island. Allen Light was the first to sound the alarm at the surprise attack and the first to reach the shore. He jumped out, turned, and fired on the foremost canoe. The Americans put up a blistering fire, Nidever remembered, and as they retreated to the highlands, they drove the attackers off. The natives had been hunting sea otter with the convoy. In the autumn of 1836, Light and Nidever made their last hunt under Captain Dana's license. In 1839 George was sea otter hunting in Baja.

Nidever continued sea otter hunting, bear hunting, farming, and piloting ships along the central coast. There are accounts of the Russian hunters driving off other hunters from Santa Cruz Island, including Captain George Nidever, whose ship once exchanged fire with a Russian vessel. Because of his many sea hunts and his vessel, *Cora*, he became widely known as Captain Nidever.

He was baptized a Catholic on January 27, 1841, and married María Sinforosa Ramona Sanchez. She was not only lovely and capable, but her family owned the 14,000-acre Rancho Santa Clara del Norte near the Mission Santa Barbara. They would have at least six children.

At the end of the Mexican American War in 1846, Nidever accompanied Frémont as interpreter to Campo de Cahuenga, where the Treaty of Cahuenga was signed. George caught the gold fever of 1849 and tried the gold fields briefly, but without much success. In early 1850, Capt. Nidever purchased a schooner in San Francisco. He also piloted the U.S. Coast survey ship *Quickstep* and assisted in the mapping of the Santa Barbara Channel.

In 1853, Nidever rescued some of the stranded passengers from the wreck of the *Winfield Scott*, a paddle-wheeler that went aground on Anacapa Island. He also purchased the right, title, and interest in San Miguel Island from Samuel Bruce. He brought 17 cattle, 45 sheep, two hogs, and seven horses to the island and built a small adobe house in an arroyo up from Cuyler Harbor. In May 1863, Nidever appeared before the 4th District Court in San Francisco and successfully bid $1,800 to satisfy a debt of Samuel Bruce that had been secured by a half-interest in San Miguel Island. Within ten years, Nidever's holdings had increased to over 200 cattle, 6,000 sheep, 100 hogs, and 32 horses. The terrible drought in 1863–1864 resulted in the death of much of his livestock and he sold his interest in the island to the Mills brothers for $10,000.

In 1850, Father Gonzáles of the Mission Santa Barbara paid Thomas Jeffries $200 to find Juana Maria, perhaps the last member of the Nicoleño people or a native woman from the north coast. She had been left behind when the rest of her tribe was evacuated from San Nicolas Island in 1835. Jeffries was unsuccessful, but Nidever launched several expeditions of his own using his schooner. After two unsuccessful attempts, one of Nidever's men, Carl Dittman, discovered human footprints on the beach and pieces of seal blubber which had been left out to dry in 1835. Further investigation led to Juana Maria's discovery. She was living in a crude hut partially constructed of whale bones, and wearing a dress made of greenish cormorant feathers. She was brought into town and treated well but soon died of dysentery.

George is listed as having property worth $15,000 in 1870—not bad for a young adventurer from Tennessee. He dictated his memoir to Edward F. Murray in 1878, *The Life and Adventures of George Nidever*. He died on March 24, 1883 and was buried at Calvary Catholic Cemetery in Santa Barbara. In 1888, his wife Sinforosa

Sanchez de Nidever was granted a widow's pension for his role in the Californio-American conflict, until she died in 1892.

YAMAMOTO OTOKICHI

Yamamoto Otokichi[78] was a 14-year-old apprentice seaman on the 150-ton cargo ship *Honjumaru* when it left port in November 1832. The ship's cargo included a sizable payload of rice, sake, one barrel of drinking water, and porcelain destined for the Shogun in Edo. Less than a day out of port the ship was caught in a typhoon, dismasted, and left without a rudder. This was not entirely by accident as the Shogun required Japanese mariners to remain in coastal waters and dictated that their ships have large rudders that would snap in the high seas encountered in the open ocean. This was designed to discourage attempts to sail to other countries. However, if vessels were caught in storms they could be left helpless. The crews would cut down their main masts and drift rudderless and unrigged across the ocean.

Yamamoto Otokichi

Caught in the current, the *Honjumaru* was carried to the east for fourteen months. The crew became *hyôryô-min*, drifting people. They lived off the ship's supply of rice, caught fish, drank rainwater and made drinking water with their still. Scurvy, exposure, and storms took their toll, and only three of the original fourteen crewmen survived to reach the west coast. As he lowered his older brother's body into the sea, 14-year-old Otokichi must have wondered what he had done to deserve such a terrible fate. The *Honjumaru* washed ashore[79] on Cape Flattery (some say Cape Alva), on what is

now the Washington coast, in December 1833; but the adventures of Otokichi, Iwakichi, and Kyukichi had just begun.

Perhaps expecting and hoping for a new chance for survival, they were no doubt disappointed when they were found, looked after, and enslaved by the Makah tribe who also plundered the ship. Fortunately, Dr. John McLoughlin, the Chief Factor and Superintendent of the Hudson's Bay Company at Fort Vancouver, heard of their plight. A rescue party of twenty men led by a voyageur was dispatched but were forced back by snow and difficult forest conditions. In June, Dr. McLoughlin ordered the HBC brig *Llama* to sail north from Fort Vancouver, stopping at the Makah villages to learn more about the three captives and to buy their freedom.

Captain William McNeill, an American, invited the Makah chief aboard the ship to trade but immediately took him hostage in exchange for the three sailors. Only two of the men could be found and their freedom was secured, but the third, Otokichi, had gone into the forest to collect berries, and the ship left without him. Imagine how he felt when he returned to the village and found his compatriots gone. Upon the ship's return, Otokichi was freed for the cost of a few colorful cotton blankets. The rescued sailors were taken to Fort Vancouver.

The three "kichis" were popular with the residents of the fort. They soon regained their health and began to learn English and the other languages spoken in this polyglot community. Kanaka Village and the fort must have been quite a shock for the insular Japanese visitors. In addition to the seven primary languages spoken at Fort

Vancouver — English, French Canadian, Chinook, Ojibway, Gaelic, Knisteneaux (Cree), Hawaiian, and more than 25 others. The Japanese could already understand the Wakashan languages after their time with the Makah.

Dr. McLoughlin realized the potential of using these unexpected visitors to open trade with the closed Japanese economy (*sakoku*), and they were sent on the brig *Eagle* to London. With this stopover in 1835, Otokichi and his shipmates were probably the first nine-teenth-century Japanese to arrive in England. Sadly, the British government did not show much interest in pursuing the open Japanese market with them. After a brief stay in London, all but one day of it confined to their ship, they were sent the rest of the way around the world to Macao. They arrived safely in June 1835 after a six-month journey. They were handed over to the German missionary and linguist Karl Friedrich August Gutzlaff. Otokichi taught him Japanese and also assisted with the translation of the Gospel of John. The first portion of the Bible in Japanese was published in Singapore in 1837 but did not reach Japan until 1859.

Otokichi's group was more than doubled when four other ship-wrecked Japanese sailors arrived. In July 1837, the seven castaways left Canton with American merchant Charles W. King onboard the merchant vessel *Morrison*. Cannons were fired from the hilltops of the Miura Peninsula as soon as the ship approached Uraga in compliance with the Shogunate's order to fire at all approaching Western ships except the Dutch. King anchored at a safe distance, out of range of the shore batteries, and several small fishing ships sailed out and sailors were allowed aboard. Sake and cookies were shared until late into the night, but by daybreak cannons had been brought closer to the seaside and were again fired at the ship. Hundreds of small boats, each with a small cannon at the front, also started to surround the ship and prepared to attack, so the *Morrison* sailed away. King then sailed to Kagoshima in Kyūshū and met with officials who took two of the castaways into custody. The following day, a fisherman came alongside and warned them to leave immediately.

As the ship was setting sails, cannons that had been secretly moved close to the ship at night opened fire. King abandoned his rescue mission and returned to Canton with the remaining castaways.

Otokichi took the name John Matthew Ottoson and converted to Christianity. He learned Chinese and was employed by the British as an interpreter during the Opium Wars of 1839 to 1842. The opening of five treaty ports in China in 1842 saw Otokichi settling in Shanghai where he was soon put in charge of the warehouse of Dent and Co. He had apparently also spent some time on ships and helped Japanese castaways return to Japan aboard Chinese or Dutch ships—the only ships allowed to visit the country. He also engaged in business on his own behalf.

He continued working for British agents and travelled extensively throughout East Asia and to Singapore. With a Chinese disguise and name, Lin Ah Tao, Otokichi landed at Uraga Port (Japan) in 1849 when he was working as a translator for the *HMS Mariner*. He assisted the Royal Navy's Vice Admiral James Stirling in forging the Peace and Amity Treaty in 1854. Stirling was not actually authorized to negotiate a treaty and the signing of the convention came about due to a series of miscommunications. This was one of the first steps in opening Japan for trade between Britain, France, and Japan. Otokichi was handsomely rewarded for this work and attained British citizenship.

Otokichi married a Scottish woman he had met in Macao, where she had worked at the Mission Press. After her death, he married Louisa Brown, a Singaporean Eurasian of German and Malay descent. She had been a coworker in Shanghai at Dent & Beale Company, one of the wealthiest British merchant firms, or *Hongs*, active in China during the 19th century.

By the late 1850s, Otokichi decided to leave Shanghai, now in the throes of the Taiping Rebellion, for Singapore, his wife's home island. Otokichi first lived on Queen Street before moving into one of the largest houses on Orchard Road, nestled in a vast nutmeg and clove plantation. He had done well in business deals in Shanghai, and the Otokichi family could afford a luxurious colonial house. They had three children, one died young but two girls survived.

When the second overseas Japanese diplomatic mission to Europe, led by Takenouchi Yasunori, governor of the Shimotsuke region, arrived in Singapore in 1862, they met with Otokichi. He took them around the island to view the sights, including his house. He probably also shared his insight in dealing with Europeans.

With complications resulting from TB and hypertension, Otokichi died at Arthur's Seat, a sanitarium located on a coconut plantation near Siglap, in January 1867. His remains were returned to Onoura, the city of his birth, in 2005, after being away for 173 years.

Dr. McLoughlin had no idea of the importance of the young Japanese man he freed from the Makah. Otokichi was instrumental in opening relations between Japan and the West. A monument honoring the three "kitchis" is now in place on the grounds of Fort Vancouver, Washington, and the fort has a leaflet about them. There was a theatrical end to Otokichi's saga. The story of the *Hojunmaru* castaways was adapted as the Japanese feature film *Kairei* in 1983, featuring American singer and actor Johnny Cash as Dr. McLoughlin, but it was poorly produced and not very successful. The sailors' odyssey has also been featured in a play called "The Tale of Otokichi" staged at Clark College in Vancouver, Washington, and at Seattle Center.

JOHN WORK, A HIGHLY MERITORIOUS MAN AND TRADER

John Work[80] was born to the family of farmer Henry Wark in Northern Ireland about 1792. He received some education but was noted for poor penmanship. He signed on as a clerk to the Hudson's Bay Company in 1814 when his name was entered incorrectly as Work. He served in the far north well enough to be made district manager. He then survived the layoffs involved in the merger of the HBC and North West Company in 1821.

He was moved to the Columbia District in 1823 and made the trip west from York Factory to the Columbia River with Peter Skene Ogden

John Work

in just three months. On his trip west he started keeping a series of excellent journals that provide some of the best descriptions of the fur trade in the inland west. He spent his first winter at Spokane House, and in 1824 he went down to Fort Astoria with Governor George Simpson. Simpson would later write that he was, "*A queer looking fellow, of Clownish Manners and address, indeed there is a good deal of simplicity approaching to idiocy in his appearance, he is nevertheless a Shrewd Sensible Man, and not deficient in firmness when necessary...*" On an exploring trip with James McMillan he discovered the Cowlitz Portage that helped link Puget Sound with the Columbia River.

Work was then sent east to manage inland operations at Fort Spokane, and then Fort Colville from 1826–1830. In 1826 he married a 17-year-old mixed-blood Spokane woman, Josette Legacé, or Little Rib. She would accompany him on many of his expeditions and bear ten children; the youngest of which was born at Fort Victoria in 1849. The marriages of his children often involved other fur traders, thus extending his influence. It was said that his constant concern was the wellbeing and happiness of his wife and children. He was afflicted with a variety of maladies and complained often of his health but carried on strenuous travels until his old age.

Work was a key player in the effort to create the "fur desert" that would slow the American advance. He left Fort Walla Walla in 1830 with 37 men, 4 hired servants, a slave, 2 youths (in all, 40 able to bear arms and armed), 29 women and 45 children (22 boys, 23 girls). This moving village of 114 went across the Blue Mountain Range and through the valleys of the Grand Ronde, Powder, and Burnt Rivers to the Snake River. From there they went on to the mouth of the Payette River, crossed over to the Boise River, and then to the Camas Plains, the Malade River, Lost River, Blackfoot River, and finally the Portneuf River. In all, they travelled almost 2,000 miles to strip beaver from the region Peter Ogden had already been through. The next year he was on the Salmon River in Idaho and returned to the Columbia as chief trader in 1831. After returning from another expedition to the Snake River country on July 27, 1832, he was ordered to make a quick turn-around and head up the outgoing California brigade and supervise a smaller California brigade under Michel LaFramboise. This expedition was to have catastrophic effects on the native people.

These fur brigades were large, well-organized, and effective at stripping beaver out of streams. They might include 100 people, including wives and children, plus 200–300 horses. The men would typically include salaried workers, freemen paid per fur, and slaves. The women played critical roles in preparing food and clothing, establishing camps, processing furs, and enabling the men to devote their time to trapping.

The 1832 brigade carried "intermittent fever" (apparently malaria) to California. This deadly disease had arrived at Fort Vancouver in 1830. A sick sailor named Jones on the American brig *Owhyhee* under Captain Dominis, was considered the cause (today he would be called Patient Zero). The initial impacts near Fort Vancouver were catastrophic in 1830–1831. Many villages were abandoned and later burned by HBC employees to dispose of the bodies. The Chinook village downstream from the fort was hard hit, with Chief Cassino losing nine wives, three children, and sixteen slaves. Thousands died, and as people fled the epidemic they helped spread it. Most Europeans were sickened but recovered thanks to quinine, better treatment, and innate resistance, but mortality ranged from 60–90% in the native population.

The first case of intermittent fever was reported at Fort Vancouver on July 5, 1832. John Work and his brigade left for California on August 17th with 26 men, 22 women (including his wife Josette), 44 children (including Work's three young girls), and six Indians.[81] As he wrote to Francis Ermantinger on July 27, "*I am going to start with my ragamuffin freemen to the South.*" Work's clerk, Francis Payette, was so sick he had to be left at Fort Nez Perce, and his illness delayed their departure. Work was dosing ten people for the fever when he left the fort and it is likely that Michel LaFramboise's smaller brigade of 63 people, which left earlier, was also spreading the disease.

Work went down the eastern route to California (Fort Nez Perce, Malheur Lake, Pit River) while LaFramboise took the central route (Willamette, Umpqua, Shasta). Both returned up the western route after trapping the Sacramento, San Joaquin, San Francisco Bay area, and Coast Range. The epidemic rose and fell within the brigades over the yearlong expedition, with almost everyone sick at some point. In August 1833, Work notes, "*Some of those who have been longest ill are a little better, the greater number of others are very bad and 7 more are taken ill during the last night and today making in all 72 ill.*" Two men, an Indian, and two children died along the way despite medicine (which ran out long before they returned) and care. Work had done an amazing job to limit the losses.

As the HBC trappers worked rivers and side streams, they met and often traded with native people and were bit by mosquitos, which also aided in the spread of the disease. In addition, an American fur trapping party under Ewing Young met the HBC brigade along the way and may have picked up the intermittent fever and spread it along their way.

The impact of the disease was clear as they returned north in the fall of 1833, still sick themselves. In his journal on August 6, 1833, Work noted, "*Some sickness prevails among the Indians on the feather*

1832-1833

—— HBC - Work and
La Framboise

Young

*river. The villages that were so populous and swarming with inhabitants
when we passed that way in Jany or Febry last seem now almost deserted
& have a desolate appearance. The few wretched Indians who remain
seem wretched they are lying apparently scarcely able to move. .... We are
unable to learn the malady or its cause.*" Dr. John McLoughlin noted in
a subsequent letter, "*Mr. Work writes me that nine-tenths of the Indian
population from here (Vancouver) to there (the Sacramento Valley) is
mostly destroyed.*" Work returned to Fort Vancouver in October 1833,
disappointed in the hunt though McLoughlin estimated the 1,023
beaver and otter skins realized a profit of £627.

In 1834 Ogden went down the west side to the Umqua River with
a dozen men, leaving on May 22, and returning on July 10. Later in
1834, Work moved to the coast, going north on the *Llama* to establish Fort Simpson, where he would spend much of his time until
1849. His travels also took him up to the Queen Charlotte Islands,

Vancouver Island, and other areas. The competition with American ships was fierce and the natives were difficult to work with. He started a garden at the fort and helped establish Cowlitz Farm to grow food for the RAC.

Work felt disregarded and frustrated with his situation and complained bitterly to friends. He was injured in falls in both 1840 and 1841 and was criticized by McLoughlin for displaying a lack of initiative and his inability to quell growing unrest. Work developed a lip cancer in 1843 but ships' doctors removed much of his upper lip in four operations, saving his life. After McLoughlin resigned in 1846, Work was made Chief Factor for the coastal trade and operation of the steamship *Beaver.*

Work moved to Victoria with his large family in 1849. He also established Fort Rupert near the new coal beds on Vancouver Island but still spent much of his time traveling or up at Fort Simpson. In 1851 he discovered gold while crossing Vancouver Island and endured the problems inherent with a minor gold rush.

He finally left Fort Simpson in 1852 and settled in at Fort Victoria with many from the former Fort Vancouver community. Many had moved to the island after the Americans overran the Columbia and Willamette Valleys and began mistreating the Canadians, particularly the Métis and natives. Work was an enterprising farmer and acquired considerable property during his lifetime. Nothing pleased him more than to gather his numerous children and grandchildren about him. He passed away in 1861. His funeral was a big affair, acknowledging his considerable role in the fur trade and the settling of the Northwest. His remarkable wife lived until 1896.

PETER SKENE OGDEN, MASTER OF THE INLAND FUR TRADE

Peter Skene[82] Ogden was born in Quebec City to Isaac Ogden, a jurist (and Loyalist) and Sarah Hanson in 1794. He was to lead a remarkable life of adventure in the fur trade. Two of his brothers were lawyers, and while Peter himself was educated, he was not suited to a desk job. After a brief spell with Astor's American Fur Company in Montreal, he moved over to the North West Company as an apprentice clerk in April of 1809.

Peter Skene Ogden

He started work at the peak of the conflict between the NWC and the HBC. He was assigned to Île-à-la-Crosse (Saskatchewan). He and an older clerk, Samuel Black,[83] were involved in a fight with Peter Fidler at the nearby HBC post in 1810. By 1814 Ogden was trading at Green Lake, once again in direct competition with a nearby HBC camp. They attacked and took their competitor's post and all their goods. Ogden was involved in the killing of a native in the fracas. The native hunter may have fired the first shot, but then he was shot and wounded. He was rescued by the HBC post only to be given up under threat. This poor soul was then, according to accounts, repeatedly shot, stabbed (by Ogden), and axed by members of the raiding party. In his defense, Ogden claimed the slain native had been wanted for murder and cannibalism, but there is no evidence of that. By 1818 an account of the incident at Green Lake was forwarded by the HBC to Lord Bathurst, Secretary of State for War in the colonies, and a murder indictment against Ogden was drawn up.

But it was too late—Ogden had been transferred to the Columbia Department in 1817 and was out of reach as he served at Fort George. He was a clerk at the Thompson's River Post from 1820–22. Although the merger of the HBC and the NWC in 1821 specifically excluded Ogden from the new organization, he remained in charge of Fort Thompson until he headed east to Montreal and then to England to request relief from the ban. The London committee of the HBC

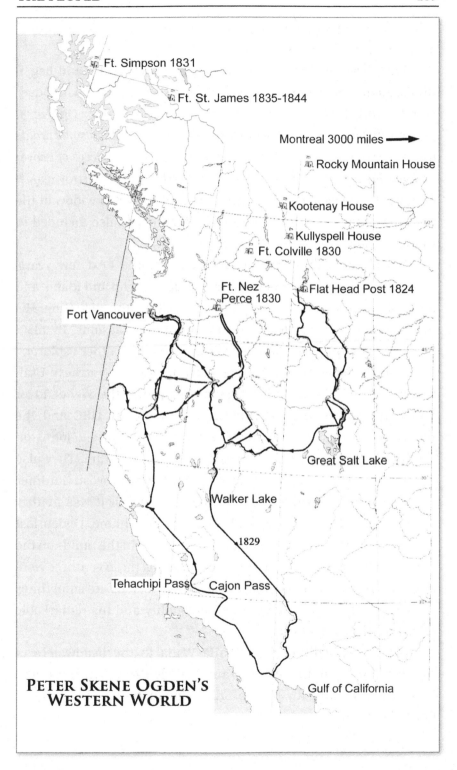

Ft. Simpson 1831

Ft. St. James 1835-1844

Montreal 3000 miles ➤

Rocky Mountain House

Kootenay House

Kullyspell House
Ft. Colville 1830

Ft. Nez
Perce 1830   Flat Head Post 1824

Fort Vancouver

Great Salt Lake

Walker Lake

1829

Tehachipi Pass   Cajon Pass

Gulf of California

PETER SKENE OGDEN'S
WESTERN WORLD

relented, and in 1823 it was agreed that Ogden should be appointed a chief trader.

Ogden was sent to Spokane House as Chief Trader and began preparations for the creation of a "fur desert" in the Snake River country. In 1824, Governor Simpson laid out his goal for Ogden: *"If properly managed no question exists that it would yield handsome profits as we have convincing proof that the country is a rich preserve of Beaver and which for political reasons we should endeavour to destroy as fast as possible."* He also took a country wife, Julia Rivet, a widow of the Spokane tribe (Seliñ, Interior Salish). Her story is also included in this collection.

Ogden would make six major trips over the next few years, exploring and trapping much of current-day Oregon and Idaho, and parts of Washington, California, Nevada, Utah, and Wyoming. His wife and children traveled with him on many occasions. By 1830, he had a better understanding of the area than any other explorer.

1824–25: Expedition to Southeastern Idaho and Northern Utah which includes Cache Valley, Ogden Valley, and the Weber River Valley, the site of the confrontation between the HBC and the Americans. He lost many of his freemen and their furs to Johnston Gardiner's party, who offered much better pay for furs. They also encountered a party from Santa Fe under Etienne Provost. Gardiner and Ogden disputed the territorial ownership, but it was neither American nor British—it was Mexican. Almost home, Ogden lost nine men, 500 furs, and his journals in an upset in the rapids on the Columbia River. Even so, the HBC was happy as these ventures were often returning 100 percent profit. Ogden's journals are sometimes cynical but attest to his tenacious personality and his remarkable efforts for the company.

1825–26: Expedition from Walla Walla to the headwaters of the Des Chutes, up the Snake to the Malade River, Raft River, and Portneuf, returning by way of the Willamette, having crossed Central Oregon.

1826–27: Expedition to the Klamath country, a part of Oregon unknown to white men at the time.

1827–28: Expedition to southeast Idaho, winter on the Snake, notes about American Parties.

1828–29: Expedition to the Snake Country. Follows Humboldt River, explores region north of Great Salt Lake.

1829–1830: On his last big expedition Ogden reached the Colorado River and the Gulf of California. His group heavily trapped the east side of the Sierras and the San Joaquin valley, leaving few beaver for American parties. His wife and children did not go on this trip.

Ogden was worn down and excused from the next trip to California. Instead he was moved up to the Northwest Coast and lighter duty. For the winter of 1830–1831 he and his family were at Fort Vancouver, and in April 1831 he was tasked with establishing a trading post on the Nass River. This was called Fort Simpson, and Ogden was the Chief Trader from 1831–1834. Ogden worked hard to gain trade against the competing American traders and the Russian American Company. He successfully countered the American maritime traders but failed to establish a post on the Stikine River.

In 1835, Ogden was promoted again and made Chief Factor of the New Caledonia District, with headquarters at Fort St. James. He spent almost nine years at home, enjoying his family time and trading without direct competition. This was a lovely post on the end of Stuart Lake. The trips to Fort Vancouver were still arduous, but less dangerous and much more predictable than the Snake River expeditions.

Ogden went to London in 1844 for discussions over the future of the Northwest. On the return trip he was accompanied by two British officers, Mervin Vavasour and Henry James Warre. They were "tourists," sent across Canada for an assessment of the political situation on the ground in the West. Warre's sketches are very good and give a detailed rendering of the forts and the overall Columbia region setting.

In 1845, Ogden was appointed to a newly formed board of management for the Columbia District, with McLoughlin and James Douglas. After he returned to Fort Vancouver in August, he carried out his instructions to purchase Cape Disappointment at the mouth of the Columbia for the HBC. He also claimed land for himself.

The Oregon Boundary Treaty of June 1846 fixed the frontier between British and American territory at the 49th parallel, placing the lower Columbia in the United States. After John McLoughlin retired Ogden, Douglas and John Work were responsible for the Columbia Department. This proved challenging as the land was now under foreign control. The scrappy and troublesome American settlers were a nuisance and their mistreatment of Métis and native people was an increasing problem. Many of the people from Kanaka Village and French Prairie chose to move to Vancouver Island; others would go south to the Gold Rush in California or east to the Grand Ronde reservation.

In December of 1847, a Cayuse tribal attack on the mission at Waiilatpu led to the death of 14 people and the taking of 47 prisoners. Ogden was never afraid of a scrape and left Fort Vancouver the morning after he heard the news. He succeeded in negotiating the release of the prisoners within two weeks.

The Oregon Census of 1850 lists Peter Skein Ogden, 56, Chief Factor HBC, Canada; Fabian Rivet, 5, Oregon Territory; Theressa Rivet, 8, Oregon Territory; Dick Owyhee, 32, steward, Sandwich Islands[84]; Learhenard[85] Owyhee, 32, cook, Sandwich Islands. Ogden's wife was living with one of her daughters in Champeog (quite nearby). She would later move with her daughter to Lac La Hache, Canada, dying at age 98.

Peter was on furlough from 1852–1853. In August 1854 he left Fort Vancouver for Oregon City. His health was failing and he died in September of that same year. He had saved and invested wisely and left a considerable estate. Governor Simpson, who had earlier worried about Ogden, noted in November 1854: *Few persons I believe knew him so well or esteemed his friendship more highly than myself.*

Ogden's will provided for a division of land, cash, and bank stock between his children, grandchildren, adopted son, and other relatives. Ogden never formalized his marriage to Julia, and despite his clear instructions, his brother Charles Richard and sister Harriet Lawrence worked hard to disinherit the Ogden/Rivet family. It was Governor Simpson who developed a compromise by which the property was divided.

Scoundrels

John Meares, an enterprising scoundrel

Captain John Meares was born about 1756. His father Charles Meares was an attorney and officer in the British Colleges of Heralds of his Majesty's Court of Exchequer in Dublin for several years. At the age of fifteen, Meares joined the British Navy as a "captain's servant" on the HMS *Cruizer,* a sloop. He studied and learned enough to pass his exam in 1778 to become commissioned as a lieutenant. It is likely that he was involved in naval action against the Americans on the Great Lakes during the Revolution. He also fought against

John Meares

the French in the West Indies. After the Peace of 1783, he entered the merchant service and captained a ship to India.

After learning of the value of furs collected on Cook's expedition, Meares and his associates organized the Bengal Fur Society in Calcutta to try their hand. They raised eighty-thousand pounds by subscription, and in 1786 the *Nootka* and smaller *Sea Otter* were purchased and sent to the coast with Meares commanding the *Nootka.* The voyage was slow and miserable with frequent fog and unfavorable winds. He was north of the Aleutians when he stumbled on the Russian settlement on Unalaska.

In late September he reached Prince William Sound where he was to join the *Sea Otter*. It was clear that the *Sea Otter* had visited the place recently and it was assumed that she had left for China; later reports suggest she foundered off Kamchatka. Meares foolishly decided to winter over in the Sound to avoid the risk of losing his crew by desertion in Hawaii. This was a costly mistake, as the ship's crew was decimated by scurvy, with over half of the complement dying. Meares noted that his first officer staved off the disease by chewing young pine needles.

On May 19, 1787, Captain George Dixon of the *Queen Charlotte* and Captain Nathaniel Portlock of *King George* arrived. They gave Meares two seamen and some supplies with the agreement that he would leave the coast. He had no choice but to head to the Hawaiian Islands. After a month to recover, he sailed for China, reaching the safe harbor of Typa[86] in the islands off Macao, on October 20, 1787. He took Ka'iana, the brother of a Hawaiian chief, as a passenger.

In January of 1788, three months after his arrival, Meares was successful in purchasing two vessels for his fur trading efforts—the *Felice Adventurer* and the *Iphigenia Nubiana*. He assumed command of the *Felice* while the latter was entrusted to Captain William Douglas. The anchor of the *Felice* was set in Friendly Cove, three months and twenty-three days from China. Meares was joined there by the *Iphigenia* in June. They brought back Ka'iana, three other Hawaiians and Comeckela (probably one of Maquinna's brothers).

On his arrival at Nootka he bought some land from Maquinna[87] to build a residence and trading post using fifty Chinese carpenters he brought. The first floor was a workshop and the second floor was a combined dining room and dormitory. A strong breastwork was built and a cannon was placed in position to command the native village.[88] His men also assembled a 40-ton schooner, *The North West America*,[89] brought from China in pieces. It was the first vessel constructed by the British on the Northwest Coast.[90]

Meares' longboat was attacked at Nitinat because the chief, Tatooche, was at war with Wickaninnish, Meares's closest ally. Meares was willing to loan Maquinna guns for a raid. Meares traded for furs from Nootka Sound south to Tillamook Bay. He sailed for China in September. His cargo included spars for ship repairs and construction in China. The *Felice, Iphigenia* and *North West America* continued trading and then wintered in the Hawaiian Islands.

Meares arrived at Macau in December 1788 and sold his furs and ship. Two vessels in the employ of Etches and Company of London made port shortly afterwards. Mr. John Etches was the supercargo and Meares probably regaled him with tales of the easy money to be made through sea otters. They formed a joint stock company, The Associated Merchants of London and India, and would use the two Etches ships. Captain James Colnett would be in charge of all the business of the company on the American Coast (including the *Iphigenia, North West America*, and the house and land at Nootka). The *Princess Royal* under Captain Hudson, and the *Argonaut* under Captain Colnett, were fully outfitted for a three-year cruise. The *Argonaut* carried a small vessel in pieces and a number of Chinese carpenters.

The Spanish frigate *Princesa* arrived in Nootka Sound in May 1789, to find the *Iphigenia*, led by Captain Douglas, and the American ship *Columbia,* led by Captain Kendrick, in port. The corvette *San Carlos* arrived soon after. After initially friendly relations, Martinez, the captain of the *Princesa*, seized Meare's ships. In July, when the *Argonaut* and the *Princess Royal* arrived, they were seized as well. The *Iphigenia* was later released under bond, but the other three craft were held. The *Argonaut* was taken to Mexico as a prize, while the other ships were reflagged and operated under Spanish authority. The *Princess Royal* was renamed the *Princess Real* and the *North West America* was renamed the *Gertrudis*.

Meares left for England when he heard about the seizures and claimed $653,433 in damages against Spain. Immediate satisfaction was demanded from Spain, but when this did not happen a fleet was organized to go to war. Thankfully, war fever subsided. In September, Meares raised his claims even higher but they were finally settled for just $210,000. It is not clear if Meares received any of the money directly or if it went to creditors.

Meares published a narrative of his adventures, but Captain George Dixon quickly contested many of his claims. Meares apparently was involved in effectively stealing William Barkley's nautical gear and his journal, and claiming credit for his discoveries. Meares also managed to persuade the owners to take Barkley's ship away and transfer the goods to him. Barkley's wife Frances later wrote that Meares, *"published and claimed the merit of my husband's discoveries therein contained, besides inventing lies of the most revolting nature tending to vilify the person he thus pilfered."* After the case was investigated, William Barkley was awarded £5000, a small part of what he was due.

Meares then dropped from sight. He was promoted to commander after returning to active duty in the Royal Navy in 1795. In May of 1796, he wrote to Evan Nepean, now under-secretary to the Admiralty, saying that he had recovered from an injury sustained while rounding up seamen for duty.

In 1796 he married Miss Mary Anne Guilleband at the Abbey Church in Bath. It appears they may have had several children, and according to his will he owned property in Jamaica. The value of his estate at the time of probate was estimated to be under £7,500 with more than £20,000 owed to him. He did not list his wife in his will (presumably, she had died) and he recognized no children.

Meares had a mixed reputation. He put forward a grand vision of a new economic network based in the Pacific, joining the Pacific Northwest, China, Japan, Hawaii, and England; he argued that breaking the monopolistic powers of the East India Company and the South Sea Company was essential. He was an innovative and enterprising man but also an egotistical, lying braggart. From his portrait we can see he was probably also a dandy. One critic noted he was never downcast, always hopeful, and could tell a bald-faced lie and then regale you with a beautiful description of some remote island, bay, native chief or woman. He seemed to get along with both Maquinna and Wickaninnish and survived challenging voyages to the North Pacific. He was persistent, and brave to a degree, but tricky and treacherous. Some critics say his navigation was questionable and his maps laughable. He remains well known only because he came so close to starting a war between England and Spain.

Joseph Burling O'Cain

JOSEPH BURLING O'CAIN, INNOVATIVE ENTREPRENEUR AND SHIPWRECK SURVIVOR

Joseph O'Cain[91] was born in 1766 in Derby, Connecticut to Jeremiah and Lauranah Johnson O'Cain. They were both from Ireland, and Joseph has often been mistakenly said to be Irish. His father fought in the Connecticut militia during the Revolutionary War. Joseph was educated and learned carpentry before sailing as a sea-man out of Boston. The early days of his seafaring are not known, but it took some time to learn the trade. He came of age during the Revolutionary War and may well have served on a privateer.[92]

He clearly was learning sailing, leadership, navigation, and survival skills by 1789 or 1790 when he was on a British ship[93] that sank in the Far East. His luck was no better in 1791 when the *Elenora*[94] sank in the Queen Charlotte Islands off the northwest coast on January first. In 1792 he was in Sitka as first mate under Captain Hugh Moore of the *Phoenix* and met the RAC's Baranov for the first time. Captain Moore presented Baranov with his own cabin boy, a Bengalese named Richard, who was destined to remain Baranov's faithful bodyguard and servant for many years.

In 1793 a Joseph Cain, carpenter, left the *Jefferson*[95] at Kaiganee[96] and signed on with the *Phoenix* again. In 1794 he was probably the first mate of the *Phoenix* again on the NW Coast to Hawaii and Canton. He would ultimately sail on eight different vessels that touched the Northwest Coast. He was responsible for devising and implementing the strategy that would lead to the destruction of the sea otters along the southern coasts.

He was one of the first non-Spanish citizens to land in California (1795) and he applied for citizenship. By some accounts he was the pilot (*pilotin habilitado*) of the Spanish ship *Sutil* and may have joined it either at Nootka Sound or San Blas. The captain of the *Sutil* was reprimanded severely for allowing O'Cain, Thomas Muir, and other English sailors on board, but he may have needed them to get back to California as his crew was sick with scurvy. O'Cain may have left the *Phoenix* in Santa Barbara or perhaps he arrived on the *Sutil* with the story modified to protect the Spanish commander. He may have stayed at his own request or after a conflict with Captain Moore.

In either case, O'Cain requested permission to stay in California and Felipe de Goycoechea wrote a very strong letter supporting his application to become a citizen. The captain noted that the young man was "*of the Boston nation, a very handsome fellow*," and "*wished to become a Christian.*[97]" This was ultimately denied, perhaps because O'Cain was traveling with Thomas Moore, a Scottish radical who had been condemned to prison in Australia for espousing democratic principles. It appears likely that O'Cain was sent to San Blas on the *Aranzazu* then rode overland to Mexico City and finally went on to Vera Cruz and perhaps to Cadiz, Spain with Muir.[98]

O'Cain managed to return to Boston by 1799 and married Abigail "Nabby" Kimball in March. They had a small house in Dorchester, near his birthplace. They would have several children that, sadly, all died young. He soon left as supercargo (trade and merchandise manager) on the brig *Betsy* under Captain Charles Winship. Winship became ill and O'Cain stayed with him in San Blas until he died. After Winship's death, O'Cain signed on as first mate of the

Enterprise under Captain Ezekiel Hubbell in 1801. The *Enterprise* was in Canton in the fall of 1802 and then traveled back to Boston. He was able to spend some rare time with his wife before leaving again in January 1803, now as Captain of the *O'Cain*. The name was probably a Winship family thank-you for his care for Charles during his fatal illness. The *O'Cain* reached Kodiak in nine months on this first voyage.

In the fall of 1803, O'Cain proposed a new system to the RAC's Baranov for sea otter collection further south on the coast. The decreasing number of otters in the north and the continued intrusions of foreigners strengthened Baranov's conviction, confirmed by Nikolai Rezanov, that new hunting grounds must be found. The Anglo-Americans must be prevented from taking away more furs and strengthening their land claims. Spanish law banned fur hunting by foreigners in California, but Baranov accepted O'Cain's idea. He did stipulate that only Russian overseers could give orders to the

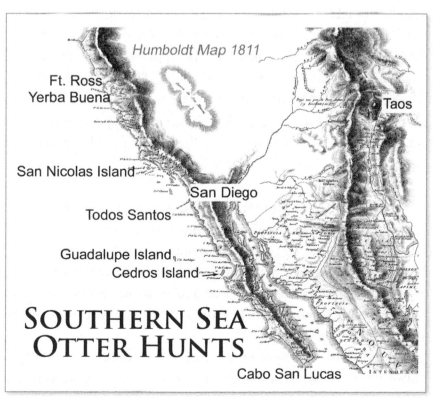

Aleuts, that the Aleuts had to be paid; and that in the event of loss of any man, his family had to be compensated at the rate of $250 Spanish.

Once terms were agreed upon, women made and repaired waterproofs for their husbands, and men whittled new paddles and repaired *baidarka* frames. *Baidarka* skins were sewed, treated, and sealed. Dried fish, whale meat, and plenty of whale oil were prepared as food for the voyage. When all was ready, seventeen *baidarkas* and forty hunters under the command of Afanasii Shvetsov were on board. O'Cain left behind twelve thousand rubles worth of merchandise as insurance. Two sailors were also left — Abraham Jones, the second mate, who became an interpreter for Baranov until Winship returned in 1806; and George Stephens, a cabin boy.

After being turned away in San Diego, the *O'Cain* headed south and was allowed to stay in San Quintin Bay for a few days to get water. The days turned into weeks while the ship stayed on in the calm waters and hunters took more otters. On March 4, 1804, Governor Arrillaga reported to the viceroy that, "*there is not an otter left from Mission Rosario to Santo Domingo.*" He repeatedly ordered O'Cain to depart, but excuses were the only reply. The *O'Cain* returned to Alaska in June 1804 with 1,100 sea otter furs collected by hunters and 700 traded from the Spanish. The crew of Unangax was intact. A profit of $80,000 Spanish was the Russian share. The money and arms O'Cain had brought would help Baranov's effort to retake Sitka from the Tlingit.

O'Cain headed down to Hawaii and then back to the Northwest Coast for more fur trading. Leaving Kodiak on October 26, he reached San Diego on December 4, Todos Santos on April 15, and then was back to Kodiak and on to Canton in January. He arrived home in July of 1805. Back in Boston he was able to spend five months with his wife before leaving again in January 1806, now as captain of the *Eclipse*.

In 1806 a new agreement was forged with Baranov. The *Eclipse* sailed down the coast to California again with even more native hunters and *baidarkas*. This time the Spanish government was determined to halt the practice. When O'Cain arrived in San Diego in June he asked for an emergency visit for water and supplies. This was denied, so he sailed down to Todos Santos. He celebrated the Fourth of July by landing twenty of his crew, fifteen well-armed, to meet with the five Spaniards sent to stop him. O'Cain told Corporal Osuna that he must have water. Following orders, Osuna refused, so O'Cain forced the Spaniards to dismount and go as prisoner/ hostages aboard his ship. Two of the soldiers were released a few days later and instructed by O'Cain to carry a strong message to Rodriguez. The pilot of the *Peacock*, who had been taken at San Juan Capistrano, had to be freed, or O'Cain would return to San Diego and demolish the fort and then the presidio.

Osuna reported that the *Boston's* crew always carried guns and the captain was ever watchful; each morning, noon, and evening, a sailor would climb the mast and closely scan the seas. However, on July 8, 1806, five of his crew were taken by the Spanish after their boat overturned in the surf at San Jose del Cabo Bay. After further time on the south coast and not many furs, he gave up and headed north to Alaska after a stop in Hawaii. He dropped off his Kodiak mistress, Barbara (*Chunagak*),[99] and replaced her with a Hawaiian girl. The *Eclipse* also picked up some stranded Japanese sailors. O'Cain then picked up furs in Alaska and headed to China.

Unfortunately, the prices and demand for furs were low in early 1807. He then stopped in Nagasaki, Japan and reached Petropavlosk, Kamchatka on August 8th. After a visit the *Eclipse* headed for Kodiak, Alaska. The *Eclipse* spotted land and then turned to the east on September 10th. About ten at night, the alarm was given that there were breakers ahead, and on the lee bow. The mate wanted to veer away but Captain O'Cain thought what they had seen was only white water, and not breakers. He ordered the helmsman to stand on course. Almost immediately the ship plunged onto Sanak Reef and struck with great violence. The large waves beat her onto the rocks and in a few minutes the rudder was unshipped, and the

stern-post forced up through the rear deck. Luckily she washed over
the reef into deep water. They dropped anchor and waited through
a cold long night. Many of the cannons were dropped overboard to
gain buoyancy.

The next morning as the dawn light came up they saw land to
leeward. Maneuvering with the sails they brought the *Eclipse* closer
to shore, grounding closer to Sanak Island about noon. Using the
ship's long boat the men were brought in safely. They set up a shelter just to the north east of Salmon Bay with sails and spars. They
gathered some food from debris off the beach and some from the
ship. They also had plentiful sea food. The crew was put to work
gathering the wreckage and salvaging what they could from the ship
using the long boat. On the 18th they made a much larger shelter
and Archibald Campbell[100] considered it a fairly comfortable village.

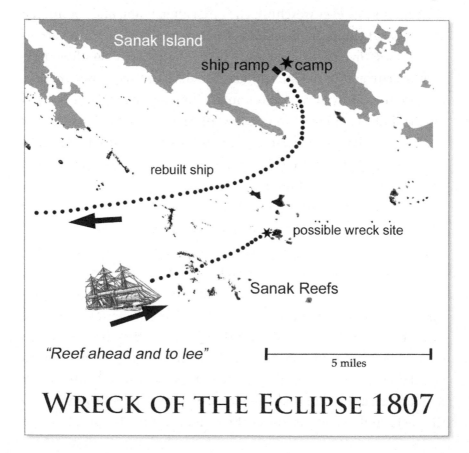

Sanak Island

ship ramp ✶camp

rebuilt ship

✶ possible wreck site

Sanak Reefs

"Reef ahead and to lee"

5 miles

WRECK OF THE ECLIPSE 1807

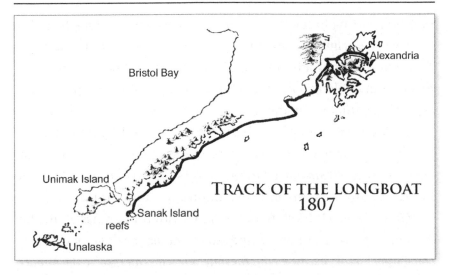

Bristol Bay

Alexandria

Unimak Island

TRACK OF THE LONGBOAT
1807

Sanak Island

reefs

Unalaska

Much of her cargo was eventually salvaged but it is not clear if a chest of coin from fur sales in China was saved.

The crew suffered from the lack of fire, but when Unangax natives arrived on the 28th they quickly started a fire with a friction drill. The crew and passengers were delighted to eat cooked sea food and warm their hands and feet. A kayaker was dispatched to Unalaska and in a remarkable kayaking voyage covered 300 miles of winter seas in about a week. After about a month the Russian leader in Unalaska, Mr. Bander, arrived. He brought about twenty natives to assist with building the new ship, salvage, and fishing. With the help of the Unangax much of the wreck was collected and salvaged.

After modifying the long boat for a winter journey with higher sides and a canvas top, and provisioning it with dried salmon, berries, and water, Mr. Campbell, Mr. Bander, the *Eclipse*'s second mate, another seven of the ship's crew, and an Unangax pilot set sail for Kodiak on the morning of November 18th. This was a daunting 500-mile voyage in a small boat[101] in severe winter conditions. Captain O'Cain and the rest of the crew stayed behind to work on building a new ship. There were no trees on Sanak Island, so salvaging the wreck was critical.

After landing in Kodiak on December 15, Bander and Campbell met with Baranov. He quickly made arrangements to outfit a Russian brig then sitting in the harbor for a voyage back to Sanak Island to retrieve the *Eclipse*'s crew and cargo. Since this would take some time, the governor advised Campbell and the others to head back to Sanak in the long boat with a Russian carpenter to help build the ship. Unfortunately, on the return trip the boat shipwrecked on the north shore of Kodiak Island in a winter storm. A desperate struggle for survival ensued. Eventually a rescue party of natives in *baidarkas* arrived and transported the survivors first to Karluk and then to Kodiak. Campbell's frostbite cost him his feet and a finger.

On October 14, 1808, Baranov had written to an assistant that he had to remain in Kodiak and was *"waiting for Captain O'Cain to come from Sanak, because I am the only one who can resolve the important question of the company's capital."* The cargo on the Eclipse was valued at about $100,000 and there was also a chest of money from fur sales in China. Baranov felt that O'Cain owed money to the RAC (perhaps the chest of money) but O'Cain was also owed money for the cargo. The initial agreement between Baranov and O'Cain split the profits on the sale of furs and provided for additional amounts per ton for freightage. Sadly, neither O'Cain nor his wife would ever see it.

After completing the new ship from salvaged materials, they set out on February 26, 1809 for Unalaska. On board were Captain O'Cain, his Hawaiian female companion, two sailors from his crew, Ivan Bubnov (the RAC sales manager), several *promyshlenniki* and a group of Unangax men who had been assisting in the construction of the ship. Off Unimak Island, the ship was pushed toward shore by high winds from the west and wrecked[102] after traveling only 30 miles. O'Cain would have tried to tack into the prevailing winds to reach Unimak Pass. Once on the north side the winds would have been less treacherous for the return to Unalaska. His rebuilt ship and inexperienced crew may not have been able to work upwind very well and it is presumed they got driven east and north onto the south shore of Unimak Island. In 1808 it is likely the sea ice came down the Bering Sea to the north side of Unimak Island (and perhaps further) but in any case the island would have had a ring of attached shore ice. O'Cain, his Hawaiian woman and the two sailors from the *Eclipse* drowned attempting to reach shore on the floating ice. Nine of the local tribesmen survived along with Ivan Bubnov and one *promyshlenniki*.

No account of the rest of the story is known. It is likely the brig did finally arrive and rescued the rest of the crew and collected the goods and money chest.

O'Cain had revolutionized the sea otter hunt, helped the RAC turn a profit, and survived three shipwrecks. Had he been allowed to stay in California in 1795 he might have done equally well and strengthened the Spanish hold on California and the north coast. His wife wouldn't know what had happened for many months. The loss of a ship at sea posed a problem for families and courts. Were the crew alive? Dead? By 1811 it was clear O'Cain had died. A Boston paper included the first legal step in 1811. *"Notice is hereby given that the subscriber has been duly appointed Administrator, de bonis non, of Joseph O'Cain, late of Dorchester, in the county of Norfolk, mariner, deceased; and has taken upon himself that trust by giving bonds, as the law directs. And all persons having demands upon the estate of said deceased are required to exhibit the same; and all persons indebted to said estate, are called upon to make payment to Wm. C. Aylwin Administrator. Boston, Dec. 3, 1811."* His brother-in-law Abraham Hardyear probated the rest of the O'Cain estate in 1823.

JOHNSTON GARDINER—TRAPPER, EXPLORER, PROVOCATEUR, AND ROBBER

Johnston Gardiner[103] was probably born a little before 1800.[104] He was not literate but his written record is rich because he made an impression on all the people he encountered. He was, by their accounts, a determined, capable trapper and trader, survivor, skilled river pilot, expert marksman, and American provocateur.

As a young man Gardiner was probably involved in the fur trade on the Ohio and Mississippi Rivers before he reached St. Louis. He was recorded going west with William Ashley in 1822. His father-in-law Joseph Laprise was also in the fur trade and his wife's uncle Francois is included in the list of men with Manuel Lisa in 1812. In 1823, Hugh Glass[105] wrote a touching letter to the parents of John S. Gardner[106] after he was killed by the Arikara. John may have been

Johnston Gardiner

Johnston's cousin and he may have known the family. In 1824 a letter to Gardiner was noted in the St. Louis newspaper as being available for pickup (whether he got it is unknown).

In 1824, Gardiner was on the Bear River accompanying John H. Weber's trapping party and working for the Rocky Mountain Fur Company of William Ashley and Andrew Henry. It was at about this time that his name may have been given to a stream on the west side of the Salt River in Wyoming, now called the Tincup. Gardiner was a free trapper working with Weber's outfit when he arrived on the international stage. In May 1825 he paid a visit to the Hudson's Bay Company's Peter Skene Ogden and his clerk William Kittson, camped on the Weber River just west of today's Mountain Green, Utah.[107] Gardiner and men arrived in a rambunctious group and loudly proclaimed, with flags waving, that the British were trespassing on U.S. territory and must leave at once.[108] As Kittson noted in his journal, *"immediately turns to me saying Sir I think you speak too bravely you better take care or I will soon settle your business. Well says I you seem to look for Blood do your worse and make it a point of dispute between our two Governments. One thing I have to say is, that you had better begin the threats you so often make use of in order that we may know the worse of this shameful business."*

Gardiner also declared that the Americans were ready to offer any of Ogden's men who chose to desert $3.50 per pound for their beaver (HBC paid about 1/5 as much, as little as 5 shillings per pelt, based on prices of goods). He added that they would also provide needed supplies at considerably lower costs. Furthermore, the Americans would fight to defend anyone who decided to join the Americans.

From Kittson's journal (with Ogden) in 1825: *Tuesday 23rd. [sic] —This morning Gardner paid a visit to our tent and had a long conversation with Mr. Ogden. The purport of which was as follows, knowing well how our party stood, he boldly asked Mr. Ogden, why he came on these Lands in order as he said to steal our money, by taking the Beaver and that if he Mr. O. knew what was good for himself and party he would return home. Mr. Ogden answered that as to the Country alluded to, he knew full well that it was still a disputed point between the two Governments and as he had received no orders from his Government to leave it, he was determined on making his best through it.*

Here Gardner was called out. Soon after Old Pierre Tevanitagon entered with two iroquois both Deserters of the year (These men had been as far south as Logan River. Their cache yielded 110 skins a few days later) he first began to state that the debts of these two villains were settled and paid to the Company by the remaining 11 Iroquois who kept true to the Concern. On his presenting notes made by himself, I interfere[d] pointed out the errors in the notes and they left us fully awared of Pierre's mistake. Mr. Ogden seing Gardner going to an Iroquois Tent (John Grey) he followed and learnt that mostly all the Freemen whites and all the Iroquois were going to leave him. I not being present cannot tell what conversation was held in the tent, however soon after percieved several tents coming down and Mr. Ogden busily employed in getting skins belonging to others who were absent. I immediately went to his assistance. A scuffle took place between Old Pierre and Mr. Ogden regarding the horses lent by that Gentleman to the old villain, who was supported by all the Americans and 13 of our scamps of Freemen (The Iroquois finally departed with their lodges and furs amounting, according to Ogden's later report, to about seven hundred skins). Mr. Ogden had me, McKay Quintal and Roy to his aid, few as we were we succeeded in getting one and the payement of the other. Soon after they left the camp together with the most part of their hunts leaveing heavy debts behind them. Three of them however paid up their debts. The following names are those that left us this day viz.

> 1 *Alexander Carson Paid up his debt*
> *Not paid*
> 2 *Charles Duford*
> 3 *Martin Miaquin*
> 4 *Pierre Tevaiiitagon*
> 5 *Jaques Osteaceroko*
> 6 *Ignace Deohdiouwassere*
> 7 *Ignace Hatchiorauquasha or Grey*
> 8 *Laurent Karahouton*
> 9 *Baptise Sawenrego*
> 10 *Lazard Kayenquaretcha*
> 11 *Joseph Perreault*
> 12 *Louis Kanota*

Although Ogden would not back down on the issue of territory, he did retreat to Flathead Post after the defection of so many of his free trappers and two workers. He was not happy about the loss of so many furs and some equipment. Gardiner got away with what was essentially a strong-armed robbery. Correspondence in the HBC files shows the managers were frustrated, but George Simpson, the pragmatist, suggested it was a sign of respect that not all men defected, given the deal they were offered. Ogden soothed his critics by bringing in 3,695 beaver pelts.

Ashley diary 1825

The next morning June 20th we continued to decend the river, at 8 miles distant Enters a small stream on the E side bg S E & N W. where we Encamped for dinner, then 3 miles farther down this river & Encamped for the night—our course to day was N W—I

*killed a mountain sheep & one Antelope. Polite a yellow man,
killed an antelope, finding that Johnson Guardner—& party
[deleted: had] of whom we are now in serch had ascended the
smalle river where we dined on the 21 June returned and followed
their trail, and after traveling about 8 miles East Encamped on
the bank of the Creek—the mountans around us to day are not
as lofty & rugged as we have had for many days—Buffalow have
been here a few days past in great numbers but [deleted: from the
Information of] they are traveling East to a mountain dividing
these & the Green River waters—we remain at this Encampment
to day June 22nd to recruit some horses. Mr. Provo who went to
the lake to trade with the Euteaw Indians returned last Evening*

The 1827 St. Louis city records show that Gardiner married Julia
Laprise in St. Louis on February 17th. The records are signed with
marks for both Johnston and Julia. Her father, Joseph Laprise[109] had
married Marie Ortiz in St. Louis in 1802. Julia was born in 1810 and
may have died in 1889. She was buried in the Calvary Cemetery, St.
Louis. It is not known if they had any children.

Gardiner remained in the northern Rocky Mountains for six
more years. He attended the 1828 rendezvous at Bear Lake. Joshua
Pilcher's fur company had lost most of their supplies to water damage in poor caches, but with their remaining goods they managed
to trade for 17 packs of beaver. Covington's comments suggest
Johnston was a free trapper with the best rifle in the company, short
of Captain Sublette. He may have accompanied the furs east, then
hired on with Sublette's supply train coming west.

Governor George Simpson of the Hudson's Bay Company, mentions that Johnston served as clerk for Joshua Pilcher at an American
trading post on Flathead Lake during the winter of 1828–1829. To
function as clerk, he must have been numerate, but he was illiterate
and this limited his ability to rise in management. He was probably
in Yellowstone Country in 1830 and the town of Gardiner, Gardner's

Hole, and the Gardner's Fork are all named for him. Misspellings are common.

When Jackson, Smith, and Sublette ended their partnership in August 1830, Johnston received a note for $1,321.48 owed to him. This was a substantial sum of money at a time when $200 a year was considered a very good wage. His contract for 1832 survived and is held at the Missouri Historical Society and can be found online.

Johnson[110] Gardner (Johnston Gardiner) Contract, 1832

Articles of agreement made and entered into at Fort Union, Upper Missouri, on the fifth day of July 1832, by and between Kenneth Mackenzie, agent of the American Fur Company, and Johnson, citizen of the United States and free hunter in the Indian country.

The said Johnson Gardner hereby agrees to sell, and the said Kenneth Mackenzie agrees to purchase, all his stock of beaver skins now en cache on the Yellowstone River, at and for the price per pound net weight of four dollars twelve and a half cents, to be delivered by the said Johnson Gardner to the agent or servants of the said Kenneth Mackenzie on the spot where it is cached, the weight thereof to be regulated and adjusted by Francis A. Chardon and James A. Hamilton on its arrival at Fort Union, the number of skins being .... and the weight now considered to be .... The said Johnson Gardner further agrees to sell, and the said Kenneth Mackenzie agrees to purchase, all his stock of castorum at and for the price per pound of three dollars, the weight thereof to be adjusted by the parties aforesaid. The said Kenneth Mackenzie hereby further agrees to and with the said Johnson Gardner to furnish and supply and equip two men to hunt and trap beaver for the fall and spring seasons next ensuing, at the entire charge and cost of the said Kenneth Mackenzie, to hunt and trap under the direction of the said Johnston; and the said Kenneth Mackenzie further agrees to furnish a third man, and at his cost and charge to supply a moiety or one-half of the requisite, necessary and usual equipment for a beaver hunter, and the said Johnson Gardner hereby agrees to supply the said third man with the other moiety or half part of the needful equipment usual for a beaver hunter, and it is hereby agreed by and between the said Kenneth Mackenzie and the said Johnson Gardner that an entire moiety or half part of the beaver skins and castorum killed, taken and secured by the united skill and exertions of the said Johnson Gardner and the said three men to be furnished as aforesaid shall be the just and lawful share of the said Kenneth Mackenzie, the other moiety or half part to be the just and lawful share of the said Johnson Gardner, and it is further agreed that the said moiety or half part which shall become the property of the said Johnson Gardner shall be purchased of him by the said Kenneth Mackenzie at and for the price of three dollars fifty cents per pound for beaver skins taken and secured in the fall approaching, and four dollars per pound for beaver skins taken and secured in the spring following, and three dollars per pound for castorum.

Signed, sealed and delivered by the said Kenneth Mackenzie and said Johnson at Fort Union[III] the day and year first above written.

> *In the presence of J.A. Hamilton.*
> *Kenneth Mackenzie, Agt. U.M.O.*
> *his mark Johnson Gardner X.*

We also know a bit about what he bought for his trading effort that year.

Johnson Gardiner Expenses for Outfit 1832

June 28

Your share of advances to Tullock & Co. $12.00

Liquor 8.00, Feast 4.00 .... 12.00

June 29

Liquor 4.00.. 4.00

June 30

Shirts 8.00, Pantaloons 5.00........................... 13.00

Liquor 11.00, Feast 2.00................................. 13.00

July 1

Feast 6.00, Suit of clothes 70.00....................76.00

Knives 4.00, Powder .75, Shoeing horse 3.00... 7.75

July 2

Tobacco .75, Cow skin 1.00 ....1.75

July 5

Liquor 3.00

July 6

Liquor 12.00

July 7

Liquor 10.00, Tea 2.00, Pork 2.00 .... 14.00

Blanket 12.00, Vinegar 1.00, Axe 6.00........... 19.00

Sugar 1.00...1.00

July 8

Thread 1.00, Biscuit 8.50.................................9.50

Salt 6.00, Pepper 4.00, Handkfs 4.00 .... 14.00

Coffee 18.00, Tea 8.00, Sugar 24.00 .... 50.00

File 1.50, Tin Pans 2.00, Kettle 5.00 ....8.50

Tin Cups 2.00, Knives 4.00, Awls 1.50............. 7.50

Tobacco 15.00, Sirsingles 112 6.00 .... 21.00

Liquor 14.00 ....14.00

July 9

Rice 4.00

Knife 2.00

Liquor and Keg 27.00

Total.. $346.00

```
----------------------------------------------------------------
|              Johnston Gardiner Equipment                      |
|                for Hunt, July 9th, 1832, viz.:                |
|  16 Traps 12.00 ............................................ $192 00 |
|  5 Horses 60.00 ............................................. 300.00 |
|  1 Horse in January, 1833 ................................ 60.00 |
|  5 Saddles and apichemons[113] ........................ 25.00 |
|  8 Trap springs 16.00, Flints 1.00 .................... 17.00 |
|  Powder 9.00, Balls 12.00, File 1.50 ............... 22.50 |
|  Knives 7.50, Kettle 5.00, Axe 3.00 ................. 15.50 |
|  Wages of 3 men ........................................... 750.00 |
|  Total ......................................................... $1382.00 |
----------------------------------------------------------------
```

John Jacob Astor's American Fur Company (AFC) built the Fort Union trading post to capture and profit from the pelts, robes, and other furs available on the plains and in the Rocky Mountains. The HBC could not ship pelts, furs, and trade goods on the Missouri and Mississippi Rivers through Spanish, French, and, after 1803, American territory. This gave the Americans a competitive edge by reducing transport costs.

Fort Union dominated the Upper Missouri fur trade soon after it was built. The post's founding manager, AFC partner Kenneth McKenzie, solidified that dominance after 1832 when he brought the first steamboat up to Fort Union. This further lowered transportation costs and benefitted the Upper Missouri Outfit (UMO), as the AFC's western department was called. This helped the UMO bring in more native traders and free traders.

Johnston shows up next on the upper Yellowstone River. In 1832 he followed a tributary of the Yellowstone into a valley he modestly called Gardner's Hole. He was one of the first to explore the Yellowstone area. There is a statement of his account at Fort Union in the summer of 1832. This is a bill of lading of furs shipped on the bull boat[114] *Antoine,* bound for Fort Union from the Crossing of the Yellowstone, dated July 18.

> *Shipped in good order four pac-tons of beaver fur*
> *marked and weighing as follows:*
>
> | No. 1 | 56 skins weighing | 73 lbs. marked J G |
> |-------|-------------------|--------------------|
> | No. 2 | 50 | 81 |
> | No. 3 | 50 | 76 |
> | No. 4 | 50 | 74 |
> | Total | 206 | 304 |
>
> N. B. 1 Otter Skin.

Fort Union, August 6, 1832

We, Francis A. Chardon and J. Archdale Hamilton, hereby certify
that we have carefully weighed two hundred and six beaver skins
purchased by the American Fur Company of Johnston and declare
the weight thereof to be two hundred and seventy-eight pounds,
as witness our hands the day and year first above written.

(Signed) F.A. Chardon

J. Archdale Hamilton

Gardiner met the Prince of Wied[115] in 1833 and from him we learn that on May 8, "*On the steamboat we were told [that] a beaver (trapper, Johnston), the (foremost) pilot of the Missouri, had gone downriver ahead of us, (but) we would catch up with him because he had a poor, heavily loaded canoe. I was advised to take him on with his load, since we would then have a very reliable helmsman. About noon we saw 's canoe ahead and soon caught up with it, (a) square leather boat loaded with furs. I suggested that he bring his cargo on board our boat and take over the helm, a proposal he accepted with pleasure, because he had little trust in his (own vessel). He had two oarsmen with him and was returning from a beaver hunt. We put ashore on the left bank (for) the (cargo) transfer.*"

Gardiner helped organize the camp against Indian assault. On May 10 he was commended for his superb skills in navigating difficult stretches of the river. On May 18 he was reported as dealing with the post sutler at Fort Leavenworth, later drunk and unloading his furs in the rain and mud.

A trading license was issued on July 3, 1833 to Johnston Gardiner by William Clark, Superintendent of Indian Affairs, St. Louis, for 13 persons to trade *"On the Cowskin (now Elk) River within about half a mile of the Missouri state line"* with the Senecas of Sandusky (in present northeastern Oklahoma).

We can see what he had been up to in September 1833 with the following credits to his account:

> **1831, July 12**
> By 53 Beaver Skins at $6.50, ...$344.50
> 1 Otter skin 2.50
>
> **1832, July 21**
> 206 Beaver skins, 278 lbs. at $4 1/8 ....1,146.75
> 1 Otter skin 2.00
> 27 1/4 lbs. Beaver skin
> (at Fort Cass) at 3.50 per100...........................95.37
> Note on Smith, Sublette and Co.................. 1321.48
>
> **1833, June 30**
> 16 beaver traps left at Fort Pierre 192.00
>
> Balance carried down.................................. 930.10
> $4,034.70

In 1833, Gardiner told the Prince of Wied about his many dangerous expeditions into Indian country and his skirmishes, including the story of the end of his friend Hugh Glass.[116] "Old Glass" (age about 50–55), Hilain Menard, and Colin Rose were hunting for meat for Fort Cass on the Yellowstone River when they were ambushed while crossing the ice-covered river. All three were shot, scalped, and robbed by a war party of about eighty Arikaras. From there, the Arikara moved to the source of the Powder River, not far from where Gardiner and twenty men were camped. They recognized Glass's gear, realized what had happened, and attacked and killed two Arikara.[117] He presented the scalp of one of the natives to the

Prince of Weid. Not too long after, Gardiner was, in turn, killed by the Arikara.

A map prepared by Capt. Washington Hood of the Corps of Topographical Engineers in 1839, showed a "Gardner's Fork" emptying into the Yellowstone River north of the lake, and the drainage of Gardner River bears the notations "Boiling Spring" and "White Sulphur Banks," the latter clearly referring to Mammoth Hot Springs.

MICHEL LAFRAMBOISE, DISOBEDIENT, LADIES' MAN, AND CAPTAIN OF THE CALIFORNIA TRAIL

Michel Laframboise was probably born in Varennes, Quebec, an off-island suburb of Montreal, in May 1791.[118] His parents were Etienne Senecal dit Laframboise and Marie Anne Amable Beique dit Lafleur. He was born into the fur trade and played an important role in the settling of the Northwest.

Michel arrived on the Northwest Coast on the *Tonquin* in 1811 and worked for the American Fur Company at Fort Astoria. While on the *Tonquin* he was noted as being a good singer, an important skill for voyageurs. He was also a carpenter and cabinet maker, a skilled boatsman, scout, and later brigade leader. He was a middleman or paddler on boats in his early years. He was described as being *"Literate, short, stout, and fond of drinking."*

Michel was adept when it came to learning languages and it was not long before he was serving as an interpreter for the Pacific Fur Company and, after the forced sale during the War of 1812, the Northwest Fur Company. After the NWC-HBC merger in 1821 he became an interpreter for

Michel Laframboise

the Hudson's Bay Company at Fort Vancouver and on expeditions from 1821–1829. He worked around the Willamette and Umpqua valleys, and his interpreting was boosted by his liaisons with many native women. In about 1827 he married Josette, in 1830 he wed Mary Tsaleel, and in 1836 he took Rose Sassette as his wife. It was sometimes suggested he had a wife in every tribe of the valley. He fathered more than twenty children.

The Hudson's Bay Company chief factor Dr. John McLoughlin never fully trusted Laframboise and kept him on a particularly tight rein from 1828 through 1832 because he had lied about the number of skins delivered for shipment in 1825. He had also disobeyed Alex McLeod's orders during the 1826–1827 trapping brigade. He was known as a poor record keeper and the HBC preferred detailed journals and accurate notes. In 1829–1830 he was the postmaster for Fort Vancouver until such time that he was sent with a small party to explore the Willamette (Umpqua) area in 1830.

In spring 1832 he led a party of 22 men to Tillamook Country to punish the natives for the murder of Pierre Kakaraguiron and Thomas Canasawarette at Beaver Creek, and to do some trapping. The two Iroquois trappers had amassed a good stock of furs by trapping without permission from the local people, sparking two Alsea men to kill and rob them. To prevent further risk to trappers, Dr. McLoughlin ordered Michel to attack *"the first Killamook group"* they came across. Six innocent Yaquina were killed, and the women and children were captured, threatened, but eventually released. They were told to instruct the remaining villagers to kill the murderers or they would face a massacre. McLoughlin's informants eventually told him that the two people involved in the initial murders were killed by relatives of those slain by Laframboise's party. There is some suggestion that many more natives may have been killed by the HBC and the Yaquina.

Later in 1832, John Work led the major trapping party to California while Michel was given a second smaller party on the western route. He was supposed to stay on the coast but switched inland. His party, like Work's, carried the intermittent fever to tribes along their route. They met up with Work's party in the Sacramento Valley where they also met American Ewing Young's trapping party. Michel started a trading post at French Camp[119] which became a place of exchange with the natives. During the annual fair hundreds of people might be around for an entire week.

Laframboise then traveled from the Bonaventura River (Sacramento River) to San Francisco and then to the missions of San José (Fremont), San Francisco Solano (Sonoma) and San Raphael Archangel (San Rafael). He noted that the San Francisco Bay abounded in beaver, and his best hunt was made in the vicinity of the missions. Chief Factor McLoughlin was furious that he had once again disobeyed orders, but a good profit eased his anger.

After his struggle with fever John Work was no longer healthy enough to lead the Southern Party so Laframboise was reluctantly given the task. He set up camp in 1834 near Sonoma, irritating the *Californios* until he was ordered away by *commandante* Mariano Vallejo. In 1835, he moved camp to the junction of Cache Creek and the Sacramento River. He trapped down the Pacific shore past the Umpqua River in 1836, reaching close to the Russian settlement at Fort Ross. He collected 2,000 beaver pelts and reassured McLoughlin that he could follow orders (sometimes). He was supposed to return by ship in 1838, but they never met up. It was in that same year that Governor Juan Alvarado asked Michel to lead a punitive strike against the interior natives who had been raiding California ranches, but he declined.

Laframboise, the Captain of the California Trail, continued to lead most of the southern parties until 1842 when his inability to discipline his men and declining profits terminated the effort. These expeditions included wives, children, and support staff—a far cry from the small groups of hard-traveling all-male American trappers. As Dr. Elijah White noted, *"The style in which they traveled was rather novel, bringing with them beds, bedding, tea, coffee, sugar,*

*bread, cakes, cheese; and not even the wine was left behind. They were
attended by a numerous suite, never forgetting the cook."*

Chief Factor John McLoughlin wrote Hudson's Bay Company
Governor George Simpson that, *"the conduct of the men was so bad that
under no consideration would Mr. Laframboise return..."* Laframboise
said that if he had not acceded to his men's requests he would have
been murdered and said he would lead no further parties.

	Laframboise Trips to California (and returns, when known)			
	Beaver			
	large	small	Other	Value
1832	755	84	152	
1834–1835	?			
1836	2000	£805		
1837	1185	251	431	£2314
1838	1361	225	884	£981
1838–1839	2300 (beaver and otter)			
1839	1404	204	695	
1839 (2nd)	1380	210	£1408	
1840–1841	?			
1842	?	£477		
1843–44	?			

Laframboise formally married Emilie Picard in 1839. She was a
Métis daughter of an Umqua native and Andre Picard, a fur company employee. Michel and Emilie had several children before
marriage and more after being wed. They settled on what became
known as the French Prairie in the Willamette Valley, about 1841. He
retired from the Hudson's Bay Company to live along the Willamette
River near Champoeg, where he built a house and barn, fenced 100
acres, and cultivated 50 acres. He also built a mill and ran about 200
horses.

In 1842–1843 Michel was still listed as a free trapper in the
Columbia District for HBC. The pressure from American settlers

led to a series of meetings over governance of the Oregon Country. These meetings led to a vote on May 2, 1843, ending in favor of forming what became the Provisional Government of Oregon. Laframboise did not vote for it.

In 1843 he worked as guide for the United States Exploring Expedition. Charles Wilkes described him as being *"of low stature, rather corpulent, but has great energy and activity of both mind and body, indomitable courage, and all the vivacity of a Frenchman... Had it not been for his proneness to dissipation I am informed he would have risen in the Company's service."* In 1843–44 the HBC lists indicate he was in charge of the California brigade.

He settled on a donation land claim north of his original claim and operated a ferry across the Willamette River between Champoeg on the south bank and the north bank from 1850 to 1857. Laframboise died of a stroke on January 28, 1861. His wife Emilie remarried and had another child following his death.

JOSEPH RUTHERFORD WALKER: TRAPPER, TRAILBLAZER, HORSE THIEF?, PROSPECTOR, RANCHER

Joseph R. Walker[120] was born on December 13, 1798 in Roane County, Tennessee. He was the fourth of seven children born to Joseph

Joseph Rutherford Walker

and Susan Willis Walker. As a young man he fought against the Creek Red Sticks with Andrew Jackson. His family and friends headed west to Missouri in 1819 and settled near Fort Osage. This was an official government trading post run by George Sibley.

Joseph was tall, powerfully built, and not easily contained in a settlement. He would later be described as *"well hardened to the hardships of the wilderness—understood the character of the Indians very well—was kind and affable to his men, but able to command without giving offence."* He would help pioneer South Pass and the primary California emigrant trail.

When he was twenty, Joseph headed west to trap beaver illegally in New Mexico. He was detained by the Spanish but released after agreeing to fight against the Pawnees. He returned to Fort Osage but then returned to Santa Fe in 1821 with his brother Joel and Stephen Cooper with the William Becknell wagon train, the first wagons to make the journey. He was likely one of the Taos trappers working south western rivers for a few years.

When President James Monroe appropriated $30,000 to survey a wagon road from Independence to Santa Fe four years later, Joseph was hired by George Sibley as a guide and hunter. Joseph helped assemble a number of Osage chiefs and people at a grove of large trees along the Neosho River about 150 miles from Fort Osage

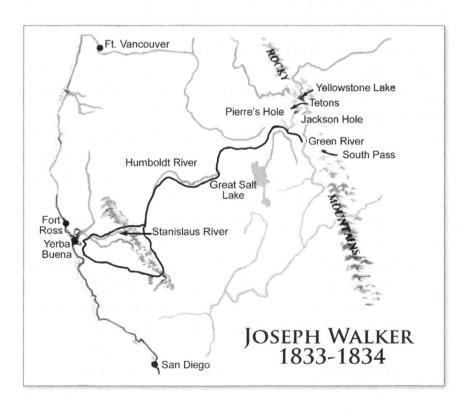

JOSEPH WALKER
1833-1834

and negotiated an easement for the route. In return, the Osage were provided with $800 in trade goods.

Walker was living in Independence, Missouri in June of 1827 and served as sheriff of Jackson County from 1827 to 1830. He then started trading horses to military outposts. In 1830, he was driving horses to Fort Gibson in Oklahoma, when he met explorer Benjamin Bonneville. In 1832, Walker signed on with Bonneville and 110 other men and traveled to the Green River in Wyoming for the rendezvous. His experience helped get the first wagons across South Pass. At the 1833 rendezvous on Horse Creek, Bonneville's 100-plus men ended up with only twenty-two-and-a-half packs of furs, most from Walker and his friends.

In January 1832 Secretary of State Edward Livingston issued passport number 2567 and a visa from the Mexican consul to Joseph R. Walker. This was delivered to Captain Benjamin Bonneville and forwarded to Walker. In 1833, Bonneville sent Walker in command of a party of men, including mountain men Zenas Leonard, old Bill Williams, Levin Mitchell, Bill Craig, George Nidever, Powell (Pauline) Weaver, and Joe and Stephen Meek. They left from the Green River to explore the Great Salt Lake and find an overland route to California. They discovered a route along the Humboldt River to the Humboldt Sink and then made their way to the Sierras. At the Humboldt Sink they encountered hundreds of Paiute, and a miscommunication led to a massacre in which 39 Paiutes were killed, with no casualties to Walker's party. They passed Mono Lake and were perhaps the first white men to see the giant sequoia trees and the Yosemite Valley. They apparently worked their way down the Stanislaus River to the San Joaquin River.

As they made their way toward the Pacific Coast they tried trapping, but few signs of beaver were found; they had been cleaned out by HBC trappers and Ewing Young. They encountered large herds of wild horses and cattle. Sighting a ship, they signaled it with blankets and it anchored. Captain Bradshaw informed Walker that San Francisco was about forty miles to the north on the south side of the

Francisco Bay, and Monterey was about sixty miles to the southwest. Bradshaw agreed to meet Walker in Monterey. Walker obtained permission from the mission to camp in the area between present-day Gilroy and Salinas.

The Walker party left the Monterey area in February 1834; six men chose to stay in California. Walker and 52 men headed east with 315 horses, 50 head of cattle, and 30 dogs. In early 1834 they crossed back over the Sierra Nevada on a pass they had learned about from natives residing in the San Joaquin Valley, now called Walker Pass.[121] They headed up Owens Valley, then up and out to the Humboldt Sink until finally returning to the Rockies the way they had come.

Captain Walker and his men crossed the Rocky Mountains to hunt and trade on the upper Missouri, Yellowstone, and in Bighorn Country. Walker's spring hunt was on the Tongue, Powder, Yellowstone, Gallatin, Clark's Fork of the Yellowstone, and the Stinkingwater (Shoshone) rivers. Walker stayed in the mountains to trap and trade with various tribes, and he married a Shoshone woman in 1836. This may have helped him get along with natives, because remarkably, he apparently lost only one man in his 34 years of leading parties in the West.

During the late 1830s and early 1840s, Walker continued trapping and made a number of return trips to California. At times he lived with the Snake tribe. He established a good business buying California horses[122] and trading them in the mountains, at Bent's Fort, and in Santa Fe. Most of the furs he obtained for his horses were marketed through Abel Stearns in Los Angles. In 1837 he met William Drummond Stewart at the rendezvous and was painted by Alfred Jacob Miller.

In 1840, Walker and a band of followers made the first known north-to-south crossing of the eastern Great Basin by Americans. Starting from Browns Park on the Green River, he and his men crossed the Wasatch Range to Sevier Lake. They then went down to the upper Virgin River and followed it to the Colorado River. From the Colorado, they crossed the Mojave Desert to Los Angeles, where

Walker sold 417 pounds of beaver pelts to Abel Stearns. Stearns was also involved in Walker's horse trading.

Walker left California with one hundred mares and an unknown number of mules. He and his wife spent the winter of 1842 with his relatives in Jackson County, Missouri. Joseph B. Chiles organized the first wagon train of California-bound emigrants in 1843 and met and hired Walker at Fort Laramie. He was to be paid $300 to guide them to California—a good price. In August, at Black's Fork of the Green River, Walker and Chiles decided to split the party because they were running short of supplies. Walker had been warmly received at Fort Hall by Hugh Grant of the Hudson's Bay Company but was refused any supplies for the wagon train. Chiles was going to cross the Sierra Nevada in the vicinity of the Truckee River, proceed to Sutter's Fort for food, and bring it back across the Sierra to Humboldt Sink where Walker and the wagon train would be waiting.[123] Once reunited, they would proceed south through the Owens Valley, along the eastern scarp of the Sierra Nevada, to a pass he believed the wagons could cross.

When it became clear that Chiles was delayed, Walker's group left the Humboldt Sink in November and traded for fish with the Paiute at what is now known as Walker Lake. The animals were too weak to pull Walker's wagons beyond Owens Lake so they proceeded on foot and crossed the Sierras going west over Walker Pass in December. They then went north and across the San Joaquin Valley to winter on the headwaters of a tributary to the Salinas River. The overland caravan had laid down the first tracks on 500 miles of what would become the California Trail.

After the expedition dispersed, Walker presented his passport to the Mexican authorities and was granted permission to trade. He left southern California with yet another herd of horses and mules in April 1844 and headed east on the Old Spanish Trail. He overtook John C. Frémont's second military topographic expedition beyond Las Vegas and traveled with him to Bent's Fort.

In 1845, by prearrangement, Walker, with his wife and retainers, joined Frémont's third government expedition as chief guide at White River (eastern Utah) bound for California and Oregon. Walker led the main body of the expedition down the Humboldt River to Walker Lake where they met Frémont and a smaller group who had taken a more southerly route after leaving Great Salt Lake.

The party again divided, with Walker taking the main body across Walker Pass in December while Frémont and a small group crossed the Sierra Nevada going up near the Truckee River and eventually reaching Sutter's Fort (now Sacramento, California). The two parties had missed their planned rendezvous along the Kings River in the San Joaquin Valley but were reunited in February 1846. Walker was very disappointed that Frémont did not get the fight against the Mexicans started.

In the winter of 1846–1847, Walker returned to Jackson County, Missouri. It is possible that his wife and children had died of cholera. He eventually started trading again and, with his nephew Frank McClellan and seven men, he went to Los Angeles and purchased another 600 horses and mules to take east over the Old Spanish Trail and on to Bent's Fort.[124] He continued horse trading, then raised cattle in Monterey County from 1851 to 1858. He also worked with Kit Carson as a guide on the Colorado River.

In 1861 he went to New Mexico and Arizona to prospect for gold. In 1862–63 he led a gold-hunting expedition of 34 men into the mountains of central Arizona, near what is now the city of Prescott. They struck gold along the Hassayampa River and Lynx Creek. The village of Walker, Arizona is named for him. The trail from the Pima villages to Prescott became known as the Walker Trail and carried freight and stagecoach traffic to and from Prescott. At some point he met Matthew Brady, who took his photograph.

Walker's nephew James T. Walker had some rancho land in Contra Costa County, and in 1868 he built a home (between present-day Walnut Creek and Mount Diablo State Park) where Joseph went to live. Nearly blind and approaching 70 years old, the intrepid mountain man remembered a single day as the best of his life and asked that a remembrance of it be carved on his tombstone: "Camped at Yosemite, Nov. 13, 1833." He died on the ranch on October 27, 1876 and was buried in the Alhambra Cemetery in Martinez, California.

Walker was a man of many firsts and contributed much to the mapping of the west, on his own and with Fremont and Bonneville. He was part of the first wagon train to Santa Fe, 1821; first wagons over South Pass, 1832; pioneering work on the California trail, 1833; discovered Walker Pass, 1834; first wagons Owens Valley, 1834; Walker Trail, 1862, discovered gold, 1861. A pass, lake and village in Arizona honor his name.

OBSERVERS

JOHN LEDYARD, THE TRAVELER

John Ledyard was born to a ship captain in Boston in 1751. His father and uncle both died of malaria in the Caribbean when he was eleven. Ledyard was passed around the family as he grew up and eventually apprenticed in a law office. He then enrolled in the newly created Dartmouth College. In the summer of 1772, the college sent him up near the Canadian border for four months to live with the Iroquois tribe in hopes of recruiting young native men to enroll at Dartmouth. He enjoyed the experience, studied them intently, and took copious notes. This experience may well have provoked his next act. He

dropped out of school and made a dugout canoe,[125] that he then paddled down the Connecticut River to a life of adventure. He tried to start a ministry but when that did not go well he gave the idea up and went to sea.

By 1776, Ledyard was in London and joined Captain Cook's third expedition as a Royal

John Ledyard

Marine. He would spend more

than four years on the trip. He was in a small boat providing support for the captain when Cook was killed in Hawaii. Ledyard noted that the relations between Cook and the Hawaiians had been problematic from the beginning. He repeatedly notes in his journal the insulting and inappropriate actions of the crew, and specifically of Cook.

Ledyard was the first American to see the tremendous demand and value of sea otter furs in China. The remarkable profits made by some sailors when the expedition members sold their furs in Canton led him to see the potential for a three-way trade from Boston to the NW Coast to China, with Hawaii as a resting point. Ledyard made it back to America on a British warship and then deserted to return home. John discovered that the British had burned down most of Groton and in a single day killed or wounded 28 members of his family.

Governor John Trumbull introduced Connecticut's newest celebrity to a small publisher, Nathaniel Patten, and a book was born. John stayed with an uncle in Hartford while he wrote up his account of travels with Cook (by memory, as no diaries were allowed off the ship) and highlighted the opportunity for a fur trade on the NW coast. Ledyard's *Journal of Captain Cook's Last Voyage* was published in 1783 and became a bestseller. John petitioned the General Assembly for copyright protection and this ultimately led to state laws that codified that right and led to the federal copyright law of 1790.

In his book he noted, *"It afterwords happened that skins which did not cost the purchaser sixpence sterling sold in China for 100 dollars. Neither did we purchase a quarter of the beaver and other furr skins we have done, and most certainly should have done had we known of meeting the opportunity of disposing of them to such an astonishing profit."*

Unable to find funding for his proposed NW fur trade in the U.S., he headed to Europe and spent time in Paris. He became friends with Thomas Jefferson, then the minister to France. Jefferson understood what John was talking about and it probably helped form the idea for the Lewis and Clark Expedition. Ledyard came frustratingly close to securing funding for a ship but the deal fell through at the last moment. Other people had heard his story, read his book, and started fitting out ships and departing for the Northwest Coast. In 1787, *Columbia Redivivia* under John Kendrick and *Lady Washington* led by Robert Gray left Boston for the NW Coast. Ledyard failed to make it aboard. He tried again for the *Harriot*, but this ship never left port. However, from 1787–1810, more than 100 American ships reached the NW Coast. Nootka Sound was humorously referred to as a suburb of Boston and the natives often referred to sailors as "Boston men." The sea otters were almost gone by 1841 when the last fur ship departed from Nootka Sound.

Jefferson may have suggested that John should travel to Russia, cross over to the Russian fur outposts in America, and from there to journey south to American territory or to find an American ship. Or it may have been entirely Ledyard's idea, as he had talked about a walk around the world. He hoped to start in Europe, proceed across Asia and the Bering Strait, and down to American territory and walk across the continent. After a grueling winter journey of almost 5,000 miles, he reached Yakutsk, Siberia. Sadly, his timing was terrible and the journey was delayed before Captain Billings[126] arrived. They then traveled together to Irkutsk, where he discovered his passport had been cancelled, and he was ordered back to Europe. Some of the Russians believed him to be a French spy, though he was perhaps really an industrial spy, but still a threat. He was rushed back across Russia and released in Poland.

Disappointed and exhausted, Ledyard arrived in Konigsburg destitute. A five-guinea draft from his friend Sir Joseph Banks enabled him to make it back to London. Banks enlisted him for an expedition to the heart of Africa. He died of dysentery (and perhaps more certainly, from the treatment for dysentery) in Cairo, Egypt in 1789. He had intended to travel the first part of the crossing of Africa with companions, but then to strike out alone.

His friends included Thomas Jefferson, Thomas Paine, the Marquis de Lafayette, and John Paul Jones. Jefferson called him *"...a man of genius, of some science, and of fearless courage and enterprise."* Thomas Paine wrote Thomas Jefferson, telling him the news as told to him by Joseph Banks: *"We have lost poor Ledyard . . . we sincerely lament his loss."*

He was curious, optimistic, cheerful, observant and in most times delighted with life despite its hardships and his many setbacks. He was the consummate traveler and enjoyed meeting and interacting with people of all races and cultures. *"Hospitality I have found as universal as the face of man."*

JOHN R. JEWITT, A SLAVE AND ETHNOGRAPHER

John Rodgers Jewitt was born in 1783 in Boston, England. Jewitt's father Edward was a blacksmith in England and moved to the coast to work on ships' ironwork. He had hoped John would become a surgeon's apprentice, but eventually relented and trained his eldest son to follow in his footsteps. As a boy, Jewitt read about the voyages of explorers such as Captain Cook, and he used his blacksmithing skills to get a position as armorer on the brig *Boston* after he and his father helped Captain John Salter with repairs. He would make $30 a year and have an adventure—little did he know.

The *Boston* arrived at Nootka Sound on the Northwest Coast in March 1803. Trading went well for several days at a small cove,

John R. Jewitt

situated about four miles north of Friendly Cove on the western shore of the sound, called *Abooksha* by the natives. On March 18th Chief Maquinna borrowed a double-barreled musket from Captain Salter to shoot ducks. He returned the next day, presenting nine ducks to Salter. He also told the captain that one of the locks on the musket had broken. The captain asked Jewitt if he could fix it and he affirmed that he could. However, the captain verbally abused the chief, who knew enough English to be outraged. This brought tempers to a boiling point, adding to the years of growing resentment he and the surrounding tribes felt for the ill treatment meted out by other fur traders, beginning with John Hanna.

Their revenge came on March 22, 1803, the day before the *Boston* intended to sail. A number of Nuu-chah-nulth came aboard to trade and were given dinner. At a prearranged signal they attacked and all but two of the white men were killed. John Jewitt was wounded in the head; the ship's sailmaker John Thompson was also kept alive. Both men became slaves but their experiences would be quite different. Thompson, from Philadelphia, despised the natives and was a bitter, resentful, occasionally violent slave kept alive only by Jewitt's careful and consistent lobbying. In order to save the sailmaker's life, Jewitt claimed that Thompson was his father. The younger, better educated, and curious Jewitt learned the language and did his best to endear himself to the chief. Maquinna enjoyed talking with him and explained that he bore no ill will toward his countrymen, but that he had been poorly treated too many times. Maquinna's wife also liked Jewitt, and her eleven-year-old boy became devoted to him. Maquinna prized Jewitt as blacksmith, armorer, and a novelty for display during trade missions to other tribes. Natives were always astonished and delighted when Jewitt could speak their language.

Jewitt was described by a native who had known him as a general favorite, owing to his good-humor and lightheartedness. He said Jewitt often recited and sang in his own language for the amusement of the community. Jewitt shared the life of the people in every way, living in Maquinna's 150-foot longhouse, taking part in fishing and hunting expeditions, raids on other villages, and in the potlatches and ceremonial feasts. He "married" the daughter of an adjacent tribal chief and fathered a child. As he noted on September 20, 1804, "*We live a great deal better since I got married, for my wife's father is always fishing.*"

Jewitt observed and recorded the yearly round, from spring and summer at Nootka, autumn in Tashees for salmon, and then winter months at Coopte for herring and sprat fishing. This annual nomadism involved packing up everything, including the planks on the outside of their longhouses, to transport in their canoes. Jewitt was an excellent observer and took notes on the Nuu-chah-nulth way of life, even measuring the lengths of dwellings and canoes, and carefully observing the complex social system. His observations are some of the best made of native life and society before diseases swept the coast.

Maquinna II. may not have been as skilled a tactician as his brother had been, but he was courageous and principled. Although he could be demanding, his relationship with Jewitt eventually took on a familial tone. He promised Jewitt that if a ship came, he could leave. However, news of the massacre had traveled far and wide to fur traders and captains, gathering horrific embellishments along the way, and no ships came to call. Maquinna's valuation of his slave was not shared by all the Nuu-chah-nulth villagers who saw the white slaves as a potential risk. Despite their marquee value and practicality, the two white slaves had been witnesses to the massacre and could bring ruin on the village.

Maquinna's many slaves ate with the family, getting the same food but in different dishes. They were generally well treated but expected to work hard. Jewitt was an inventive blacksmith and developed a new type of harpoon for whale hunts, and various other weapons and implements that pleased the chief. Maquinna allowed Jewitt to undertake work for others and he used this privilege to make bracelets, fishhooks, and other items to trade with the villagers and visitors. Other chiefs including Wickaninnish of the Tla-o-qui-aht, attempted to buy Jewitt, but he was not for sale.

In July of 1805, the brig *Lydia* arrived in Nootka Sound and came to his rescue. Captain Samuel Hill had received one of the sixteen letters that Jewitt had written and attempted to send to passing ships. When the *Lydia* arrived at Nootka Sound, Maquinna asked

Jewitt if it would be safe for him to go aboard. He not so wisely asked Jewitt to write a letter of recommendation to the captain to ensure safe passage. Instead, John asked the captain to hold Maquinna securely, to exchange for himself and Thompson. The captain put Maquinna in irons but allowed him to speak to one of his men; after some tense moments, the exchange was safely made.

When Jewitt came onboard the *Lydia* he was painted red and black, wrapped in a bearskin, and had green leaves stuck through his topknot. Captain Hill welcomed him and soon learned what had happened. The captain was inclined to execute Maquinna but Jewitt persuaded him that doing so would lead to further attacks on ships visiting the coast. Jewitt negotiated for the return of what little property remained of the *Boston* including cannons, anchors, remnants of cargo, and the ship's papers, which Jewitt had secured in a chest. Once everything was onboard, Maquinna was released, and the brig weighed anchor and departed.

Jewitt was not able to return home as quickly as he wished. The *Lydia* continued trading to the north along the coast for four months, then dropped down to the Columbia River for spar timber. They missed Lewis and Clark because Hill did not follow up on a letter they sent. In November, the *Lydia* returned to Nootka to trade more furs. John felt the toxic atmosphere on Hill's ship was almost worse than being a slave. Rather remarkably, he was able to have a friendly visit with the chief. Maquinna promised to raise Jewitt's son (then five months old) as his own.

Jewitt understood that the acts of others had cost the crew of the *Boston* dearly. He could see that the innocent too frequently suffered for the wrongs of the guilty. Few of the natives discriminated between persons of the same general appearance, more especially when speaking the same language. Maquinna repeatedly told Jewitt that it was not his wish to hurt a white man, and that he never should have done it, though ever so much in his power, had they not injured him. More than a year after his release from slavery, John finally left the coast in August 1806.

The *Lydia* took four months to reach China, trading at Macao and Canton. The ship left China in February 1807, returning to Boston 114 days later. Jewitt quickly published his *Journal Kept at Nootka Sound*. He married Hester Jones in Boston on Christmas Day in 1809, and they had four or five children. Jewitt worked hard to support his family by selling his books, speaking and other activities. On one sales trip, all of his books were stolen. His head wound continued to bother him. An expanded version of his book written with a more skilled author appeared in 1815 with publication of *A Narrative of the Adventures and Sufferings of John R. Jewitt, only survivor of the crew of the ship Boston, during a captivity of nearly three years among the savages of Nootka Sound: with an account of the manners, mode of living, and religious opinions of the natives.*

Jewitt spent the rest of his life playing the role of himself as captive, regularly singing his signature song, "The Poor Armourer Boy," and even playing himself in a production of James Nelson Barker's play "The Armourer's Escape." He also performed *Nootkan* songs and dances in a circus. His larger book was republished in the U.S. as well as in London and Germany. Jewitt died in Hartford, Connecticut at the age of 37, but his descendants, including John R. Jewitt IV., V., and VI. were located by a reporter in 1988. Jewitt's wife outlived him by 15 years.

Sir William Drummond Stewart, Gay Fur Trade Tourist

William Drummond Stewart was born at Murthly Castle, Scotland to Sir George Stewart and Catherine Drummond in 1795. As the second of six children and the second son he was free of responsibility at the home holdings. For his 17th birthday his father bought him an appointment to a lieutenancy in the 15th King's Hussars. This unit was already in action in the Peninsular Wars and he saw combat there, serving with distinction in the Waterloo Campaign of 1815. In 1820 he was promoted to captain and retired on half pay. He

Sir William Drummond Stewart

impregnated a maid in 1830 and had a son, who he later legitimized by marrying the mother.

As a gay man in Scotland, Stewart was at risk of arrest, punishment, and scandal, and was perhaps encouraged by his family to go to America. He was 36 when he set foot on American soil in 1832. He was described as slightly taller than average with dark curly hair, a florid complexion (partly from drink), and a mustache beneath a pronounced hawk-like nose. He had a stiff military bearing and a violent temper but got along well with most of the leaders of the fur traders and mountain men. He became the first tourist to visit much of the West, arriving in 1832, and traveling around the area on and off for almost eleven years. He developed his wilderness skills and was, at times, involved in managing supply trains and night guards.

When Stewart arrived in St. Louis in 1832, he checked into the finest hotel and presented his letter of introduction to fur traders William Sublette and Robert Campbell. He offered them $500 to allow him to accompany them on their journey to the 1833 rendezvous. They agreed, and he accompanied Robert Campbell[127] to the Green River Valley. Here, he met Métis hunter Antoine Clement, who would be his partner off and on for more than a decade. He may have found the native tribes' tolerance of homosexuality of interest. The two spirit[128] men were often well regarded and held special ceremonial roles in some tribes. He would also have relations with other men, including European visitors, during his visits to America.

While traveling with Thomas Fitzpatrick, Stewart was left in charge of camp when Fitzpatrick met with the Crow chief. A band of younger braves stormed the camp and took the furs, while Stewart stood by, uncertain about what to do. It later turned out that they had been encouraged to rob the camp by a rival fur company. Stewart then visited the Big Horn Mountains, wintered at Taos, and attended the following year's rendezvous on Ham's Fork. American businessman Nathaniel Wyeth met him in July 1834. *"We were joined at the rendezvous by a Captain Stewart, an English gentleman of noble family, who is traveling for amusement, and in search of adventure."* That summer, Stewart traveled west with Wyeth, naturalists John Kirk Townsend and Thomas Nuttall, and the missionary Lee family.

Stewart enjoyed his wilderness adventures to the fullest. He and his companions made their way to the HBC's Fort Nez Perce. From there Stewart, Wyeth, and the Lees hired a large barge to travel down the Columbia River to The Dalles, walked around the falls, and boated down to Fort Vancouver. Chief Factor Dr. John McLoughlin warmly welcomed them to the fort. Wyeth noted, *"The dinner was very good and served in as good style as in any gentleman's house in the east. Fine muskmelons and water melons and apples were set before us which were, indeed, a luxury after the dry living we have had for some time. After dinner took a turn in the garden and was astonished to find it in such a high state of cultivation. The orchard is young, but the quantity of fruit is so great that many of the branches [would] break if they were not prevented by props."*

McLoughlin mentioned him in dispatches: *"Captain Stewart is an Officer of the British army... He says he intends (according to the means of conveyance he may find) to go to Canada or St. Louis on the Mississippi next spring."* Stewart spent the winter of 1834 -1835 in the fort's bachelor's quarters, eating at the mess, and no doubt enjoying McLoughlin's hospitality and conversations.

In early February of 1835, Stewart joined Francis Ermatinger to head upriver with three heavily laden canoes to Fort Colville and Fort Hall. Stewart then turned south to the summer's rendezvous in Wyoming. He enjoyed the 1835 rendezvous at the mouth of New Fork River before returning to St. Louis, while Clement travelled partway back, and then returned to the mountains. Stewart found his older brother had failed to forward his share of the estate left when their father died. To raise some cash, Stewart dropped down to New Orleans and speculated in cotton to recoup his losses,[129] and then sailed to Cuba for some winter warmth.

In May 1836 he was back for yet another rendezvous, this time on Horse Creek with Antoine Clement. On the way to the rendezvous he traveled in style with two wagons full of luxury goods including canned meats and sardines, plum pudding, preserved fruits, coffee, fine tobacco, cheeses, and a selection of brandies, whisky, and wines. He had three servants, two dogs, and two racehorses for this excursion. He then dropped downriver and wintered over in New Orleans and St. Louis. He made more money speculating in cotton and was feeling flush for his next adventure.

We are most grateful that Stewart hired Alfred Jacob Miller as his documentary artist in 1837. Miller would travel to the rendezvous on the Popo Agie River. Miller's detailed and lovely paintings provide some of our best looks at life in the fur trade in the West. His sketches and later oil paintings provide detailed views of life on the fur frontier. Stewart secretly brought out a steel breastplate and ornate helmet of the Life Guards, an elite British unit, and presented them to mountain man Jim Bridger. Stewart spent the winter in St. Louis and New Orleans, and converted to Catholicism at the old St. Louis Cathedral.

In March 1838 Stewart returned to St. Louis by steamship and travelled with the supply train of the Pratte, Chouteau Company to the 1838 rendezvous. Stewart and Clement assisted with the management of the supply train. August Johann Sutter, who would later build Sutter's Fort in California and buy Fort Ross, was also along on this trip west. The rendezvous this year was held on the Wind River.

Stewart's older brother died in 1838 and Stewart became the 7th Baronet. He returned to Murthly Castle in July 1839 with Antoine Clement. Seven bison were caught, driven to the Missouri and shipped to Scotland. Some were for a present to the Marquis of Breadalbane and some for Murthly Castle. His artist, Miller, arrived later with his sketches and continued work on the paintings. Antoine found the climate and social situation unpleasant as he had to pretend to be a servant. One story has a drunken Clement and the two natives hitching two bison to a boat perched on a set of wheels and tearing through town screeching like natives on the war path. As a break, Stewart took Clement for an extended tour in the Middle East, but it was not a satisfying setup.

Stewart sold one of the family's estates to pay off his brother's debts and to finance another trip to the West. Traveling in 1842 with Antoine and the two natives,[130] he made it to the United States. He loaned $4,000 to William Sublette and Robert Campbell, who were experiencing a cash crunch. With help from Sublette, Stewart arranged for an outrageous trek in 1843 that would culminate with a costume party on Fremont Lake. He was trying to recreate the spirit of the now-ended fur rendezvous one last time. Before they left, Stewart was staying at the Planter's House (the newest and finest hotel in St. Louis, costing more than ten dollars a week). He had arrived in 1843 on the steamboat *Julia Chouteau* after surviving the sinking of the steamer *J. M. White* when it struck a rock forty miles above the mouth of the Ohio. It sank in just four minutes, but only one life was lost and almost all the baggage was saved.

The journalist Matt Field had also journeyed up from New Orleans to be a member of this adventure... a prospect, thought the reporter in advance, "*of a most exciting and truly delightful travel.*" When the Stewart party left St. Louis aboard the *Weston*, thousands of friends and curious spectators congregated on the levee to cheer. This extravagant party was co-hosted by his friend William Sublette, who noted that they had, "*Some of the armey. Some professional gentlemen. Some on a trip for pleasure. Some for health, etc., etc. So, we have Doctors, Lawyers, botanists, Bugg Ketchers, Hunters and men of nearly all professions, etc., etc.*" Most had servants and support staff. The travel out was challenging with considerable rain, high water in rivers and streams, and cold. Stewart was leading the trip and his overbearing personality also caused some trouble with his gentlemen travelers. On the way to Fremont Lake, Antoine's younger brother Francois (age 15) died of an accidental chest wound. In a letter to his paper Mr. Field described it as an accident caused when Francois pulled a rifle out of a tent and accidentally snapped the lock, firing a ball into his chest. During that sad day, Francois was comforted by his brother and Father de Vos as he died. Although they did take some trade goods, it was primarily an excursion for pleasure rather than a business deal. The two-week-plus party included an array of European finery of velvet and lace used to create a medieval pageant. There was heavy drinking from many kegs of alcohol, feasting, hunting, horse races, and gambling. The festivities also included a visiting group of Shoshone people. We can only imagine what they were thinking. After the party, Stewart returned to St. Louis, spent a month at his friend William Sublette's farm, and then continued on to New York and Scotland.

Stewart returned to duty as the Laird of Grandtully and the Baronet of Murthly and Blair. He lived in Dalpowie Lodge and rented the castle. The rest of his life was less satisfying, but he kept busy, transforming the estate into a wilder, more romantic setting. He sowed buffalo grass seed brought from the west for his "buffalo park." The bison herd grew and was seen by Queen Victoria. This remarkable eccentric lived surrounded by Miller's paintings and a vast collection of artifacts he had picked up during his extensive American travels. His son William survived the charge of the Light Brigade in the Crimea, the India Campaign, and won a Victoria's Cross[131] for bravery in the defense of the Residency in Lucknow. Sadly, like his father, he was overly fond of drinking and taking risks, so it was of little surprise that he died from an injury caused by a drunken sword-swallowing demonstration.

Laird Stewart died of pneumonia in 1871. He had seen a great part of the West, met almost every man of importance involved in the exploration and exploitation of the beaver, and left a remarkable record in the paintings he commissioned.

The National Archives of Scotland include a number of letters to Stewart from "friends" he had made in America, many of them "young men asking for money." After his death, his adopted son Franc Nichols Stewart (a young Texan and perhaps sex partner) lost the estate. He was the executor of disposables but the property reverted to William's brother Archibald through entailed rights of primogeniture.[132] Nichols did sell off and disperse many of the paintings, furnishings, and collected artifacts; but he was freed of responsibility for repairs to tenants' farms in a related legal case.

ANTOINE CLÉMENT, HUNTER

Stewart's companion, Antoine Michel Clement was born in 1811. His father, also Antoine, was in the fur trade and was working for the NWC at Fort des Prairies in 1804. His father was probably on David Thompson's special express canoe crew for many years. After the Hudson's Bay Company bought out the North West Company (1821) Antoine's parents settled on a small farm just northwest of St. Louis. Here, young Antoine grew to be a crack shot and hunter. The career of choice in St. Louis was the fur trade and he came of age just in time for the great explorations and profits from the heyday (1822–1840).

Antoine Clement (or perhaps his father[133]) was with Peter Skene Ogden in Utah in 1825. He defected to the American party under Johnston Gardiner with many other free men on the promise of more than four times as much for their furs. On May 25th Kittson notes, *"Soon after Mr. Montour, Clement & Prudhomme came forward & told me they intended joining the Americans; that they were free & not indebted ... as for Clement he has a Balce in the Compys. Book; go we will where we shall be paid for our Furs & not be imposed & cheated*

Antoine Clément

as we are in the Columbia—they were immediately Surrounded by the Americans who assisted them in loading & like all Villains appeared to exult in their Villany."

Twenty-two-year-old Antoine appears in records for certain in 1833 when he was at the rendezvous working for the Rocky Mountain Fur Company. Here he met William Drummond Stewart; at some point they became lovers and would remain partners off and on for many years. Both were renowned for drinking and quick, violent tempers. What precisely they meant to each other remains unknown and unknowable. Was Antoine an equal and lover? An exploiter or the exploited?

Antoine was with Stewart again at the 1835 rendezvous at the New Fork River. They traveled together during the winter of 1836–1837 to New Orleans. They made it back to the 1837 rendezvous at Green River and the 1838 rendezvous on the Popo Agie River. Here, Stewart's artist, Alfred Jacob Miller, sketched and painted him several times. Antoine saved Miller from a charging bison on one occasion.

Antoine returned to Scotland with Stewart in 1839 and Miller soon arrived. We learn a bit more about Antoine in the artist's correspondence. In a letter Miller wrote, *"Clement had metamorphosed into a Scotch valet and waits on the table in a full suit of black... I am told that while in the mountains he was twice instrumental in saving his master's life, and for this reason I have no doubt he indulges him. He presented him the other day a full Highland suit which cost fifty pounds — that he may attend the balls the peasantry hold in the neighborhood."* Here a large section of the original letter was cut away, perhaps thought too scandalous to keep.

Antoine Clement makes other appearances in Miller's letters, usually as a mischievous figure testing the limits of his ambiguous status in the castle. Miller writes, *"...yesterday Antoine put on my Indian chief's dress and made his appearance in the drawing room, to the astonishment and delight of the company, for the dress became him admirably. Afterwards he made his debut in the servant's hall to the great wonderment of the butlers and valets and to the horror of the ladies' maids.*" One story recounts that Clement and the natives became very drunk one night, hitched two bison to a boat on wheels, and careened through the streets of nearby Dunkeld, piercing the night with savage war cries. It is likely Antoine was bored and chafing at the restrictions of the charade that Stewart was asking him to play. Here he was not a coequal or the superior hunter. Stewart took Antoine to the MidEast, breaking away from the Scottish weather and reaching a society where homosexuality was tolerated.

The two men may have shared the night in the privacy of Dalpowie Lodge, but during the day Antoine was expected to appear as a properly obsequious servant. He had to cut his long hair and wear servant's clothes. He chafed at this role and would trespass into the drawing room to astonish and amuse the aristocratic guests but would then be banished to the servants' quarters. The servants, with sensitivity honed by years of scrutiny and understanding of "precedence and proper conduct," could clearly see that Antoine had never been in service and was ill-suited for it.

Antoine returned to America in 1842 for Stewart's last western journey and outrageous 1843 costume party on Fremont Lake. Jean Baptiste Charbonneau, the son of Sacagawea of the Lewis and Clark Expedition, took care of the mule train. The excursion went on after Antoine's brother's death. The 2-plus-week party was cohosted by Stewart's friend William Sublette, and they tried to recreate the spirit of the now-ended fur rendezvous. This included excessive drinking, feasting, gambling, wrestling, sharp shooting, and horse races. The party included costumes for the gentlemen in satin and lace medieval styles. After returning to St. Louis, Stewart returned home without Antoine. Perhaps Antoine refused to go because his brother had died?

Stewart missed him and wanted Clement back in Scotland but he apparently never went. In April 1844 Stewart asked Robert Campbell to help him get Antoine to Scotland. Campbell wrote back to Stewart, "*Antoine Clement called upon me and left with me your letters proposing his return to Murthly... He wishes me to furnish him with money to bear his expenses to Scotland. I am led to believe that you wish to have him to Murthly, but I confess I have some fears that Antoine might be led to squander the money...and that you might regret his having started."*

Clement may have truly wished to return to Murthly, or he may have simply seen the prospect as a way of raising cash. He did get some travel money but spent it all on alcohol and partying. Clement was still a relatively young man at the age of 32 and a skilled hunter and interpreter, but perhaps also an alcoholic. His preference for going on a "drunken frolic" instead of meeting Campbell's conditions for the trip to Scotland may reflect an attempt to balance the power in the relationship.

Antoine next shows up, quite surprisingly, as an Army private in the Battalion of Missouri Volunteers. This was an element of the Army of the West during the Mexican War of 1846–1847. Men for this group were largely recruited from St. Louis. One of the field officers was William Clark's son Meriwether. Antoine was in Battery A of the artillery. From June 1846 to June 1847, the Missouri volunteers embarked on a 5,500-mile trek from Fort Leavenworth, Kansas to Santa Fe, south to El Paso, Chihuahua, and Matamoros, before returning to Missouri. Antoine is noted as having regaled men with his tales of adventures with natives, bison, grizzlies, and the fur trade. His skills as a hunter helped provide meat for the soldiers' stomachs on the hard march west to Santa Fe. He was described as having suffered severely on the march to Bent's Fort. He may have stopped there or in Santa Fe, or perhaps he went all the way. An Antoine Clement died in 1852, and it may have been him.

XIE QINGGAO 谢清高, SAILOR AND AUTHOR

Xie Qinggao was born about 1765 in Jiaying (now Meizhou City), eastern Guangdong. This region was visited by traders, and Xie set out from home to seek his fortune. The year he turned eighteen, the ship he was sailing on was caught in a storm and sank.

He was rescued by a foreign merchant ship (probably Portuguese) and joined its crew, which led him to foreign countries on business. He later crewed on Portuguese-flagged and other European ships for more than 14 years (~1782 to 1796). His story was recorded in a book first published in 1820 by Yang Bingnan, a junior scholar from Jiaying. Since then the book has been reprinted many times.

Xie visited America, Brazil, Zanzibar, Holland, Spain, Portugal, England, Guinea Bissau, and the Northwest Coast. In his book, *Hai Lu* 海錄 (*Maritime Journals*), he mentions ninety-five countries and regions that he either visited or heard about in the fourteen years he spent at sea. His biographer describes what he experienced in a manner that suggests he was talking directly with Xie.

The last section in his book describes a place called Kai-yu. The Ingaliks[134] on the lower Yukon River referred to themselves as the Kaiyu-Khotana. The harbor was probably the Yukon River mouth. He may have been on one of John Meare's Portuguese flagged ships, or perhaps went to work with the Chinese workers building the outpost on Nootka Sound. He might have helped by speaking up in Portuguese, if and when the English ship was stopped.

Xie Qinggao

Meares was not the only one flying Portuguese flags to ease trade in Macao and China. Xie notes that they reached Kai-yu after three months of travel north from Hawaii. The ship was there to buy sea otter, fox, and other skins. It was freezing cold with snow and icebergs. The native people came out in *baidarkas* to lead the way into the harbor. Some people onboard Xie's ship could speak their language, and he heard the name of the place pronounced something like 'kai-yu.'

Xie thought the native people looked much like the Chinese and he noted that they ate dried fish. Every day the sun could be seen very close to the horizon and it would set between one and two o'clock in the afternoon; this suggests they were far to the north. When he first arrived, he suffered some frostbite on his hands and feet. He went on to observe that the natives loved well-made Chinese leather chests and traded furs for them. He once went ashore and entered a native home with more than ten leather chests.

From Kai-yu they sailed further north over several weeks to reach another harbor, perhaps on the Kobuk River. This was in Inupiat territory. Here they fired a cannon but no one came. He heard from other crew members that north of it was the "Ice Sea."[135]

Xie was losing his vision[136] so he left the sea and settled in Macao, a Portuguese colony, where he was an interpreter and a merchant with a small shop. When he was 41 he had a dispute with his Portuguese landlord over his unpaid loan to the landlord's nephew. This dispute made it into the records of the National Archives in Lisbon.

Xie died in 1821 at the age of 56, at his home in Guangdong Province. One Chinese scholar called him "the Chinese Fernão Mendes Pinto," comparing him to the sixteenth-century Portuguese adventurer who wrote up his adventures in the Far East in *Peregrinação* (Pilgrimage). In writing what he did, saw, and heard over the course of his life, he thought he could become immortal, and so he is.

GABRIEL FRANCHÈRE, FUR TRADE DIARIST

Gabriel Franchère was a fur trader, born in Montreal in 1786. He was the son of a merchant and port master, Gabriel Franchère, and Félicité Morin. He had certainly had some education and perhaps experience in the fur trade before he joined the Pacific Fur Company.

Hoping to advance himself in the proposed enterprise of John Jacob Astor on the Columbia River, he signed on as clerk for the PFC and set sail from New York in 1810 on an adventure that would determine the course of his life. His account of the voyage on the *Tonquin* and the creation of Astoria provided useful details of the adventure. Franchère, a mere clerk, was a member of the Duncan McDougall party, making the difficult voyage around Cape Horn to the Columbia in 1810 under the deranged Captain Jonathan Thorn of the *Tonquin*.

Franchère demonstrated his ability and common sense in the daily struggles at the outpost, observing the competition between the HBC and NWC. Fort Astoria was established in 1811 but the prospect of hostilities after war with Britain broke out in 1812 and the aggressive competition of the North West Company forced the sale of the assets of the Pacific Fur Company to the NWC in October of 1813.

Franchère returned to Canada with some of the survivors of the Astor enterprise and a party of NorthWesters in 1814. He was described as being "*of very simple and correct habits, which insured him good health and cheerful spirits. He possessed a blithe disposition, veined with a kindly humour; was very active and intelligent, exceedingly kind-hearted, true to his adopted country, and had a firm faith in the Christian religion.*"

Franchère kept a diary with the intention of describing precisely, for family and friends, "what I had seen and learned." He prepared a manuscript, *Narrative of a Voyage to the Northwest Coast of America*, for publication five years after the events on the *Tonquin* and at Astoria. This 284-page book was published in French in 1820 and soon became a valued item in Canada; it established Franchère's reputation as a traveler and writer.

In 1815 he married Sophie Routhier (who waited for him) at the basilica de Notre Dame in Montreal. He remained around Montreal for many years and was the chief agent of the American Fur Company from 1828 to 1834. The company enjoyed great success in these years, earning close to $200,000 in profits annually, and the Montreal office played a modest part by supplying some of the 400 to 500 *engagés* who worked for Astor at $80 to $200 per year. Franchère advertised for men, travelled to towns to enlist them, paid notaries to draw up contracts, and arranged the purchase of supplies for the voyage to the west. He also dealt with the inevitable problems of search and arrest associated with the many "deserters and delinquents" who accepted cash advances and then disap-

Gabriel Franchère

peared. Astorian Ramsay Crooks assumed control of the American Fur Company in 1834, and asked Franchère to direct the company's agency at Sault Ste Marie.

Gabriel and Sophie had eight children; six of them survived childhood. Sophie died at Sault St. Marie in 1837. Gabriel then met and married a widow, Charlotte Prince, in 1839. In 1842 he became the New York agent for Pierre Chouteau, Jr. and Company.

His book would play a part in the debates in the Congress of the United States over the Oregon boundary in 1846. Franchère was invited to Washington by Senator Thomas Hart Benton to discuss the book. It was frequently cited as a record of the fur trade's relations with native people. The Oregon dispute and the appearance of narratives of Astoria, not only by Irving but also by Ross Cox and Alexander Ross, prompted an English translation of his book published in 1854.

In 1853 he was given a public welcome on a visit to Montreal and an address signed by 100 leading citizens for his work as president of the Société Saint-Jean-Baptiste in New York. He founded his own fur commission house in Brooklyn in 1857 and was probably engaged in this business when he died in 1863 at the home of his stepson in Minnesota.

CHAPTER 3

Multi-ethnic Communities

*A*midst the disease, displacement, violence, and sorrow, there were two Fur War communities that worked surprisingly well. One, Kanaka Village, was under the HBC, and the other, Fort Ross Village, was under the RAC. Both succeeded in bringing people from many cultures together in a remarkably harmonious manner, much like many cities on the west coast today.

KANAKA VILLAGE AT FORT VANCOUVER

Fort Vancouver became the economic hub of the fur trade. The Chief Factor Dr. John McLoughlin created a thriving international business community that involved natural resources, agricultural commodities, and manufactured goods. The fort dealt in furs, lumber, salted salmon, crops, dairy products, livestock, wood, iron and tin tools, household goods, and trade goods. These products and services reached Hawaii, Alaska, Spanish California, and many First Nations; they also reached London, Montreal, and a remarkable number of fur-trading posts.

A surprisingly harmonious multicultural village developed outside the fort under McLoughlin's leadership. Kanaka Village was described in almost idyllic terms by visitors—quite a contrast to the native villages nearby that were decimated by disease, loss of resources and despair. By 1840 Kanaka Village had about 800 residents, with more than 200 working for the HBC at the fort. The village included French Canadians, Scots, Hawaiians, English, Iroquois, Cree, and dozens of different local tribal members. The

babel of languages was quite entertaining. Although a few languages were dominant, more than thirty were spoken.

Dr. McLoughlin supported a school and it proved to be quite a challenge for the schoolmaster. In addition to the many languages spoken, some of the children would be gone for months or years at a time as they accompanied their parents on the fur brigades. Many teachers today can appreciate the challenge. Mornings in the classroom were devoted to basic studies; afternoons were devoted to manual training. Boys worked in the fort's large garden and workshops while girls learned sewing and housekeeping. The fort officers also took in orphans, abandoned women, and widows from time to time. Métis and native children from outside the fort community could live at the fort or village at the request of their parents.

The fort required a remarkable array of skills to manage the all-important fur trade, sawmill, grist mill, boatbuilding facility, smithy, gun repair shop, and farrier, along with maintaining operations in gardening, dairy, fishing, fish drying and salting, cooperage (barrels and pipes), bakery, orchards, and tending to the flocks of chickens, and herds of pigs and cattle. These all supported the fur trade operations. In later years, the production of food, timber, and other products contributed to the bottom line. In 1828, just three years after the first crops were planted, workers harvested 1,300 bushels of wheat, 300 bushels of peas, 4,000 bushels of potatoes, and 1,000 bushels of barley.

The gardens included strawberries, carrots, turnips, cabbages, potatoes, squash, parsnips, cucumbers, peas, tomatoes, beets, and a variety of fruits. They grew flowers, including roses and dahlias. By 1836 the garden had grown to five acres. Notably, the garden was not reserved for the officers and gentlemen of the fort. Many sailors in from long voyages relished the fresh fruit and vegetables. From the late 1820s (or early 1830s) to 1849, the principal gardener was William Bruce, a Scot. When Jedediah Smith reached Fort Vancouver in August 1828, he found *"some small apple trees and grape vines"* growing at the establishment; the first cultivated fruits in the region. By March 1829 the cattle herd had grown to 153 head. Before long, citrus and pomegranates were being grown as well as many medicinal plants. Salt pork, butter, wheat, potatoes, and other foods were shipped to Hawaii, Alaska, and California.

People in Kanaka Village built their own homes and had to buy or gather the materials needed for foundations, walls, roofs, and chimneys. With the help of friends and some of the fort's craftsmen, the families constructed their own one- to three-room homes. When John Kirk Townsend visited Fort Vancouver in 1832, he described the village as *"very neat and beautiful."*

Many workers at the fort married women from the Cowlitz, Upper Chinook, and Chehalis tribes. With advice from friends, the men would observe the tribal traditions of marriage, including the proper approach to the girl's older male relatives and the exchange of gifts. Men often made provisions for their families in case they were killed. They supported the schooling of their children and helped with apprenticeships for their sons and domestic training and marriage of their daughters. Many of the marriages were long-lasting and helped lay the foundation for the settlement of Oregon. The mix of people varied over time as policies and markets changed. In addition to the residents, it was common to have many tents and camps of visitors outside the fort and village.

Table 3.1—Ethnicity at Kanaka Village

Ethnicity	1827–28	1830–31	1837	1838–39	1842	1843
French-Canadian	117	53	30	29	54	44
Hawaiian	18	14	32	35	77	78
Native (not Iroquois)	17	3	4	5	25	25
Unknown	15	20	5	7	16	9
Iroquois	14	4	4	4	5	7
Anglo-Saxon	10	6	24	22	27	28

THE HAWAIIANS

The village was called Kanaka Village because the Hawaiians were often the most numerous culture. Many were engaged at the fort rather than out on brigades. They were in particular demand because they worked hard, learned new skills quickly, were skillful paddlers, good swimmers and excellent divers. They also knew how to sail. They were good in combat and fearless. However, they could be "too independent" and a challenge to manage on the fur brigades.

The *kanakas* found the cold damp climate difficult at first, but many became successful winter travelers. The first Hawaiians came on the *Tonquin* for Astor's Pacific Fur Company in 1810. His company, and later the NWC, paid them with room and board and a few goods. Most switched over when the HBC offered pay. *Kanakas* often came on a three-year contract, perhaps rented out by the king of Hawaii, but some stayed to work and settle in the area following their service.

Between 1827 and 1842, about half of the Hawaiians were engaged in water-based occupations. The HBC paid them ten to nineteen pounds a year, plus food—largely smoked salmon and sea biscuits. The smoked salmon quickly became a staple and was called *lomi lomi* salmon. *Kanakas* with extra skills were paid more. In his later years, Naukane, the well-traveled Hawaiian, managed the pig farm for the fort. Hawaiians also served food, cooked, and acted as servants for the HBC officers. In McLoughlin's later years the census records show him having two *kanakas* at his house.

After the malaria epidemic struck and devastated the native workers, the *kanakas* became even more important. A third of the labor force may have been Hawaiian in the 1830s. In 1836, there were 28 Hawaiians working in the sawmill cutting and shipping lumber. Much of the wood went to Hawaii. In 1840, a visitor wrote, "*the Islanders are felling the pines and dragging them to the mill. Using oxen and horses, sets of hands are plying two gangs of saws by night and day, nine hundred thousand feet per annum are constantly being shipped to foreign ports.*" By 1841 they were being paid £17 a year at the company sawmills.

THE IROQUOIS

The hiring of Iroquois and other natives from the east brought well developed skills to bear on the fur trade enterprise in the west. These trappers and workers tended to be tall, strong, and very capable. They were experienced beaver trappers and knew how to use steel traps. Many early writers were impressed by the strength, courage, and frontier competence of the Iroquois they met. Men from outside the region also had few competing local loyalties and limited family or tribal attachments that might compete with their commitment to the NWC or HBC. However, they were sometimes seen as less than obedient because they maintained a sense of internal loyalty that sometimes trumped their loyalties to the fur companies.

The North West Company began recruiting Iroquois labor in 1815 from the vicinity of its headquarters in Montreal. Some were sent to the far west to work. Their boat handling and trapping skills had been developed over decades or generations of working for the fur companies in the east. The HBC also recruited a modest number of Iroquois employees before Fort Vancouver was built. After the merger of the NWC and HBC, the Iroquois could be found throughout the region. Marriage to native women provided added benefits for the fur companies by establishing a bond that would encourage better treatment and protection. More than ten Iroquois men married in the Catholic church and their children show up in baptismal records.

OTHER TRIBES

From accounts and records of marriages, baptisms, and burials, we know that the following people were involved with Fort Vancouver and many lived in Kanaka Village: Métis with tribal affiliations across Canada, Achomawi, Atsugewi, Carrier, Cascades, Cathlamet, Cayapooya (Kalapuya?), Cayuse, Clackamas, Cowichan, Cowlitz, Kalama, Kathlamet, Klallam, Klickitat, Knisteneau (Cree), Mollala, Multnomah, Nez Perce, Nipissing, Nisqually, Nuu-chah-nulth, Okanagan, Pend d'Orielles, Umatilla, Nisqually, Quinalt, Salish, Shasta, Skillute, Snake, Snohomish, Spokane, Stikene, Twaliwalla, Tillamook, Umatilla, Umpqua, Walla Walla, Wasco, Willamette, Wishram, and Yakama. Communication was certainly a challenge at times but *Chinook wawa* became the common language.

SLAVES

There were also slaves from various tribes in the village, at the fort, fur outposts, and on brigades. They worked in near-conventional servants' roles in the fort. Outside the fort they worked for their owner, and their treatment depended on the relationship. Slaves were employed to cut wood, hunt, and fish for the families of the men employed by the HBC. This helped provide for the families when the men were away for months or sometimes years. The HBC census of 1838 showed that slaves made up more than 25% of the population of nearby villages.

MANY BENEFITS BUT SOME CHALLENGES

Communication could be an issue on the job, on the trail, or coursing down a wild river. As George Simpson noted on one of his trips, *"Our bateau carried as curious a muster of races and languages as perhaps had ever been congregated within the same compass in any part of the world. Our crew of ten men contained Iroquois, who spoke their*

own tongue; a Cree half-breed of French origin who appeared to have bor-
rowed his dialect from both his parents; a North Briton, who understood
only the Gaelic of his native hills; Canadians who of course knew French;
and Sandwich Islanders who jabbered a medley of Chinook, English, &c.
and their own vernacular jargon."

The varied languages and skills provided benefits as well and
eased relations with local tribes. Many of the smaller outposts
included a variety of different cultures, and the larger posts were
often similar to Kanaka Village. As Modeste Demers described Fort
Langley in 1841, "*About twenty men are employed there at agricultural*
activities, of whom eight are Canadians, one an Iroquois, and the other
Kanakas, inhabitants of the Sandwich Islands; all having wives and chil-
dren after the fashion of the country."

HARMONY AND HEALTH

The HBC supported two hospitals, one in the fort and one near the
village, and provided free care and medicine as needed. Religious
support was also provided for Catholics, the Church of England, and
Hawaiian services.

Music probably played a big role in the community with the voyageur songs, Hawaiian songs, native music, and traditional English
and Scottish tunes. In the 1840s, Anne and Richard Covington were
hired to teach the children of Fort Vancouver's employees. They
were talented musicians and had a guitar, violin, and the first piano
in the Northwest.

As the American settlements grew in the 1830s they fostered
ill-treatment of the natives, *kanakas*, and mixed-race families and
children, and the village gradually melted away. Many Hawaiians
went home; other workers moved to Vancouver Island or other HBC
posts. The French Canadians were among the first permanent settlers of Oregon. They developed a small colony on French Prairie
including several small towns including St. Paul, Champoeg, St.
Louis, and Gervais. Many others also made land claims and eventually became American citizens.

The Russians at Fort Ross

The Russians had been successful hunting sea otters on the California coast and staying in Bodega Bay when they decided to build a southern outpost. Between 1808 and 1811, Ivan Kuskov made several voyages to California seeking a location for a new colony. By 1812 the site for the Russian outpost of Fort Ross was chosen. Timofei Tarakanov conducted the negotiations for the purchase of land for Fort Ross and played such a pivotal role that the Miwok thought he was the captain of the Russians. Two separate transactions were completed, one with the Kashaya Pomo chief at Fort Ross (Pánac-úccux) for an actual transfer of property, and a use permit from Ióllo, chief of the Bodega Bay Miwok. The land purchase was formalized in a treaty in 1817 to improve claims against the Spanish or Americans.

Ivan Kuskov, his crew, and 86 Aleuts with 40 *baidarkas* sailed down the coast to start construction. Hunting expeditions soon began as well, and whenever the Aleuts could be spared, they were hunting. They would go as far north as Cape Mendocino but rarely further south than Drake's Bay due to Spanish resistance—although sea otter hunts by *baidarka* were conducted into San Francisco Bay. They also established a work group on the fur-rich Farallon Islands. This barren, rocky, and storm-tossed outpost did not have a reliable fresh water supply. It was windy, often wet from sea spray, and cold. Consignment to the islands was sometimes used to punish people who misbehaved at Fort Ross.

Kuskov's wife Ekatarina mastered the native languages of tribes living near Fort Ross and she established extremely friendly relations with them. She taught native children the Russian language and other subjects. Their piano must have led to many evenings of music and song. Russian soldiers and settlers from the fort could roam the surrounding woods without fear of being killed by the natives.

The goals of making Fort Ross a center for sea otter and seal hunting, manufacturing, ship building, and husbandry were not

realized. The harvesting of pelts slowed quickly from over-hunt-
ing and the hope of a successful manufacturing and ship building
enterprise was derailed by lack of skills and competition from afar.
The climate and topography were not ideal for agriculture and the
lack of labor and limited expertise further hindered the effort to
transform Fort Ross into a granary that would supply the RAC outposts and cities. However the people in the community worked well
together.

Compared to the Alaska outposts, it was paradise and most
Russians fully appreciated it. One wrote, *"Ross is blest with an abundance of the finest wood for building. The sea provides it with the most
delicious fish, the land with an inexhaustible quantity of the best kinds
of game; and, notwithstanding the want of a good harbor, the northern
settlements might easily find in this a plentiful magazine for the supply
of all their wants."* A visiting Bostonian in 1832 reported, *"There are a
number of work-shops outside the walls, in which many different trades
are pursued; and in a small place near the sea are huts of the Kodiacs. I
should think there were about 300 inhabitants of all descriptions. They
cultivate about 400 acres of wheat and raise many vegetables and some
fruits."*

At the time of the sale to John Sutter in 1841, Fort Ross included
more than 40 buildings, 75 fenced acres, corrals, two cattle barns,
an orchard, smithy, mill, brick making, sauna, and foundry. The
Russian orchard on a hillside included apples, peaches, grapes,
cherries, and several types of pears. The fort also had two ranches.

Three brigs and a schooner were built at the shipyard but the green oak they used did not hold up well.

The fort was built near the Pomo village of Meteni, and local natives worked closely with the Russians throughout its tenure. In 1833 the community included 60 Russians, 88 *kreols*, 92 natives, and 53 Aleuts. The natives included Pomo, Miwok, Eskimo (Yupik/Inupiat?), Yakuts, Chugach, Tlingit, Tanaina, and others. At its peak Fort Ross included 260 people: 120 Russians, 51 *kreols*, 50 Kodiak (including several tribes), and 39 local natives.

Peter Stepanovich Kostromitinov spent seven years at the fort and described the local natives as follows: *"The Indians are of medium stature, but one also finds tall individuals among them; they are rather well-proportioned, the color of their skin is brownish, but this color is caused by the sun rather than being innate; eyes and hair are black, the latter is straight... Both sexes are of robust build; one rarely finds crippled people among them; but as a result of the climate and their mode of life they do not reach old age. The physiognomy of the Indians in general bears an expression of good nature rather than savagery and one often encounters charming faces, among males as well as females. They are gentle and peaceful and very clever... The Bodega [Miwok] Indians have no artificial coloration on their body; the Northerners [Pomo], on the other hand, tattoo their faces, breasts and hands with various figures, and apply an herbal extract to their bodies, which gives their skin a dark blue color, which is permanent."*

The treaty with the local tribe provided security for the Russians by adding native allies. This would be helpful if Spanish enmity turned to violence. It also provided some protection for the native people who had the Russians on their side. The Russians saw that they could protect the local people from the *"attacks of savages under control of the Spaniards"* without much difficulty or cost to the Company. Fort Ross itself served as a formidable deterrent to Spanish hostility. The settlement was never threatened by outside attack.

Many of the Russian observers were sympathetic to the plight of Native Californians. The climate was mild yet invigorating, and the beauty of the surroundings imparted a sense of well-being recorded by many who were there. Manager Alexander Rotchev and his wife Helena looked back nostalgically at the time spent in this "enchanting land" as the "best years" of their lives.

The many ethnicities got along well. Ekaterina Prokhorovna, Kuskov's Tlingit wife, is given credit for getting things off to a good start. Over the life of the colony a number of Russians and Alaskan natives married Kashaya, Coast Miwok, and Southern Pomo women with the consent of tribes and the RAC. *Kreol* and native families had many children, and by the mid-1830s children made up about a third of the residents; most were considered *kreols*, born of ethnically mixed unions. It was a healthy place with relatively few deaths.

The last manager at Fort Ross was Alexander Rotchev and a new house was built for him, his wife Elena, and their three children, Olga, Elena, and Konstantin. Rotchev was a well-educated, and well-traveled man of the arts, and a poet. His wife, Princess Elena Pavlovna Gagarina, was a descendant of the titled nobility, accomplished in the arts and sciences and conversant in several languages. The Rotchev House was considered a refined and properly furnished residence with a good library, piano, and scores of Mozart's music. Their hospitality was widely known and appreciated.

Fr. Veniaminov visited the fort in 1836 and performed a number of weddings, baptisms, and other services. He noted that about 15 percent of the settlement's population, then numbering 260, consisted of Indians baptized in the Eastern Orthodox faith, but there were also residents who were Lutheran and Catholic.

As in many other places, the Russian workers were not well paid and were charged high prices for goods. At first the native workers were volunteers; later they were usually paid, but when a labor shortage developed some were forced to work on the farm. Although it was not a good place to make a living, it was a good place to live— particularly compared to the Spanish missions or Alaskan outposts.

After thirty years the fort was sold to John Sutter but he was very slow to pay. On January 1, 1842, Rotchev and about one hundred colonists sailed from Bodega Bay on the last Russian ship bound for Sitka. Many Russian men took their country wives, but others were abandoned. In 1841 there were 50 Indian buildings outside the fort's palisade. A decade after the sale of Fort Ross there was still a population of about 500 Southwestern Pomo and Coast Miwok along the coast from Fort Ross to San Francisco Bay.

RECAP

These two villages show what could be done with good management. People from many backgrounds and races worked and lived well together. Elsewhere the native people were often treated as inferior, and in some cases subhuman, but here they were treated better. The RAC workers were also treated more fairly, but still not as well as one might hope. In both cases the more harmonious relations improved the quality of life and morale and reduced the cost

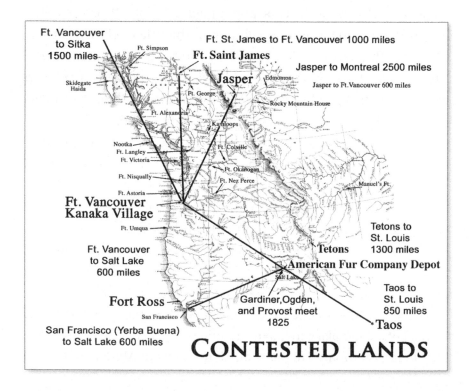

of operations. Both villages faded away as the fur trade declined and the Americans moved in, mistreating and abusing the native people.

We still have much to learn but it is clear we can live together if we try.

CHAPTER 4

Lessons Not Yet Learned

We can learn a great deal from the experiences of the fur trade. Key lessons include the need for true cost accounting and better understanding of the linkages between people and the environment across time. We can also recognize the need for much greater investment in integrated studies of resource management and cultural survival. And we can learn from the unsung heroes of the struggle for power and wealth along the Fur Coast.

KEY LESSONS

TRUE COST ACCOUNTING

The fur trade demonstrates the damage caused by the failure to count the true or full costs. The HBC fur brigades of 1832–33 are a good example. John Work and Michel Laframboise carried malaria south into California; they returned to Fort Vancouver with a fair number of beaver and made a modest profit, but it came with the death of tens of thousands of women, men, and children.

It was clear when they left the fort in 1832 that they had disease in their ranks. Sadly they did not, at that time, fully understand what the disease was and how it was spread. But the impact of the disease was clear as they returned north in the fall of 1833, still sick themselves. In a journal entry dated August 6, 1833, Work noted, *"The villages that were so populous and swarming with inhabitants when we passed that way in Jany or Febry last seem now almost deserted & have a desolate appearance. The few wretched Indians who remain seem wretched they are lying apparently scarcely able to move."* As George Yount later recalled, *"The bodies of untold thousands lay whitening the plains and fertile valleys.... Deserted and desolated village sat tenantless all over the valleys..."* Jonathan Warner remembered, *"The banks of the Sacramento River, in its whole course through the valley, were studded with Indian Villages, the houses of which, in the spring, during the day time were red with the salmon the aborigines were curing... On our return, late in the summer of 1833, we found the valleys depopulated. From the head of the Sacramento to the great bend and slough of the San Joaquin, we did not see more than six or eight live Indians, while large numbers of their skulls and dead bodies were to be seen under almost every shade tree, near the water, where the uninhabited and deserted villages had been converted into graveyards."* As many as 50,000 people may have died for 2,000 beaver worth about $4,000. This is less than 8¢ for everyone that died. Today we face many equally unknown and dangerous risks[1] yet blunder forward without careful consideration of "What can possible go wrong?"

THE INTER-LINKAGES BETWEEN HUMANS AND NATURE

The destruction of so many native people resulted in significant changes to the plant and animal communities. The removal of the sea otter triggered loss of the rich kelp ecosystems and resulting declines in fisheries and shellfish that continue to today. The removal of the beaver triggered significant hydrologic changes. Streams that once flowed in the summer, dried up. Increased flood intensity led to channel deepening and accelerated erosion, resulting in declining water tables and loss of riparian habitat. Changes in these wetlands in turn affect a wide range of plant, insect, animal, and bird species. These are described in more detail in Volume 1: *Fur War - the Political, Economic, Cultural and Ecological Impacts of the Western Fur Trade 1765–1840* and in my earlier book *A Guide for Desert and Dryland Restoration.*

THE STIFLING POWER OF BUREAUCRACY AND RED TAPE

Spanish fur trader Vincent Vasadre and many of the British fur traders were burdened with bureaucratic obstacles that plagued their enterprises. Vasadre was defeated by the Philippine Company and Spanish bureaucracy. The British were dragged down by The East India Company and sometimes also the South Sea Company— each demanding fees and power. They were less hampered by the British government because they had developed working relationships over the years since the founding of the HBC in 1670.

THE NEED FOR MORE INTEGRATED LONG TERM STUDIES

As environmental historians and landscape ecologists, we need to better understand what happened in order to more accurately comprehend what we see today. This can enable us to develop better management strategies for a more sustainable future. Ecological restoration provides opportunities to create mutually beneficial relationships between ourselves and the non-human landscape. The old notion of wilderness must be replaced with an understanding that the people and non-human entities are dancing in a continuous co-evolution. If we pay attention, we can improve the way we do business and live well while we improve the quality of life for all.

The return of sea otters to some areas has benefitted the kelp and improved the productivity and value of many harvests from the sea. The remarkable recovery of Monterey Bay once otters returned was striking. The re-establishment of the wolves in Yellowstone has enabled riparian plants to prosper and enabled the beaver to recover. The natural expansion of beaver ranges and introduction of beaver to old haunts have revealed the enormous benefits for water conservation, wildlife habitat, and recreational opportunities.

Although the eco-sciences have made many strides, there is still much we do not know. Most critically, we do not know what the west coast ecosystems were like before they were damaged. We do not fully understand the systems today and we are even less sure of the long-term effects of pollution and climate change. We can be sure these will offer unwelcome surprises.

There is so much we need to learn. Wherever we look, research and investigation soon show us how incomplete our knowledge is, even of the things with which we are most familiar. We need to learn more with long term field work. We also need to listen carefully to the tribal elders. We need to more forcefully ask how any given action or project contributes to, or detracts from, sustainability from a long-term ecological and cultural perspective. We need to better understand and consider the long term risks, costs and benefits.

More research on sustainability is urgently needed. Fortunately, much of the research is not costly, requiring little more than secure long term funding for managers and volunteers' time, travel and supplies.[2] We should reach out to locally-trained volunteers and university students, as well as to specially trained para-ecologists, -sociologists, and -accountants, asking them to undertake fieldwork under the supervision of experts. College, high school, and even middle school students can also provide meaningful research while gaining invaluable experience.

Long-term interdisciplinary research projects are critically important yet remain quite rare. The National Science Foundation's Long-Term Ecological Research sites are, unfortunately, almost unique. They are woefully underfunded, with about $20 million each year spread over 26 sites. Each site can easily use $5 million to $10 million of base funding, and there should be hundreds of them to cover a wider range of wild ecosystems, agroecosystems and urban/suburban ecosystems.

Research should be multidisciplinary and involve a range of scientists, engineers, economists, anthropologists, first nations, psychologists, artists, designers, marketers, managers, and students who are working on common problems. Research on the successes and failures of existing ecological restoration projects is also needed. The benefits of restoration on biodiversity and ecosystem structure and function should be evaluated carefully. The importance of protecting cultural diversity to maintain biological diversity needs to be better understood as well.

A Long-Term Cultural Knowledge Research program can be developed to focus on the cultural challenges now facing the First Nations and rural communities along the fur coast. Research agendas for long-term cultural research sites would include a wide range of problems that have proven intractable due to incomplete cost accounting and a lack of focus on sustainability.

WORTH REMEMBERING AND HONORING

Although some of the people involved in the fur trade were greedy, cruel, and even vicious, there are also examples of people who succeeded by being better. Both men and women were courageous, intelligent, and persevered under the most extreme trials. Four people who few have heard of are worth getting to know: William Sturgis, Alexander Kashevarov, Maquinna the elder, and Vasadre Vega.

THE MORAL CAPITALIST

William Sturgis did better by being moral, fair, and respectful of other cultures. He was well-regarded by his crews, never lost a man in conflict, or had a fight with the natives. His business model should be known by all students in environmental science and business because he got rich without being evil. He also helped resolve the boundary dispute between the U.S. and Britain. He suggested the Northwest Coast should be governed by the native people. Imagine how rich the cultural diversity and productivity of the coast could have been if his idea had been implemented. Imagine how much we would enjoy seeing thousands of sea otters, and plentiful whales and seals as we took the ferry up the coast while stopping at the prosperous towns of the Haida-Gwaii, Hinya Kwáan, Sheey At'iká Kwáan, Xunaa Kwáan, and Gunaaxoo Kwáan for seafood and salmon feasts before stopping in Yakutat.

THE KREOL COMMANDER

Alexander Kashevarov made a remarkable climb from being a mixed-race youngster in Alaska to commander and map maker for the Russian Navy. He advocated for the *kreols* and natives; and clearly saw and described the ecological collapse of sea otters, fur seals, sea lions, and other fur-bearing animals. Before the fur trade, all of these animals had lived and multiplied while providing generally sustainable resources for the native people for thousands of years. He argued that only the natives understood the animals well enough to manage them and thus should be ceded control over Alaska's environment.

MAQUINNA THE LEADER AND DIPLOMAT

The Maqinna who led during the critical first period of the fur trade (1778–1795) was remarkably astute and effective. He worked particularly closely with the Spanish, but also dealt with the British and American captains. He was able to take advantage of the popularity of Nootka Sound to manipulate competition between traders to increase the prices paid for his furs. Maquinna also saw opportunity in extending his hold over a larger area. He tried to ensure that all furs traded at Nootka passed through his hands and by 1792 he controlled a trading network with the Kwakiutl on the east coast of Vancouver Island. The trader John Hoskins reported that his profits as a broker were considerable.

THE ECONOMIST

Vincente Vasadre was a well-educated, thoughtful observer, and a very innovative thinker. He was business-oriented and always trying to improve the management of people and resources. Vasadre correctly saw the possible reciprocal trade of furs for quicksilver (mercury) for use in processing gold ore at the mines in New Spain. His inability to move entrenched bureaucracies is also a lesson for us all, being right does not inevitably lead to the preferred outcome or action. Vasadre was very knowledgeable about the societal problems and the flaws in the Spanish and colonial economies. He was a successful administrator in Venezuela and the Philippines. He was a forthright advocate for free markets and fair treatment, and in 1799 he noted that free trade would mark a glorious epoch for posterity. His efforts to support the Galician independence movement would cost him his freedom.

We can learn from these men and from Aldo Leopold — an avid hunter, land manager, and later in life, restoration ecologist. His writing should be required reading for all students, as he came to realize...

A thing is right when it tends to preserve the integrity, stability, and beauty of the biotic community. It is wrong when it does otherwise. —Aldo Leopold (1949)

Further Reading

1. GEOPOLITICS

See Volume 1. Fur War and supplemental materials at
www.furwar.com.

- Dolin, J. 2010. *Fur, Fortune and Empire*. W.W. Norton.
- Gibson, J. 1992. *Otter Skins, Boston Ships, and China Goods*.
  McGill-Queens University Press. (excellent)
- Giraldez, A., J. Sobredo, D. O. Flynn, eds. 2017 [2002]. *Studies in Pacific History: Economics, Politics and Migration*. CRC Press.
- Gutiérrez, R. and R.J. Orsi, eds. 1998. *Contested Eden: California before the Gold Rush*. UC Press.
- Mackie, R. 1997. *Trading Beyond the Mountains*. University of British Columbia Press.
- Vinkovetsky, I. 2011. *Russian America*. Oxford.

2. MORE ABOUT THE PEOPLE OF THE FUR TRADE

The best sources of information are the personal diaries and journals. The HBC journals are often very detailed. Most key individuals have had biographies published, although the quality is very uneven. There have been some excellent dissertations in recent years, with many of them leading to journal articles. For a wider range of characters and hints to start sleuthing from, try:

- Anderson, M.K. 2013. *Tending the Wild*. UC Press. (exceptional)

- Barman, J. and B.M. Watson. 2006. *Leaving Paradise: Indigenous Hawaiians in the Pacific Northwest 1787–1898.* University of Hawaii Press.
- Black, L.T. 2004. *Russians in Alaska.* University of Alaska Press. (exceptional)
- Chittenden, H.M. 1986 [1935]. *The American Fur Trade of the West, 2 volumes.* Bison Books.
- Cleland, R.G. 1963. *This Reckless Breed of Men: The Trappers and Fur Traders of the Southwest.* Alfred A. Knopf,
- Curtis, E.S. 2005 [1907–1930]. *The North American Indian.* Taschen.
- Gamble, L.H. 2008. *The Chumash World at European Contact.* UC Press. (exceptional)
- Hafen, L.R. 1965. *Trappers of the Far West.* Bison Books.
- Heizer, R.F. and M.A. Whipple. 1972. *The California Indians: A Source Book.* UC Press.
- Powers, S. 1976 [1877]. *Tribes of California.* UC Press.
- Langdon, S. 2013. *Native People of Alaska, Traditional Living in a Northern Land.* 5th Ed. Greatland Graphics.
- Lewis, A.B. 2016 [1907]. *Tribes of the Columbia Valley and the coast of Washington and Oregon.* (now also on Kindle)
- Muckle, R.J. 2014. *First Nations of British Columbia.* UBC Press.
- Newman, P.C. 2005. [1985]. *Company of Adventurers.* Penguin.
- Weber, D.J. 1971. *The Taos Trappers.* University of Oklahoma Press.
- Williams, Maria Sháa Tláa, Editor. 2009. *The Alaska Native Reader: History, Culture, Politics.* The World Readers.

3. MULTI-ETHNIC VILLAGES

- Duer, D. 2012. *An Ethnohistorical Overview of Groups with Ties to Fort Vancouver National Historic Site.* College of Forest Resources, University of Washington and Pacific Northwest Cooperative Ecosystem Studies Unit National Park Service, Pacific West Region Seattle, Washington. 362 pages.
- Mitchell, K.E. 1984. *Fort Ross, Russian Colony in California, 1811–1841.* MA Thesis, Portland State University.

- Nicks, T. 1980. *The Iroquois and the Fur Trade in Western Canada*. In Carol M. Judd and Arthur J. Ray, eds. *Old Trails and New Directions*. Pp. 85–101. Toronto: University of Toronto Press.
- Osborn, S.K. 1997. *Death in the Daily Life of Fort Ross*. PhD thesis. University of Wisconsin, Milwaukee.

4. LESSONS YET UNLEARNED

- Arkema, K.K., L.A. Rogers, J. Toft, A. Mesher, K.H. Wyatt, S. Albury-Smith, S. Moultrie, M.H. Ruckelshaus, and J. Samhouri. 2019. *Integrating fisheries management into sustainable development planning*. Ecology and Society 24(2):1.
- Bainbridge, D.A. 2006. *Adding ecological considerations to "environmental" accounting*. Bulletin of the Ecological Society of America. October. 8(4):335–340.
- Bainbridge, D.A. 2020. *True Cost Accounting*. www.truecostalways.com
- Barg, S. and D. Swanson. 2004. *Full Cost Accounting for Agriculture*. International Institute for Sustainable Development. Winnipeg.
- Brodie Rudolph, T., M. Ruckelshaus, M. Swilling, et al. 2020. *A transition to sustainable ocean governance*. Nature Communications 11(1):1–13 https://doi.org/10.1038/s41467-020-17410-2
- Cone, M. 2000. *Mystery: Why is the Aleutian ecosystem collapsing?* Worldcatch News Nov 7, Center for Biological Diversity. https://www.biologicaldiversity.org/species/birds/spectacled_eider/worldcatch.html
- Elkington, J. 1999. *Cannibals with Forks: The Triple Bottom Line of 21st Century Business*. Capstone, Oxford.
- Goldfarb, B. 2018. *Eager—the surprising secret lives of beaver and why they matter*. Chelsea Green.
- Leopold, A. 1949. *A Sand County Almanac*: And Sketches Here and There. Oxford University Press. (exceptional)

Acknowledgements

First, my thanks to the journal keepers and diarists, as well as the people who preserved these records and the diligent librarians and genealogists who have digitized so many original sources. Google Earth has been very helpful in understanding the relations between historical events, trading posts, and fur trails.

Thanks also to the information aggregators, H.H. Bancroft, H.M. Chittenden, Canadian biography, Wikis from several countries, encyclopedias, fur trade journals and blogs, web page developers, and others.

I also appreciate the writers who have led the way: Harold L. Innis, Stephen R. Brown, James R. Gibson, Richard Somerset Mackie, Ilya Vinkovetsky, Lydia T. Black, Lynn H. Gamble, Mary Malloy, and so many others. As the great environmental historian George Perkins Marsh said, "*I shall steal pretty much, but I do know some things myself.*"

The artists who did such amazing work under often difficult conditions help us understand the places and events. Louis Choris, John Webber, Paul Kane, José Cardero, Mikhail Tikhanov, Ilya

Gavrilovich Voznsensky, Yuri Fyodorovich Lisyanski, Luka Voronin, Gavril Sarychev, Henry J. Warre, Alfred Jacob Miller, J. M. Alden, and Henry Wood Elliott were especially helpful. Mark Myers has done a series of superb historical paintings of the Fur War ships and Bill Holm has provided detailed paintings of the First Nations. More information on the artists in the supplemental notes at www.fur-war.com.

I have been fortunate to visit many of the fur outposts, to paddle on the Columbia headwaters and British Columbia lakes and rivers up to Fort St. James; to visit, hike, and paddle in Alaska and to hike and camp in the Rockies, Sierras, San Juans, and other mountains as well as the deserts of North America. I have always been interested in ecology, ecological restoration, and environmental history. This book enabled me to bring these all together.

Thanks also to family, colleagues, and friends who contributed to my understanding of ecosystems and ecological restoration. Many have also supplied support, encouragement, information, editing, and a variety of images and documents for this book that I may otherwise have never seen.

I would also like to thank Sutton Mason and Laurie Lippitt for their editorial assistance and Manon Wogahn for design suggestions and manuscript preparation.

David Bainbridge

San Diego 2020

Notes

GEOPOLITICS

1. I found discussions of more than 100 epidemics on the fur coast from 1765–1840
2. Nakba in Arabic: النكبة, al-Nakbah: disaster, catastrophe, or cataclysm.
3. some open boats similar to the Viking long ships
4. or a bit earlier
5. kayaks with one, two, or three cockpits, sometimes incorrectly called canoes. The fur trade model had three cockpits - two for men and one for the catch or for a Russian passenger. For pictures see supplemental notes at https://www.furwar.com.
6. It had already been rebuilt once—*Rediviva* in Latin. Ships could deteriorate quickly if not well maintained or run on to too many reefs or sand bars.

THE PEOPLE

1. also sometimes Kotlian, Katlian, Qatya'n, Kotlean
2. Some suggest the attack was instigated by the HBC in 1801 with an offering of guns and powder in exchange for exclusive future fur-trading rights. Others blame the British Captain Barber or perhaps most likely, the American Captain William Cunningham of the *Globe*.
3. the names of a chief might be a son or grandson
4. A hieromonk is a monk who is also a priest in the Orthodox Church
5. Ya'aihlstohsmahhlneh, Ya'aistohsmalni, Wikinanish, Wickananish, Wee-ka-na-nish, Wicananich, Huiquinanichi, Huiquinani, Quiquinanis, also known as Hiyoua. Suggested meaning: "No one goes before him." Name transferred as leadership changes took place.
6. by comparison, St. Louis had only 1,100 people in 1786
7. one of the Nuu-chah-nulth tribes
8. fifteen, according to the navy
9. rebuilt and modified in 1787
10. the fifth mate assists the second mate, a job shadow or apprenticeship
11. a yellowish cotton cloth

12. Zhou?
13. A hydrographer measures and describes the physical features of oceans, seas, coastal areas, rivers and lakes.
14. Other notes suggest O'Cain joined the *Sutil* in San Blas, but I think that was to minimize the role of the non-Spanish sailors.
15. Country wives were native women without a church marriage, often left behind or traded. Some were clearly happy companionable marriages and some were eventually legalized.
16. A second lieutenant in the Russian Ekaterinburg regiment, fluent in Russian, built a ship in Okhotsk for the Shelikhov Company, and in 1792 sailed it to Kodiak Island with a supply of rigging and hardware for the construction of a new frigate.
17. This was a standard practice but it was both difficult and dangerous. Exposed to new diseases and loneliness far from home, many died in Russia. This effort yielded one trained mariner a year.
18. By most accounts, the men who attacked the fort in 1855 were found and killed long before word reached St. Petersburg.
19. he is commonly referred to as Bodega y Quadra, his mother might not have approved. In Spanish tradition a person's name consists of a given name (simple or composite) followed by two surnames. Historically, the first surname was the father's first surname, and the second the mother's first surname. Joseph Burling O'Cain was sometimes referred to as Burling.
20. alias *Nueva Galicia*
21. aliases *Felicidad, Nuestra Señora de Guadalupe*
22. Port Etches is a bay in the south-central part Alaska on the west side of Hinchinbrook Island.
23. sometimes Basadre
24. an important port city and provincial capital
25. king of Spain and the Spanish Indies (1759–1788) helped lead Spain to a brief cultural and economic revival
26. or perhaps still in Spain
27. or 1785
28. One of only six people who were awarded American citizenship; Vasadre was recognized for supporting the Americans in the Revolutionary War after he led Spanish forces that defeated the British in Florida.
29. Vasadre may have been over-estimating the opportunity based on the sea otter take from the NW Coast and an optimistic view of the possibility of adding new Spanish ports to the north.
30. officer in charge, elected by his fellow officers

31. these furs would be worth $40–90 or more in Canton in 1787–1788 but only $15–30 in the following years. The dollar, or real of eight, was also called a peso. It was the standard of international exchange in China.
32. perhaps with the chance to avenge his mistreatment
33. Venezuela's main port, now the capital city of the Venezuelan state of Vargas
34. the war would go on for 13 more years
35. "I have lost all happiness in my life…"
36. founder of Los Angeles, later governor of both Baja and Alta California
37. or six
38. God-parenting was sanctioned by the Russian Orthodox Church, and at baptism, a native person could use the name of his or her Russian godparent.
39. Muquinna, Mukwina, Maquina, Maquilla, "the possessor of the pebbles"
40. Tahsees
41. Cooptee
42. more than forty men were killed in the conflicts between NWC and HBC
43. the area around Hudson's Bay
44. He also acknowledged two out-of-wedlock children in England
45. *à la façon du pays*; according to the custom of the country as a temporary and often disposable common-law wife
46. 1802?
47. or 12, or 14
48. skins stretched over a framework of branches
49. some suggest as many as 2,000
50. or 1811
51. Solovieoff, Soloviev, Solovioff, Solovyov
52. the atlatl adds to the lever arm of throwing. Record distance for atlatl is 848 ft, javelin 340.
53. Becherin himself may have been tortured as part of the investigation
54. Solovei is a name for Nightingale in Russian and Solovei the Brigand was in epic poetry
55. Irkutsk improbably had one of the first centers for smallpox inoculation in the world
56. now part of Maine
57. The *Lydia* was about 80 feet long, 180 tons, owned by the Lyman family
58. Alternatively, he was in on the plot. He later tried to stir up trouble along the Columbia River.
59. woods runner, typically an independent trader, trapper, voyageur

60. Another story says he helped construct a canoe and went back downstream as far as an Arikara village before joining an expedition with Manuel Lisa.

61. one source suggests she sat this one out, but the sons probably went along

62. this was not uncommon, to bring a country marriage into legal status

63. Francois' good friend Philippe Degie had died in 1847 at a reported age of 108.

64. Marie Aioe Dorion Vernier Toupin, Marie Laguivoise (Aioe may also be Ohiose - her daughter's baptismal name)

65. listed as Aiouez in a 1718 map, also called Iowa, Ioway. One of the Sioux tribes.

66. Pierre Dorion Sr. had been an interpreter for the Lewis and Clark expedition

67. In April 1807, about a year after the end of the Lewis and Clark expedition, the Charbonneau family moved to St. Louis. Toussaint Charbonneau and Sacagawea departed for the Mandan villages in April 1809 but returned to St. Louis in November 1809. The interpreter community was small.

68. or Fort George (Astoria) - there are several versions of this story embellished by various authors. Fort Nez Perce is closer, just about 25 miles away, and makes the most sense.

69. perhaps Vagnier

70. often Osipovich; also Vasiliy Petrovich

71. *baidarshchik*

72. on the north side of Kodiak Island

73. Aleut was used generically, perhaps Koniags

74. near La Push, Washington

75. They called him Talacani as there is no r, f, or v in Miwok

76. named after the famous Russian Orthodox Alaskan clergyman Veniaminov's mother

77. In the fur trade a sutler

78. 音吉 or 乙吉) also. John Matthew Ottoson, J. M. Otterson, Lin Ah Tao

79. Not as unusual as you might think; the Chinook had a name for Japanese sailors: "the washed ashore people." They ended up in California, Russia, Alaska, the Philippines, and other places.

80. originally Wark

81. probably Iroquois, Cree, Nippissing

82. baptized Skeene, he also used Skein and Skeen

83. Black was almost 40, Peter just 20. They remained friends. G. Simpson called Black, "the strangest man I ever met." A big bully but able adventurer, eventually killed for mistreating natives.

84. Hawaii

85. probably misspelling of the Hawaiian *Le'a rhe ard* — he does not rush

86. often an area for smuggling, something Meares may have done

87. Maquinna later denied this

88. It seems possible Meares was working for Prime Minister William Pitt, laying claim for the crown but as a private person so the government could disavow him if needed.

89. relatively small, at around 45 feet long with a beam of 20–24 feet and a draft of 4–6 feet

90. the Russians had been building ships in Alaska for some time

91. José Burling, José Burling O'Cain, Josef O'Cain, Ocayne, O'Quin, O'Keen, O'Keane, O'Kain and O'Kenn.

92. 626 letters of marque were issued in Massachusetts, a key part of the American private navy

93. noted as the *Britisher*, but ships from a given country were often called generically by origin. A British East India ship, the *Vansittart* went down in 1789 near Bangka Island on a London to Canton run. Most of the crew were saved and taken to Canton where Capt. Bligh saw them.

94. Nautical Archeology Shipwreck Survey. 1986. There may be a mistake, or two ships were named *Elenora*. Metcalf was back on the coast in an Elenora 1789, 1790, 1791 & 1794.

95. *Jefferson* out of Boston, owned by J. and T. Lamb and associates. Master, Josiah Roberts, Bernard Magee, first mate, prefab ship built in the Marquesas.

96. a native village on the NW coast, or less likely, Kawaihae, Hawaii.

97. Catholic

98. 1796 Reserve letter No. 351 from the Viceroy of New Spain to the Prince of Peace, gives an account of the arrival in Mexico of the Scotsman Muir and José Burling: of the continuation of his trip to Veracruz and of the state of the English sailors.

99. She was able to serve as an interpreter as she spoke Aleut, Russian, and some English. She was left at Honolulu when Kamehameha was ruling and she became a companion to Kamehameha's wives and accompanied them to Kailua when the royal settlement was moved there.

100. What we know about the wreck is primarily from Campbell's narrative of his voyage around the world.

101. An open boat of 22 feet with a sail and six oars. This voyage is in some ways comparable to Shackleton's similar 800-mile voyage from Elephant Island to South Georgia Island.

102. O'Cain was a good seaman, it is likely the rebuilt ship was not handling well. His crew was also inexperienced with only two sailors from the *Eclipse.*

103. Ogden called him Johnson Gardner, others used Johnson or Johnston Gardiner

104. possible from near Scranton. He would have come down the Ohio river.

105. Hugh Glass was later recorded as Johnston's friend. Glass apparently fled a gunsmith's apprenticeship in Pittsburg in 1795, stealing a rifle. He probably went down the Ohio and Mississippi rivers to New Orleans where he worked with the smuggler/privateer/pirate brothers Jean and Pierre Laffite.

106. possibly Virginian

107. Etienne Provost out of Santa Fe was also there with a small group of trappers

108. It is unclear if they were encouraged to challenge the Canadians by William Clark or John Quincy Adams. Clark negotiated 37 treaties with the natives. They were aware of the HBC efforts to build new forts and take the beaver first.

109. Joseph Laprise probate 1822, the circumstances of his death not known

110. often misspelled

111. Fort Union Trading Post was built near the junction of the Missouri and Yellowstone rivers in 1828. It was a 220 by 240-foot quadrangle enclosed by vertical logs with bastions at the northeast and southwest. Fort Union also installed a distillery in 1832.

112. Surcingles

113. epishemores, a blanket or buffalo hide pad under the saddle — often slept on

114. a skin boat, typically with willow frame and hide covering

115. The German naturalist Prince Maximilian of Wied in 1832–34 led the first scientific exploration of the Missouri River's upper reaches since the epic journey of Lewis and Clark almost thirty years earlier.

116. It is possible Gardiner may have known Hugh Glass back in Pennsylvania.

117. Jim Beckwourth (or his biographer) claimed they were bound and thrown into a fire and burned alive to the frustration of his native allies who wanted scalps.

118. or July 1786.

119. not too far from today's Stockton
120. sometimes Reddeford
121. name attached by Fremont
122. called by some a land-pirate with a penchant for stealing the best California horses
123. This seems a bit odd since Walker knew the route and was more proficient.
124. Horses were worth $50–150 in the mountains but inexpensive or free in California. A good horse could sell for 10–20 beaver pelts.
125. still celebrated yearly by Dartmouth College with a boat trip from Hanover, NH to Old Saybrook, CT
126. also on Cook's ship but now working for the tsarina as leader of a round-the-world naval expedition
127. he developed a fine bromance with Campbell and remained friends for life
128. often referred to as berdache in earlier writing, considered pejorative today. Among several hundred tribes in the country the consideration and treatment for these men varied widely. Women who assumed the role of men were often accepted as well.
129. or perhaps gambled and won
130. or perhaps more likely they both died of disease and were buried by the Tay River as local historians suggest.
131. equivalent to the Medal of Honor
132. the first-born legitimate son to inherit his parent's entire or main estate
133. his father would have been 60, not impossible, although a 14- or 15-year-old is more likely
134. Deg Hitan
135. probably the Beaufort Sea
136. cataracts are common in some Chinese populations

Lessons Not Yet Learned
137. For example the nuclear meltdowns at Fukushima and Chernobyl, global warming and the cornona virus.
138. It may cost more than half a million dollars for the equipment for a modern biology lab, but only a few thousand dollars to set up a field studies program. Field staff costs and funding for travel and training need to be adequate and secure for many years to ensure continuity. Many grants are just 2 or 3 years but field work should be funded for 10, 20 or even 50 years.

Illustration Credits

Cover: Man of Nootka Sound 1778 J. Webber
Fronts-piece detail from Nootka types 1778 J. Webber
Hanna's ship *Sea Otter* adapted from C. Brooking
Nuu-chah-nulth women paddlers E. Curtis
US Army barracks/Ft. Vancouver G. Sohon
Kanaka Village by G. Gibbs
Fort Ross from a Russian stamp by A. Polotnova
Sloop *Union* H. Jackson
Maps and others by author

John Webber (1751–1793) was apprenticed to Swiss artist Johann Aberli, a popular, landscape artist, when he was 16. He spent three years in Aberli's studio and four years in Paris at the Académie Royale before returning to London to continue his studies at the Royal Academy. He was just twenty-four when he was  offered a place as expedition artist with Captain James Cook on his third voyage of exploration to the Pacific and witnessed Cook's death in Hawaii. Webber was popular with his shipmates and put his subjects at ease. He was a rare artist, equally skilled at both landscapes and portraits, and able to do his own etchings. His reputation as an artist was thoroughly established by his work on the expedition. For the rest of his life he made regular tours to draw landscapes and continued painting portraits. He was one of the first artists to make and sell prints of his own works. He was elected Associate of the Royal Academy of Arts in 1785 and Royal Academician in 1791. When he died in 1793 he left a considerable fortune.

Don't miss Volume 1:

Fur War: The Political, Economic, Cultural and Ecological Impacts of the Western Fur Trade 1765–1840

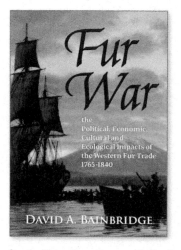

"The fur trade played a key role in the development and ultimate ownership of lands and resources on the West Coast of North America," explains Bainbridge, an environmental historian with degrees in Earth Sciences and Ecology. "Yet it is often neglected in histories and understanding of the west. In California classrooms, it is skipped almost entirely."

In this book, readers will discover how Russia, Great Britain, America, France, Spain, Mexico, and Hawaii contested for furs and power, and how the many First Nations fought to maintain their communities. The book reveals how - with just a few minor changes in government response or markets - the North Americans on the West Coast might speak Spanish or Russian and how Tlingit, Haida, and Mowachaht Nations might dominate the North Coast.

Much like the *narco traficantes* today, the fur trade was risky, often illegal, but could be incredibly profitable. The catastrophic impacts have been severe for the First Nations whose lands were invaded, and for the ecosystems that were stripped of wildlife. Epidemics devastated the First Nations and the fur trade's impacts are still evident today along the coast and rivers of Alaska, Canada and the American west. Many groups and institutions are working to restore the Fur Coast and this compelling book makes it clear that everyone can play a part. Teachers can access free lesson plans, supplemental illustrations, and added text online at **www.furwar.com**.

eBook, $2.99 | ISBN 978-1-7351492-1-9

Paperback, $9.99 | ISBN 978-1-7351492-2-6

Made in the USA
Las Vegas, NV
28 January 2021